SoHo

The Rise and Fall of an Artists' Colony

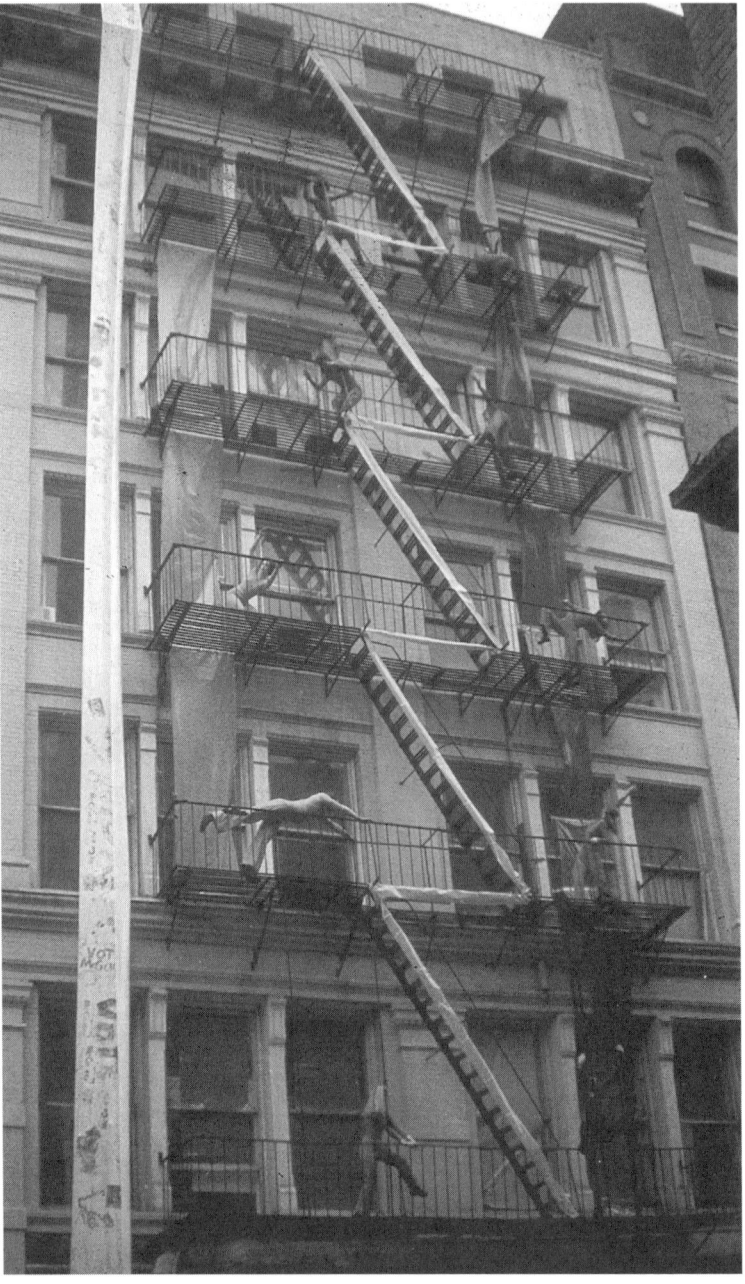

SoHo

The Rise and Fall of an Artists' Colony

Richard Kostelanetz

Routledge   New York London

Published in 2003 by
Routledge
29 West 35th Street
New York, NY 10001
www.routledge-ny.com

Published in Great Britain by
Routledge
11 New Fetter Lane
London EC4P 4EE
www.routledge.co.uk

Routledge is an imprint of the Taylor & Francis Group.

Printed in the United States of America on acid-free paper.

10 9 8 7 6 5 4 3 2 1

Library of Congress Cataloging-in-Publication Data

Kostelanetz, Richard.
Soho : the rise and fall of an artists' colony : a critical memoir / Richard Kostelanetz.
        p. cm.
ISBN 0-415-96572-1 (hardback : alk. paper)
1. Art, American—New York (State)—New York—20th century. 2. Artist colonies—
New York (State)—New York. 3. Artists—New York (State)—New York. 4.
Bohemianism—New York (State)—New York. 5. SoHo (New York, N.Y.) I. Title.

N6535.N5K67 2003
709'.747'1—dc21   2003002694

Frontispiece: Marilyn Wood and the Celebration Group performing "SoHo Fire
Escape Dance" at the Soho Arts Festival, October 22, 1972. Photo by Robert E. Wood.
Courtesy of Marilyn Wood, Celebrations.

The text of this book was composed in Electra with Hellenic display face. Book design
by Dutton & Sherman Design. Printed and bound in the United States of America by
Sheridan Books, Inc.

*To the memory of George Maciunas, our founder,
and for my partners in Good Deal Realty Corp.*

In the 1840s and 1850s, when Broadway between Canal and Houston streets emerged as the city's grand shopping and entertainment boulevard, New York's bawdy houses trekked northward too. They clustered directly behind the commercial strip, in the small cobbled streets of Mercer, Greene, Howard, and Wooster—present-day SoHo.

—Edward G. Burrows and Mike Wallace, *Gotham* (1999)

For seventy-five dollars a month we got raw space: no elevator or sprinklers, just exposed wooden beams, brick walls, and wooden floors, big windows at either end, a toilet, and a sink. We were working artists, living in lofts zoned for light manufacturing in the center of the raw fabric district, bounded by produce and meat-packing warehouses with carcasses hanging from their canopies. The neighborhood was a residential desert.

There were no subdivisions in our life. We did not leave to go to work: that would have been bourgeois. It felt good to be persecuted; everyone knew real artists had to pay dearly for their freedom. When we moved in, our downstairs neighbor, Bob Huot, a painter, told us to tear up our envelopes so no one could track our address and to distribute our garbage in *all* the neighborhood trash baskets, not just the one on our own corner, lest we draw attention to the fact that someone was living in the building.

—Twyla Tharp, *Push Comes to Shove* (1992)

The thing that I worry about, not just about the Kitchen but about New York, is its remaining a community of artists who work together, artists who see each other's work, artists who are influenced by each others' work, and artists who can create a community of other artists who, together, create the kind of art that we've identified with New York and with the United States.

—Philip Glass, in a press conference for the Kitchen (1987)

Some Keys to Artists' SoHo

(Page numbers indicate principal occurrence. Full index in back.)

Preface

This book brings together two long-standing interests of mine: avant-garde arts, about which I've written much before, and New York City, the sound of which was the subject and theme of my longest electro-acoustic audiotape composition. Better yet, it takes place in downtown Manhattan, where I went to elementary school and have lived most of my life, where my parents still live, and an area I continue to love even as I'm leaving it. Since my roots remain in downtown Manhattan, I've tried to speak of SoHo as though I still lived there, preferring "here" over "there."

This panoramic essay in intimate cultural history mixes the spatial with the sequential, as well as the personal with the general, in a series of interrelated episodes about various phenomena, individuals, and issues. As the book's title is its theme, most of its text is a continuous elaboration, which is meant to be read sequentially. Rather than a table of contents, the book opens with a selective index, identifying exactly where discussions of key subjects can be found. What is more important to one reader may be less consequential to another.

Of the many people who generously helped, mostly by responding to e-mailed questions and drafts, I'm grateful to Avis Berman, Davidson Gigliotti, Robert C. Morgan, Charles Doria, Larry Qualls, Daryl Chin, George Waterman, and especially, Douglas Puchowski. The first draft was written between ocean swims during a post-residency respite at the Atlantic Center for the Arts in New Smryna Beach, Florida. Some chapters previously appeared in NY Arts. Richard Carlin and Shannon McLachlan used a keen knife on the manuscript before it went to the copy editor.

As this cultural history covers a terrain about which much has been forgotten or has disappeared, I welcome not only correction of details but additional information for a possible second edition, should there be enough support for this book to warrant a publisher commissioning it. If you think your activity or a friend's needlessly slighted, don't deprecate the book or its subject. Be thoughtful, if not self-interested, and, instead, please create preconditions for an appropriate revision, writing me through www.richardkostelanetz.com or PO Box 454, Rockaway Beach, NY 11693.

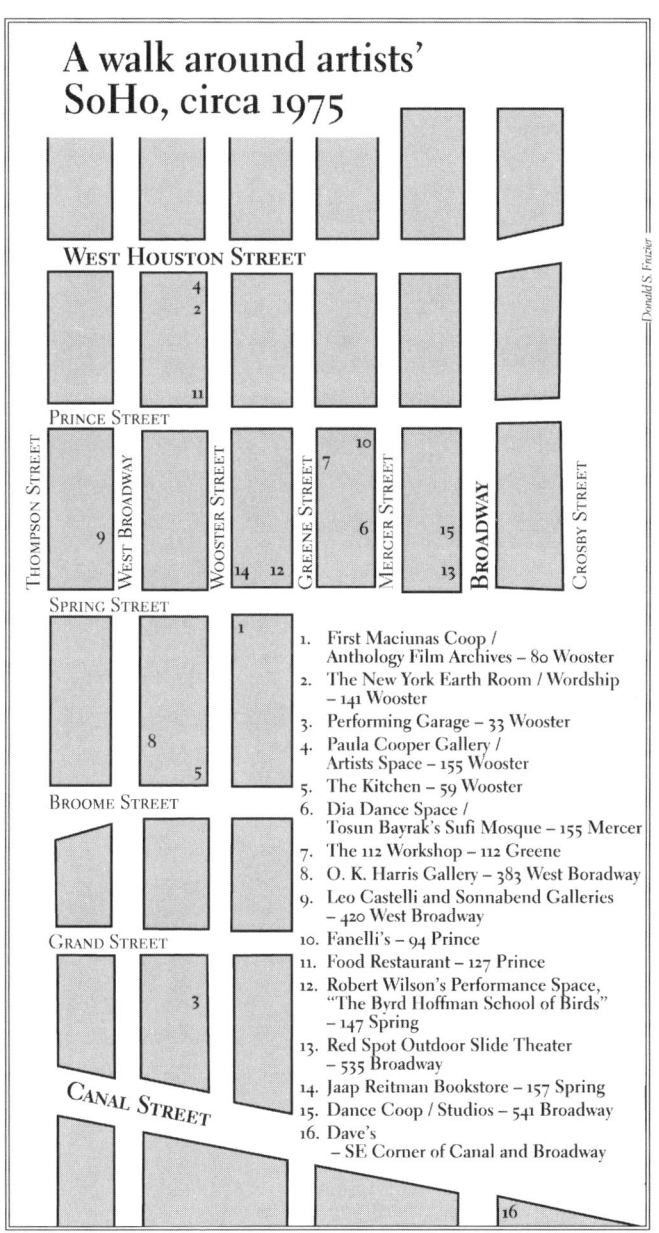

A walk around artists' SoHo, circa 1975

WEST HOUSTON STREET

PRINCE STREET

THOMPSON STREET

WEST BROADWAY

WOOSTER STREET

GREENE STREET

MERCER STREET

BROADWAY

CROSBY STREET

SPRING STREET

BROOME STREET

GRAND STREET

CANAL STREET

Donald S. Frazier

1. First Maciunas Coop /
   Anthology Film Archives – 80 Wooster
2. The New York Earth Room / Wordship
   – 141 Wooster
3. Performing Garage – 33 Wooster
4. Paula Cooper Gallery /
   Artists Space – 155 Wooster
5. The Kitchen – 59 Wooster
6. Dia Dance Space /
   Tosun Bayrak's Sufi Mosque – 155 Mercer
7. The 112 Workshop – 112 Greene
8. O. K. Harris Gallery – 383 West Boradway
9. Leo Castelli and Sonnabend Galleries
   – 420 West Broadway
10. Fanelli's – 94 Prince
11. Food Restaurant – 127 Prince
12. Robert Wilson's Performance Space,
    "The Byrd Hoffman School of Birds"
    – 147 Spring
13. Red Spot Outdoor Slide Theater
    – 535 Broadway
14. Jaap Reitman Bookstore – 157 Spring
15. Dance Coop / Studios – 541 Broadway
16. Dave's
    – SE Corner of Canal and Broadway

A walk around artists' SoHo, circa 1975.

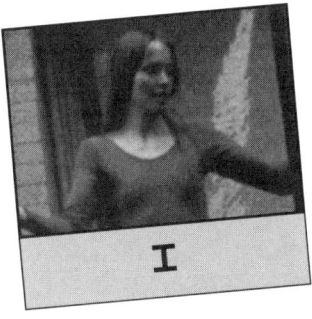

I

Choosing a place to live has been for the American artist a problem of the first order.

—Harold Rosenberg, "Tenth Street" (1954)

WHEN I CAME BACK to New York City from college in 1962, the area below Houston Street was an industrial slum that I might have walked through reluctantly on the way from Greenwich Village to its north or Chinatown to its east. Industrial debris littered streets that were clogged with trucks and truckers during the working daytimes but deserted at night. Its streets were not numbers typical of most of Manhattan but names: Mercer, Greene, Wooster, Crosby running from north/south; Prince, Spring, Broome, and Grand running from east/west. Its geometry differed from that typical elsewhere in the city. Its rectangular blocks, though roughly observing a perpendicular grid, were far longer from north to south than from east to west. The area immediately to its north on Houston Street, running between Mercer Street on the east and upper West Broadway on the west (later called La Guardia Place) and then as far uptown as West Third Street was roughly similar to proto-SoHo until condemned by the city in the early 1950s, its industrial detritus demolished and some of its paved streets eliminated. In its place came an impressive residential urban renewal complex called Washington Square Village with a private garden unusually large for Manhattan above a car garage. Having built too much on the available property, the builder Paul Tishman was persuaded to give it to a "community institution" that was permitted to exceed the rules.

The most feasible choice was New York University, on whose board Tishman incidentally served. NYU has used the buildings since the early 1960s to rent mostly to its faculty and staff. No private real estate developer ever again tried anything so big in the downtown neighborhood between Fourth Street on the north and Canal Street on the south. For that "dead" area, city planners repeatedly proposed during the 1960s a ten-laned Lower Manhattan (aka Broome Street) Expressway that would link the East River bridges on the east with the Holland Tunnel on the west.

"In the 1700s, the land that is now the SoHo district," according to Charles R. Simpson, "was largely a portion of the Bayard family farm, which stretched over hills and meadows from Canal Street up to Bleecker Street. During the Revolutionary War period, wooden palisades were built across the Bayard farm, and two forts were erected in 1776 on hills situated at the present site of Grand Street, marking the northern defensible limits of the city. The War left Nicholas Bayard, the farm's owner, financially devastated, and he soon after was forced to mortgage one hundred acres west of the unimproved wagon road that was to become Broadway. This tract of farm land, comprising most of what became the SoHo district, was subsequently laid out in streets and sold in lots."

A century and a half ago, this area below Houston Street attracted wealthy New Yorkers, who patronized elegant stores and theaters on Broadway. "This was the Fifth Avenue of its day," according to one guidebook. In the wake of minstrel halls came gambling casinos and eventually brothels, especially on the side streets. Walt Whitman wrote in 1857: "After dark any man passing along Broadway, between Houston and Fulton streets, finds the western sidewalks full of prostitutes, jaunting up and down here, by ones, twos, or three—on the look-out for customers." From the *Directory of the Seraglios in New York* comes this entry for Miss Clara Gordon at 119 Mercer Street: "We cannot too highly recommend this house, the lady herself is a perfect Venus: beautiful, entertaining, and supremely seductive. Her aides-de-camp are really charming and irresistible, and altogether honest and honorable. Miss G. is a great belle, and her mansion is patronized by Southern merchants and planters principally. She is highly accomplished, skillful, and prudent, and sees [that] her visitors are well entertained." The historian Timothy J. Gilfoyle, in his classic about New York City prostitution *City of Eros* (1991), writes: "Directly behind the hotels and theaters on both sides of Broadway, Mercer, Greene, Wooster, and Crosby streets were known for their rich collection of brothels." In the 1870s, according to Gilfoyle, Wooster Street had twenty-seven whorehouses while fifty-two were on Greene (not even art galleries were as numerous a century later.) Before long, these brothels too moved further uptown.

Most of the cast-iron buildings that came to mark the neighborhood for architectural historians were constructed between 1840 and 1880, generally for use by the textile industry. Beginning in 1890, a street car pulled by horses came from the East River across Delancy Street and the Lower East Side, taking immigrant workers across Spring Street past Broadway and then West Broadway to Broome Street and the Hudson River, and then taking them back in the evening on two-way streets. In 1913, according to Joseph R. Brennan, battery-driven cars replaced the horses on the route that ran until 1931, except for during 1919–1920. Once much of this textile industry succumbed to southern and foreign competition after World War II, printers and warehousing moved into the large empty interior spaces that could be rented for as little as $100 per month through the 1940s into the 1960s. Charles R. Simpson quotes a pamphlet published in October 1962 by the City Club, ominously titled *The Wastelands of New York City*: "The report found 15.4 percent of the spaces vacant, 50 percent of the buildings renting for the low rate of $0.75 for square foot per year or less, and some space available at the distress rate of only $0.13 per square foot per year. The very inexpensive lofts were used for 'dead storage,' that is, or long-term warehousing of bulky, inexpensive materials such as rag and waste paper bales." Need I calculate that $0.75 becomes for 1,600 square feet, say, only $1,200 per year or $100 per month; $0.13 becomes roughly $200 per year. No wonder that fires were frequent in this area.

I first became aware of someone actually residing in the nineteenth-century industrial slum in 1965 when I was introduced on Canal Street to a Korean artist who had just arrived in America and

rented a nearby "loft," which was a word new to me at the time, referring to the upper floors, customarily open spaces, of a factory or warehouse. Already prominent in European avant-garde circles, Nam June
Paik had come to New York to further his career. I later learned about
such urban pioneers as Alison Knowles, who, in the late 1950s, had
rented space in an industrial building on Broadway just north of
Canal Street, where she lived with her husband-to-be, Dick Higgins,
who decades later became my closest professional colleague. The
industrial supply stores then on Canal Street seemed a long way, culturally, from my apartment on the edge of Harlem, down the hill
from Columbia University, where I was then a graduate student. So
did the cast-iron palaces that stood out from the smaller, shabbier,
mostly older buildings that were never more than a few stories high.

Whether prostitution or any other legally vulnerable activities
(other than the Gay Firehouse) continued into current times in SoHo
is an interesting question. On the one hand, consider that underpo-
liced, anonymous buildings provide incomparable opportunities for
sub-rosa activities; on the other hand, no one can remember any
arrests for prostitution (or gambling or large-scale drug-dealing) in
SoHo. The last observation could mean either that none existed, that
no arrest happened, or that no arrest ever got publicity. Actually,
"artistic prostitution" was a greater threat to SoHoites. Drug-dealing
was also rare in SoHo per se, which didn't have enough street traffic
except Saturday afternoon to interest professional drug-dealers, who
tended instead to favor Washington Square to the north or the Lower
East Side.

By the time I relocated downtown, first to the East Village in
1966 (and incidentally changed my cultural outlook from academic
to bohemian—from "uptown" to "downtown"), I became aware of
artists who had rented large open spaces in which they worked and,
incidentally, lived. Around the corner from me on Second Avenue at
that time, Yoko Ono, later famous, had a loft briefly above a store. A
young California woman I knew that year, the daughter of a poet, had
rented on Warren Street, yet farther downtown, just west of City Hall,
part of a loft sloppily divided, as I recall, from another woman who
had already lived there for several years. I wish I could find my friend

now, because I'd like to know how someone new to New York at that time had made such an unusual move. I visited Robert Rauschenberg's on Broadway around 12th Street, which was the loft center for a previous generation. In Calvin Tomkins's classic description of it written in 1964 (and reprinted in *Off the Wall*):

> The loft was about a hundred feet long by thirty wide [or 3,000 square feet—a measure to keep in mind]. A row of supporting columns ran down the middle, but otherwise it was clear, unobstructed space. Tall, grimy windows let in the distinctively white light of downtown New York—also the roar of trucks on Broadway. [Within the space] stood a group of large objects—a car door, a window frame, a roof ventilator mounted on sheets—components of an unfinished five-part sculpture.
>
> Paintings, combines, and sculptures from the recently concluded Jewish Museum retrospective were stacked against the wall father alone. There was a big table in the middle of the room, its surface cluttered with magazines, pictures clipped from magazines, felt pens and pencils, and tubes of painting and other materials. Toward the back of the room, a counter projected from the end wall formed an alcove for the refrigerator, the electric stove, and the bed—a mattress laid on the floor. All the rest of the loft was workspace.

So impressive to writers was this loft at the time that the fiction writer Donald Barthelme in 1980 told an interviewer, "I looked out the windows, and they were dirty, very much the tonality of [Rauschenberg's gray] pictures." Barthelme continued, "They were very much New York Lower Broadway windows." (Later, Rauschenberg purchased, on upper Lafayette Street, an abandoned orphanage with several floors of open space along with, in the back, a former chapel that could be used for tall work or performances.) Ceilings more than ten feet high were rare in New York City residences. In the 1960s, I recall visiting New York nonartists residing in apartments with double-height living rooms on West 67th Street between Central Park West and Columbus Avenues and on 9th Street near University Place and coming away impressed.

Walking south of Houston Street at the time I noticed in certain upper-story windows houseplants or interior lights shining into the night, both signifying that someone might be residing there. However, the area between Houston and Canal Streets was still largely terra incognita. Taxi drivers at the time customarily didn't know the names Wooster Street, Greene Street, or Mercer Street and had to be guided block by block. Sometime around 1969 I first heard the epithet SoHo to define an area south of Houston Street, the capital H meant crucially to distinguish this Manhattan neighborhood from London's Soho, which was (and is) a neighborhood of social venues and small apartments resembling New York's Greenwich Village.

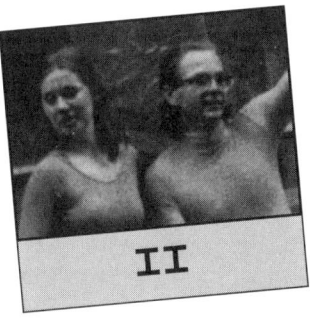

II

SoHo barely existed when I moved there in '67. There were maybe 10 people living between Canal and Houston Streets. I first lived down on Greene between Canal and Grand. Then, around '69, I moved to a building where the restaurant Jerry's is now. During the week there were trucks, rats, and rags, garbage trucks, because it was part of the carting area, so rats were just running everywhere. And the streets were filled with bales of rags and stuff like that.

—Chuck Close, in *5000 Artists Return to Artists Space: 25 Years* (1998)

PRIOR TO SoHo, many ambitious American artists preferred to live in "artist colonies," as they were called, where a dozen or two artists, customarily colleagues already, purchased empty land and constructed studios. Other purposeful artists settled in sparsely populated retreats, such as Fire Island, Provincetown, or Woodstock, establishing in those communities a culture more sympathetic to art and artists than could be found elsewhere in America. These artist colonies differ crucially from bohemias, which are communities, usually within an urban setting, hospitable to counter-bourgeois living. Indicatively, political radicals, often prominent in bohemias, are scarce in artists' colonies.

Within New York City, artists tended to create sympathetic pockets mostly in lower Manhattan. For nearly a century beginning in 1858, a building at 51 West 10th Street offered twenty-five studios, ranging in size from 300 to 600 square feet each, and a communal

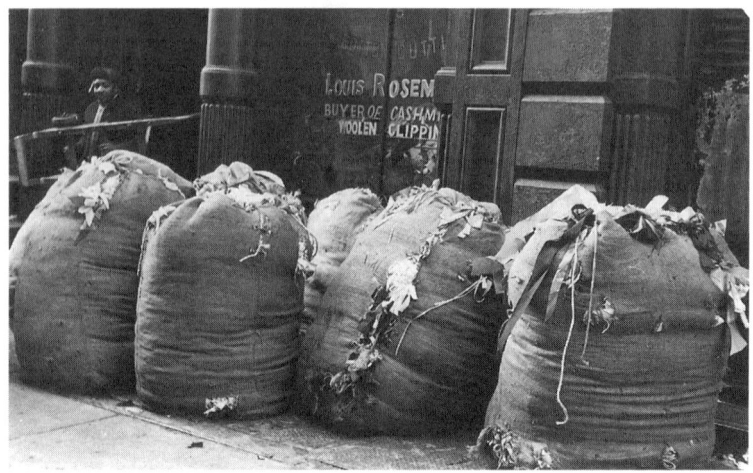

Burlap bags with remnants of cashmere, woolen, and cotton clippings in front of 75 Greene Street, January 1966. Copyright Fred W. McDarrah

gallery that was very useful not only for displaying but also for selling. Among the more prominent working and sometimes living at this address were William Merrit Chase, Frederic Church, and Winslow Homer. Nearby on Washington Square North, Edward Hopper long had a studio. The writer Thomas Wolfe (1900–1938) briefly shared a loft with his paramour, the theater designer Aline Bernstein, at 13 East 8th Street. "The fourth floor had recently served as a sweatshop, but it could easily be cleaned up, and those skylights, they were ideal!" writes Ross Wetzteon. "So in January 1926 they moved in, Tom insisting on sharing the $35–a-month rent." Artists in twentieth-century Paris, by contrast, tended to work in small but well-lit ateliers on the top floors of residential buildings—penthouses to some; attics to others—often residing in an apartment immediately below. These Parisian ateliers were perceived to be so attractive that non-artists eventually wanted them as well, sometimes opening up the floor to create a living room twice the height of their bedrooms

When the New York-born writer Henry Miller visited the painter Beauford Delaney one evening in the early 1940s at 181 Greene

Street, east of Washington Square and north of Houston Street, he found "streets which seem commemorated to the pangs and frustrations of the artist; having nothing to do with art. Shunned by all living as soon as the work of day is done, they are invested with the sinister shadows of crime and with prowling alley cats which thrive on the garbage and ordure that litter the gutters and pavements." Once inside Delaney's top floor studio, Miller was overwhelmed by chill, even at the beginning of the fall: "In a few moments, the fire died out—and remained dead for the rest of the evening. In about twenty minutes the floor became icy cold, the dead cold of cold storage in which cadavers are preserved in the morgue. We sat in our overcoats, collars turned up, hats pulled down over our ears, our hands stuffed deep in our pockets." Sometime after I first read this, a quarter century later, I had similar negative responses to my first forays both inside and outside downtown artists' lofts.

In the years just before World War II, according to a unique unpublished history by the artist/writer Elliott Barowitz, an artists' community took shape in the east Greenwich Village area around 10th Street just east of Broadway—to be exact, between Sixth Avenue on the west, First Avenue on the east, 8th Street on the south, and 12th Street on the north. Galleries as well as studios were located in walk-up buildings scarcely 25 feet wide. On their ground floors were retail stores, sometimes a few steps down from the street; on their second floors, showrooms with large windows displaying goods; above them, open spaces or apartments. Scarcely unique to this neighborhood, this kind of modest multiuse building can still be found elsewhere in the city, especially on Madison and Lexington Avenues on the Upper East Side on blocks that haven't fallen to wreckers. I once imagined that well-lit second floors would give artists a good deal of natural light, but Pat Pasloff, a veteran painter who came of age after World War II, recently assured me that any space that could be rented for retail would have been too expensive for emerging artists at that time. Instead, artists worked and resided in the floor(s) yet above, customarily around 1,000 square feet, with rents under $100 per month, often adding wood or coal stoves, or kerosene heaters, to keep themselves warm at night and on weekends. Even if the space was not zoned for legal residence, the working artist could still spend the night surreptitiously. The rules allowed a shower, but not a bathtub; a hotplate, but not a stove; and anything resembling a bed needed to be hidden away if a city buildings' inspector knocked.

Because their galleries were at 79, 80, 88, 89, and 90 East 10th Street, many of these downtown artists were exhibiting in their own neighborhood—in a model duplicated decades later in SoHo (but not yet in West Chelsea, say). The critic Harold Rosenberg, whose enthusiasm for his neighbors' best work was hugely influential, resided only a few blocks away, on 10th Street between Second and Third Avenues. Nearby as well was both the Cedar Street Tavern, where artists liked to talk and drink (and often fight, as some recall), and the Whitney Museum, then located on West 8th Street, where some exhibited, because it, unlike the Museum of Modern Art, was exclusively devoted to American work. Many lofts in this area were torn down for "urban renewal" in 1961, which, as Barowitz notes, "coincidentally marks the demise of the Abstract Expressionist movement." Compared to what became SoHo, 10th Street was a remarkably tiny scene.

In the 1950s, some artists lived in modest lofts on lower Park Avenue, such as 49 East 19th Street. Around Coenties Slip, then on the lower East River south of Wall Street, several painters lived who a decade later became more prominent, including Robert Indiana, Jack Youngerman, Ellsworth Kelly, Agnes Martin, and Fred Mitchell. A building on Monroe Street on the far-eastern Lower East Side offered cheap rents to the composer John Cage and the sculptor Richard Lippold, among others. So did Chinatown, which was said to be the immediate source of the gigantic laundry bags Lee Bontecou incorporated into her sculptures, which seemed so impressive around 1960. The poet and anthologist Oscar Williams, residentially more adventurous than his literary colleagues, lived after World War II with his wife, the artist Gene Derwood, in the penthouse of an office building on Water Street, south of the Brooklyn Bridge, surrounded by "seedy bars all around and dozens of woebegone drunks," John Gruen wrote. "Visiting the Williamses was something of a trauma, particularly since we had to wait for several very long minutes before Gene Derwood made her way down in the manually operated elevator to unlock the front doors of the building." In the 1950s, some artists wishing to work where they lived, chose large Upper West Side apartments, then less fashionable than they became, customarily reserving one of many rooms, such as a master bedroom or a dining room, perhaps as large as 600 square feet, for their work.

In the early 1960s, an informal group calling itself the Artists Tenants Association petitioned the office of New York City's mayor at the time, Robert Wagner, whose brother was an artist, for permission to reside—not just work—in districts not officially zoned for residential use or in buildings lacking a residential Certificate of Occupancy, customarily called a C of O. The city agreed that no more than two artists could live in such a building and that their presence would be announced on the front of the building with a sign six inches square with large letters declaring "A.I.R." for "artist in residence" and identifying the residential floors with numerals. The assumption was that the A.I.R. signs would alert firemen arriving on the scene to rescue the residents first. The buildings designated at the time for partial artist residency were largely in the West Village, the Lower East Side, the Bowery, and further uptown in Chelsea/Clinton (west 20s and 30s) and Murray Hill (east 30s). "The artists themselves did not enroll en masse, partly because they could not afford the improvements required to gain legal residential status for their lofts," notes James R. Hudson. "The artists' reluctance to participate in a program designed for their benefit and protection certainly made public officials question their willingness to be responsible citizens, to meet acceptable standards of conduct as loft tenants. Artists, after all, were [thought to be] a rather unstable lot at best, with little capital or other power to rebuild an urban area."

"Ironically," Barowitz writes, "few if any of these units were in SoHo or as it was then called 'Hell's Hundred Acres,' a reference to its many fires. Alternatively, this distinct was known as 'the Valley' or 'The Cast-Iron District.'" Compared to the other neighborhoods, this one appeared less conducive to habitation: the buildings were too big, the spaces too large and too industrial, for individual artist's studios. As the buildings were individually constructed, often in disregard of those beside them, little in SoHo resembled the uniformity of, say, a row of residential brownstones. Indeed, while my coop building has eight stories with roughly 7,000 square feet on each floor, as does another resembling mine two buildings away, the structure between us has only three stories with roughly 2,000 square feet apiece. SoHo also had no grocery stores, no dry cleaners, no schools, no pharmacies, no libraries, no churches, and no synagogues (ever since Shereath Isreal had closed its doors on Broadway a century before). The only "restaurants" were workers' luncheonettes that closed before sundown. For residential needs, the neighborhood was a desert. "When artists moved into SoHo loft spaces, few if any of those responsible for 'saving the city' recognized that their individual efforts could significantly change land-use patterns," notes James R. Hudson. "The entire ideology of 1950s urban renewal was based on large-scale development. The illegal conversion of lofts did not have any place on the agenda."

Many of the loft-based businesses were owned and managed by people whose heirs were disinterested. Sometimes these proprietors were indivduals; other times, partners. Some had owned their buildings and businesses since the 1930s (like my relatives mentioned ahead) and, indeed, had never located anywhere else. Because the neighborhood was regarded as decaying, newer entrepreneurs desiring newer premises or more acceptable addresses tended to locate elsewhere in the city; turnover in proto-SoHo was scarce. The workers came mostly from the tenement neighborhoods of the Lower East Side, some of them taking city bus number 12 that even in the mid-1970s conveniently came across Prince Street only in the mornings and went back only in the afternnoons across Spring Street to Delancy Street and the East River, essentially duplicating the earlier horse and battery trolleys. Once the owners retired or their marginally profitable businesses were forced to close, new commercial or industrial tenants were hard to find. This was particularly true for the narrower buildings that lacked elevators or could not accommodate businesses that required larger horizontal spaces. Another factor keeping prices low was the threat of a proposed Lower Manhattan Expresssway. Owners of SoHo buildings feared they might be insufficiently com-

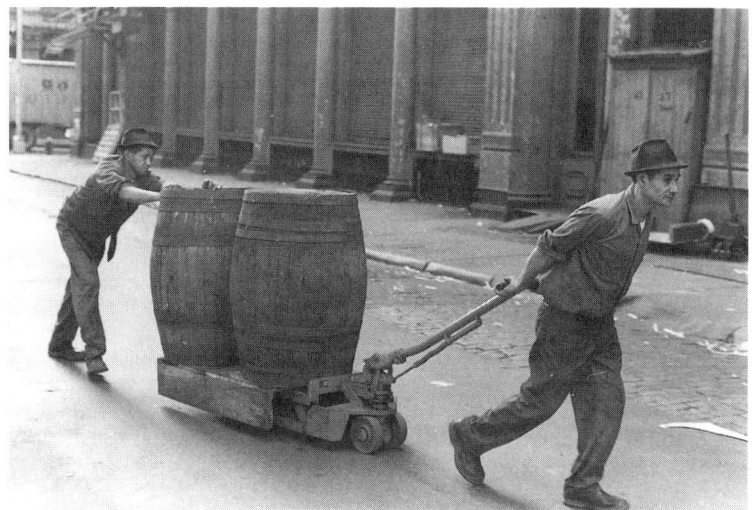

Workmen moving barrels on Greene Street, October 1969. Copyright Fred W. McDarrah

pensated were their properties to be demolished, much as the owners of industrial real estate in the South Bronx were ripped off only a few years before, when construction of the Bruckner Expressway destroyed their neighborhoods.

Other downtown businessesmen simply moved their operations uptown. My immigrant maternal grandfather's youngest (and thus most assimilated) brother owned from the 1930s into the 1960s the loft building at 99 Hudson Street, at the corner of Franklin Street, out of which he ran an olive oil importing business. His nephew, my mother's cousin, went to work there after World War II, eventually specializing in the importation of cashew nuts. He once told me in the 1970s that he would arrive at work at six in the morning to learn what he might have to sell that day. He would then walk down Franklin Street knocking on doors, so to speak, and expect to unload his available inventory by noon. In the 1960s, his business, like others, moved into midtown, which was closer to Grand Central Station that took him home to Westchester; and instead of touring Franklin Street, my cousin spent all day on the telephone, which he regarded as considerably less fun. After my great-uncle died prematurely in a plane crash in 1965, the olive oil business moved into Westchester, and the building was sold off. (Too large to be residential, it now houses a sports bar and film production companies.) So far away were my relatives from their old working neighborhood that I was the first to tell them in the 1980s about the new residents and the renovations that they made.

One element rescuing SoHo-to-be from the lower Manhattan wrecking machine mentioned before was the "Rapkin Study" prepared in 1962 by Chester Rapkin, then New York City's commissioner of planning. As a professor at Columbia University, he had recently coauthored a book titled *Residential Renewal in the Urban Core* (1963). In the report, officially titled "The South Houston Industrial Area," he noted that the number of business establishments in the area had declined from 651 in 1962 to 459 in 1963, and the number of employees from 12,671 to 8,394. Nonetheless, Rapkin advised the city not to destroy the "Renaissance-style" buildings that, though visibly dingy, employed people in garment, rag, and hat industries that were incidentally important sources of tax revenues. When Rapkin died in 2001, obituaries credited him with coining the epithet SoHo in this report, although others have likewise been credited with a christening that stuck.

So eager were the aging downtown landlords to rent or, better, to sell their decrepit properties that some gave the new artist owners a "purchase mortgage," as it was called, which was repaid directly to the seller. This saved the buyers a trip to a bank that, assessing the neighborhood's or artists' low-level commercial reputation, might have declined any loan. After all, even the mortgage program of the Federal Housing Administration refused in the late 1960s to back buildings in Hell's Hundred Acres while neighborhood banks were reluctant to lend to any building, let alone an artists' cooperative, that lacked a Certificate of Occupancy. (Our co-op had its first mortgage from the building's previous owners and its second mortgage from the co-op's sponsor; only after receiving a C of O did we petition banks.) Landlords unable to sell were relieved to have tenants of any sort for empty spaces, often at rents that now seem ridiculously cheap, some of them cynically assuming that artists residing illegally could be easily evicted. In that last assumption they were wrong. One proposal common around 1975 was called "a net lease," for, say, five to ten years, which differed from the customary rentals in making tenants fully responsible for everything except the mortgage (if there was one): maintenance, insurance, repair, heat, taxes both past and current, and so on. To a landlord owning a problematic building, perhaps with building department violations or a leaky roof, this arrangement gave the landlord modest income while retaining ownership. Two strategic assumptions were that the artists, "good with their hands," knew how to make such spaces habitable and that the landlord could confiscate much-improved space once the lease ended. In a Crosby Street building, the tenants simply took possession by paying off back taxes on which the landlord had defaulted, turning it into a co-op, not before they resided there, as was more customary, but afterward.

A few pioneering artists moved into these buildings, notwithstanding M1–5 zoning (light manufacturing) that made residence illegal. "Raw space" was the epithet for a loft with cracked walls and ceilings, broken or leaky windows, an abundance of garbage, and lumpy floors. "Renovation" was the name of the procedures necessary to make it usable, if not livable. Under the discouraging surface, some artists envisioned larger workspaces and hardwood floors more sturdy than those around East 10th Street; others appreciated the existence of elevators, even if their operators kept workday hours.

"In 1964," Barowitz continues, "the State Legislature amended Article 7–b to the State Multiple Dwelling to permit local municipalities to zone living work space for artists in the 'visual fine arts.' Inventive arguments were made that artists indeed were 'light manufacturers' and that they were living in (so to speak) the back of the store." The next steps included expanding the definition of an artist to include those involved with theater or dance, but excluding, to Barowitz, "the so-called commercial arts—graphic design, fashion, photography, architecture, etc., i.e., professions that normally use work for hire and performed work in an office-like setting." Writers who only wrote were also excluded. Likewise turned away were actors who weren't, say, directors or stage designers as well. The SoHo lawyer Margaret Baisley recalled that in 1987 the chief of city artists' accreditations told her that "she would not certify any rap musicians because she did not consider their work to be music or art." "The Department of Cultural Affairs once denied certification to a photographer client of mine," Barowitz continues, "because she was 'too young' at age 22 to be a 'serious' artist, even though her work had shown publicly. The nebulous edict that you must be a 'serious and committed' fine arts artist is difficult to quantify. So an unrecognized Picasso has no hope of success with the DCA. He must wait for his NEA grant or for discovery by an art gallery. What happens to the spouse of an artist who dies in his loft? She must be evicted, according to the Department of Cultural Affairs, because the certification is not in her name. There are many inequities."

Partly to protect the light manufacturing businesses, the city ruled that lofts with more than 3,500 square feet or less than 1,200 square feet were not available for individual artists. Likewise unavailable for residency were those located on the "Broadway corridor" between Houston and Canal Streets, which were meant to be reserved for manufacturers (and later for favored retailers and the small high-tech corporations that by the 1990s gave this stretch of Broadway a new identity as "Silicon Alley"). After the early 1970s, the area from the west side of Mercer Street to the east side of West Broadway (and also north of Broome) acquired a slightly different zoning from the areas east of Mercer Street (to Lafayette Street) and south of Broome Street (to Canal Street). Whereas the former was M1–5a, the latter was M1–5b. The difference in the last letter was crucial. Whereas retail spaces could occupy the ground floors in northwest SoHo (M1–5a), as we'll call it, as could bars and restaurants, ground floors in the other parts of SoHo (M1–5b) were reserved for light manufacturing and wholesale outlets. The fact that many galleries and restaurants nonetheless opened to streets designated M1–5b reflected either an outlaw mentality or the successful efforts of a pricey lawyer. Even as late as 2002, a savings bank purportedly in New York City refused to give me a residential co-op home loan on the grounds that SoHo is still zoned for light manufacturing. As indeed it is, residential neighbors all around me notwithstanding.

Another development was empowering New York City's Department of Cultural Affairs to form an Artist Certification Committee composed of twenty people—mostly artists to be sure, but including others involved in the arts or housing. Only those applicants who could explain why their work "demands a lage space for its creation," to quote the application, could obtain a "variance" legally to reside in the A.I.R. buildings, initially in SoHo and later in a designated zone north of Houston Street, conveniently called NoHo. (Look on the street maps reprinted in Caroline Ware's 1934 sociological study *Greenwich Village, 1920–1930*, and you can see that all these areas east of West Broadway are off the map, to so speak.) As a member of the committee, Barowitz recalls, "While over the years many non-artists slipped through and were certified, the artist members of the Certification Committee knew many of the applicants. Potential 'cheaters' were exposed when labels peeled off slides revealed other names or dates or work did not agree with those printed on the slide mounts. Such discoveries must have been amusing. Also, while aesthetic considerations were not a factor in certification, knowledge of the field churned up the rank amateurs. When the committee was uncertain as to who was an artist and how the space was or might be used, we would often try to setup a studio visit. If no appointment could be made, then no Certification was issued. This often happened." Though the committee couldn't evict frauds and the city rarely did, "the banks became the enforcers by requiring certification affidavits for mortgage loans." So did the city's Department of Buildings by requiring documents whenever a landlord or co-op applied for a new or revised Certificate of Occupancy. Approximately 3,500 people received certification. No artists' colony in the United States was ever so populous, or even half as populous.

Once the New York City Landmark Preservation Commission declared the largest cast-iron gathering in the world to be an "Historic District" in 1973, nothing could be torn down or even altered without advance clearance by the tight-assed commission. One early threat was a proposal to build a twenty-story sports complex between Canal and Grand, Wooster and West Broadway, mostly in a parking lot that still remains empty. When the cobblestones on my street had to be

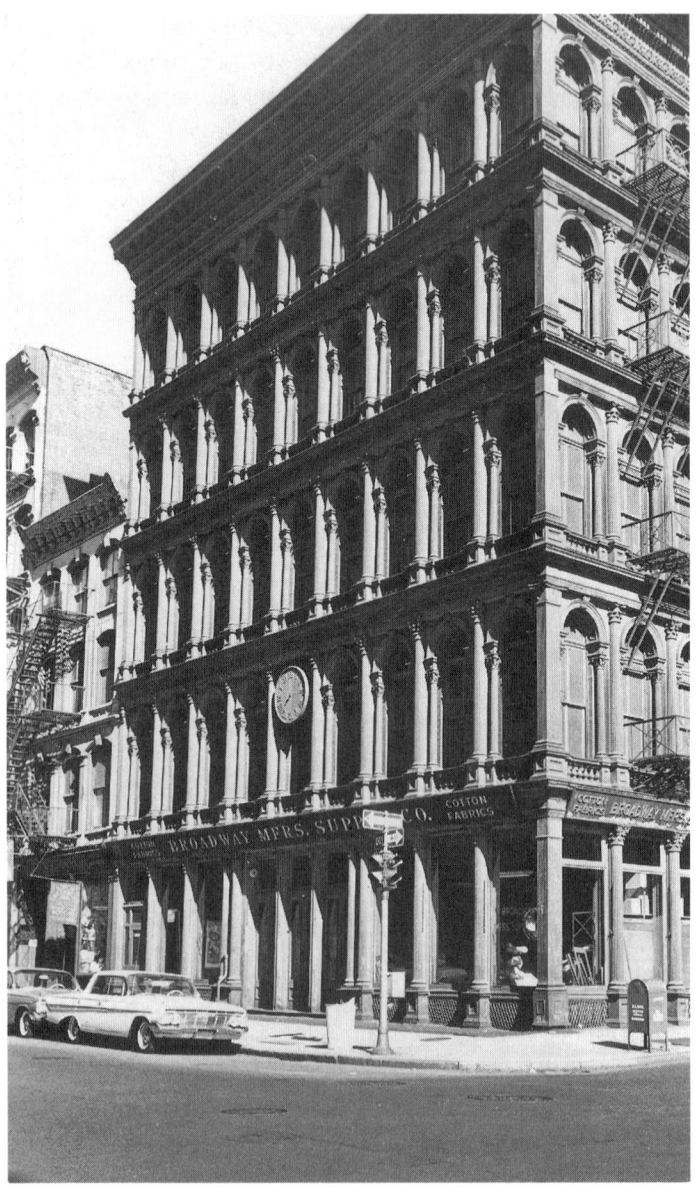

488 Broadway, Houghwout Building, cast-iron architecture and first building with Otis passenger elevator, September 1965. Copyright Fred W. McDarrah

replaced, only new cobblestones were acceptable, in contrast to the normal urban ideal of continuous paving; we witnessed the comedy of city street-construction workers trying to do a job for which they were not adequately prepared. After initially wanting the city to leave them alone, artists preemptorily learned how to get local politicians to support artists' aims.

By limiting SoHo's industrial buildings only to wholesalers or light manufacturers, who were scarce, and artists, who were more plentiful (while legally discouraging other potential residents), the city had made SoHo spaces artificially cheap, inadvertently creating the preconditions for an artists' colony whose setting was urban, not rural, with buildings that were renovated, rather than built from scratch. One element contributing to sophisticated taste for nine-teenth-century industrial buildings was a critical enthusiasm initiated by the Swiss historian Siegfried Giedion, the most influential writer on modern architecture, in his widely read *Space, Time and Architecture* (1941) and continued by Ada Louise Huxtable, among others, decades later. Only when nonartists wanted to live in SoHo, the restrictions forbidding them notwithstanding, did the prices rise, eventually astronomically. Few have noticed, then or now, that this model for contemporary "urban renewal," to recall a "planning" slo-gan popular at the time, cost New York City little beyond the exces-sive price of cobblestone replacement.

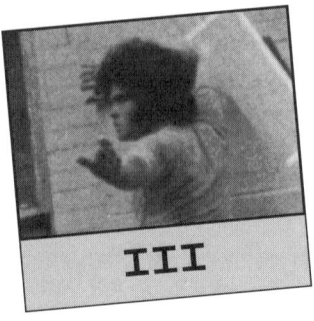

III

These 20 blocks between Canal and Houston ("how-ston") Streets, West Broadway and Broadway are a rich architectural resource, a high point in urban commercial architectural history. They are, largely, not to be noticed as individual monuments, but as parties to whole streets and blocks that, together, make the most glorious urban commercial groupings that New York has ever seen.

—Norval White and Elliot Willensky, *AIA Guide to New York City* (revised edition, 1978)

D URING THE 1960S, I began to visit SoHo more often. By 1968, the Performance Group, led by a professor new to New York University, had acquired a truck garage on lower Wooster Street, a block and a half north of Canal. In its cavernous space, the company staged, among other works, *Dionysus in '69* (1968), which I saw more than once, impressed not only with the performance but with the arena, which was not a sometime church or moviehouse, like many off-Broadway theaters, but a single-story building devoid not only of interior pillars but any stages as well. Though the Performing Garage (as it was called, and still is) lacked chairs, usually every night was sold out. The Dionysus performance typically concluded with the actors leading the audience out the front door into a neighborhood unfamiliar to most of us, concluding at a workingman's bar on the southeast corner of Broome Street and West Broadway. Looking north from this corner, up SoHo's widest street, one had a framed portrait of the Empire State Building. From the same corner looking south, one had a magnificent earthbound view of the World Trade Center.

By the early 1970s, I learned to visit SoHo art galleries. A painter friend invited me to conclude our gallery tour one Saturday at another workingman's tavern on the corner of Prince and Mercer Streets called Fanelli's that had photographs of boxers on its walls. Jonas Mekas opened the Film-Makers' Cinematheque in the ground floor of 80 Wooster Street, and the theater artist Richard Foreman, since more prominent, used this space for several weeks to present one of his plays. Around 1970, I remember observing a stream of men, usually in pairs, going down Wooster Street to the "GAA [Gay Activist Alliance] Firehouse" at number 99. Larry Qualls, later my co-op partner, remembered it later as the first gay dance hall and meeting place that was not connected to a university, a gangster-controlled tavern, or a church. In addition to offering dances, the Firehouse had, on its upper floor, offices and classrooms. Wherever artists went in America, homosexuals often followed, both desiring some distance, if only a few blocks, from the straight-laced world.

A few years before, I heard of George Maciunas, initially as the originator of an American artists' group called Fluxus. In addition, he was purchasing buildings that artists divided among themselves in a kind of cooperative venture. Some of those involved with Maciunas's first co-op, at 80 Wooster, which he typically called Fluxhouse Cooperative II, paid less then $10,000 for an entire floor of 4,000 square feet that, once renovated and securely occupied, would escalate in value over the years to $2 million or so. Half-floors went for less than $5,000. In retrospect, Maciunas became one of the crucial people who made artists' SoHo possible.

Another crucial figure was a commercial real estate agent named Jack Klein who persuaded the neighborhood landlords, burdened with empty loft spaces, to rent to artists. Two other major early movers were Paula Cooper and Ivan Karp. The former, a strikingly handsome woman then about thirty, established in 1968 a gallery in a second-floor space on Prince Street. Previously, she had managed an artists' cooperative gallery north of Houston Street. Karp, a frustrated novelist who had previously worked with the prominent art dealer Leo

Castelli at the latter's gallery in the 1970s on the Upper East Side, took the more audacious step of putting his O.K. Harris gallery on the street level of West Broadway, which is the neighborhood's widest thoroughfare (wider than the others as the Sixth Avenue elevated train formerly ran above it). Soon afterward, Cooper opened a ground-floor space on the northern tip of Wooster Street (incidentally on the other side of the same SoHo block as the first O.K. Harris). Although working independently, Karp and Cooper together demonstrated that new art could not only be exhibited but, more crucially, be sold in this newly credible neighborhood. None of these developments—renting, purchasing, exhibiting, selling—would have been obvious in this neighborhood only a few years before; none. (Some historians credit Richard Feigen, essentially an Upper East Side art dealer, with opening the first SoHo gallery in 1968. What he did, in truth, was briefly open his SoHo warehouse to the public before closing it soon afterward.) Cooper and Karp, among others, also established for SoHo gallerists less formal styles of office attire than their uptown colleagues, who tended to dress like morticians.

If Houston Street was the northern boundary of the new neighborhood, Canal Street was its southern end, with its dense traffic moving in and out of the Holland Tunnel (and New Jersey). Canal Street also had a wealth of retailers with the lowest prices in town for, say, stationery, motors, plastic displays, used office furniture, art supplies, and so on. West Broadway and Lafayette Street were both natural boundaries on the west and east, respectively, because in each case the neighborhood on the other side of it was predominantly residential with an abundance of small apartments. One factor initially making SoHo safe at night, even to women walking alone in the evening, was its location between Little Italy to the east and a mostly Italian-American turf to the west, as New York street thugs customarily avoid neighborhoods whose streets are carefully watched. Once safe, it never became unsafe. Indeed, for reasons never entirely clear to me, women friends told me in the 1970s that the street harassment they might suffer in midtown, say, rarely if ever happened in SoHo. On the other hand, cars left on the street overnight, again taking advantage of industrial parking hours, were frequently broken into, I think because the absence of doormen, along with the paucity of residents, meant that few were watching the streets at, say, 3 A.M.

As industrial buildings didn't have doorbells, an upstairs artist often installed a bell near the front door and ran a wire directly into his loft. However, since the resident lacked an electrical connection to open the floor door, he or she had to run downstairs to open the building's front door or, more conveniently, throw a key customarily inserted in a thick sock. Then he and his guest had to decide whether they wanted to be responsible for the elevator. Those residents lacking a front doorbell told prospective visitors to shout from the street. If not heard, they were advised to go to the nearest pay telephone to alert their host. The hazards seemed implicitly designed to scare off those who didn't belong in SoHo, such as building inspectors, process servers, and, needless to say perhaps, an artist's parents.

Most of the buildings had manually operated, oversized freight elevators manned only during working hours. The elevator operators tended to be martinets in their own cabs. Davidson Gigliotti remembers that in the late 1960s, "Our [daytime] elevator-man was a guy named Morris who, with his World War II buddy Max, who ran the coffee stand on Mercer Street, was heavily involved in the selling of various goods from broken boxes that had fallen off the back of trucks that frequented the area. His war cry, 'Cock ya moon,' could be heard at least two dozen times a day." Some of these elevators had modest motors activated by moving a handle across a kind of bell-shaped fixture within the cab. Others, more delicately balanced, depended upon pulling on a vertical rope that passed through the cab to an array of levers. In both cases, only those inside the elevator could make it move. For after-hours, the residents necessarily agreed that whoever last used the elevator to get to his or her floor would be responsible for answering the next bell, taking the elevator to whichever floor demanded it. The person on that latter floor would then first take the previous user back to his or her former floor before proceeding to his destination. People waiting downstairs would necessarily wait on the street, often anxiously, as in the memoir of visiting the poet Oscar Williams quoted before, while the building's occupants moved the slow elevator about. Once the freight elevator was returned to the ground floor, especially at night, individual responsibility ended. If someone came home late at night, he or she simply climbed the stairs. What seemed a huge nuisance to outsiders was acceptable to young residents of such buildings. Some of these freight elevators opened directly onto the street, without even a lobby in between, better to facilitate working heavy stuff into the industrial building. Even now, I'm still surprised by an elevator that lacks any lobby. Once a building with an archaic elevator was co-oped, one of the first major expenses was installing an "automatic" cab that could be summoned to a floor by pressing a button on the floor. In buildings lacking elevators, the stairways were invariably rickety, their steps uneven in height and not parallel to each other, which is to say slanted, often to bothersome degrees.

Picking not only furniture but art materials off the street was a neighborhood game. Once I moved to SoHo, I found many of my bookcases on Friday evenings, which has been the designated time for putting out larger trash in my neighborhoods. Almost every evening I could find skids to keep certain furniture off the floors and tubes varying in length and thickness for mailing posters and other large-format papers. The theater artist Terry O'Reilly mentions seeing a film projector lying on the street with a card attached reading, "It works," to make sure an artist would get it before the trashmen.

Dumpsters along the sidewalks, which were necessary for interior renovation, were also rich sources for materials that could be turned to artistic uses. "Picking over the discards from [SoHo] businesses became a regular nocturnal activity for those living in SoHo," writes James R. Hudson. "There even developed a certain etiquette governing the process of pawing through the discards. The first rule was not to approach any trash containers while someone else was selecting objects. It was also *de rigueur* to put the trash back into the containers when one had finished making choices." Well into the 1970s the streets of SoHo were filled with piles of industrial stuff: wood, metal, rubber, textiles, construction material, and whatever—the sorts of stuff that sloppy truckers leave behind. Even into the 1980s, there was a classic workman's Puerto Rican bodega on the northwest corner of Prince and West Broadway. Not for uptown culturati was this sort of venue.

Gigliotti also recalls how Fanelli's became a central part of the early SoHo social scene. Originally it "was a beer and a shot bar, if you take my meaning. A guy, small and well-built, who I think unloaded trucks in the neighborhood, came in and looked neither to the right nor to the left. He made eye-contact only with the bartender, and the bartender immediately set out a shot glass and filled it to the brim with whisky. He then drew a short beer and set it down next to the shot glass. The guy picked up the shot glass, looked at it just for a second, and tossed it down. He then passed his hand across his nose, sniffed, picked up the beer and took it in three chugs, set the glass down, and walked out of the place, again looking neither to the left nor the right. He didn't pay either, as far as I could see."

One turning point in the development of Artists' SoHo came in the wake of the Joe Frazier–Mohammed Ali fight of March 8, 1971, which could be seen only at the fight itself or over closed-circuit TV. As the Videofreex, a local artistic collective, were hired to provide a backup video projector at a local movie theater, one of them surreptitiously recorded the entire fight on early videotape. "So we asked Mike Fanelli," Gigliotti recalls, "if he thought it would be a good idea if we set up a big monitor behind the bar just before lunch, and played the videotape of a fight that most would be seeing for the first time. Mike, being quick on the uptake, didn't think about it too long. Well, you couldn't get into Fanelli's from 11 A.M. to at least 5 in the afternoon. They had to send out for an emergency beer delivery. Our money was no good at all in Fanelli's for about two weeks. We enjoyed our lunchtime pasta e fagioli and salad for free. Fanelli's had become an artists' bar at last." It remained so as long as Mike Fanelli lived, hospitable into his nineties. Once sold to a new owner in the mid-1980s, Fanelli's became what I would call, for lack of a better epithet, a yuppie bar where well-dressed young people visibly came alone and sometimes departed together.

Because most of SoHo was zoned to "protect" (favor) light manufacturing, artists preferring to sleep where they also worked were forced to resort to subterfuges. I saw with my own eyes lavatories with showers but no bathtubs; kitchens with electric hot plates but no gas stoves. Beds were folded away. To alleviate such residential inconveniences, the city in the mid-1970s began, as noted before, requiring artists needing space to obtain variances to live legally in the lofts where they also worked. Visual artists were encouraged to apply, along with playwrights and composers, on the grounds that they too needed extra living/working space. Literary writers, such as myself, mostly could not qualify. Fortunately, I did visual art as well as designing books. When my own application was questioned, as it was, I could offer slides along with a history of exhibitions, earning official permission. When fellow writers came to visit, admiring all the interior space for my bookshelves, "No, no," I would need to reply. "Look at my pictures above them." Only in 1985 was my cover blown, when my apartment was featured on the front page of the Thursday Home section of the daily *New York Times* under the heading, "Living with Too Many Books." As no mention was made of my visual art, I feared that my variance might be revoked. Fortunately, it wasn't, perhaps because few of my SoHo neighbors read the *Times* or any other uptown papers.

Large open spaces were conducive to populous parties, especially in the wake of something requiring celebration, such as an art opening or a birthday, and I remember going to many of them in the 1960s and 1970s, entering a space with attractively high ceilings, an absence of partitions, and usually an unadorned mattress on which I would lay my coat. I thought about living in SoHo in the late 1960s, but most of the lofts I visited were too chilly in the wintertime, especially on weekends, when a commercial landlord wasn't required to provide heat, reminding me of Henry Miller's nightmare in Beauford Delaney's studio. Many of these SoHo lofts were also too noisy, not only because of trucking on the streets but also because only tin sheeting beneath a single piece of wood separated one floor from another. One friend with large windows told me about the trucking garage across the street whose drivers gathered at 4 A.M. every morning and exchanged profanities for a half-hour before commencing their weekday rounds. These inconveniences were not for me.

People living near a thriving bakery smelled every night too much sweet-tooth stimulus. Their neighbor Lucy Lippard wrote at the time a description of her typical day, "12 P.M.–3 A.M.: Wake several

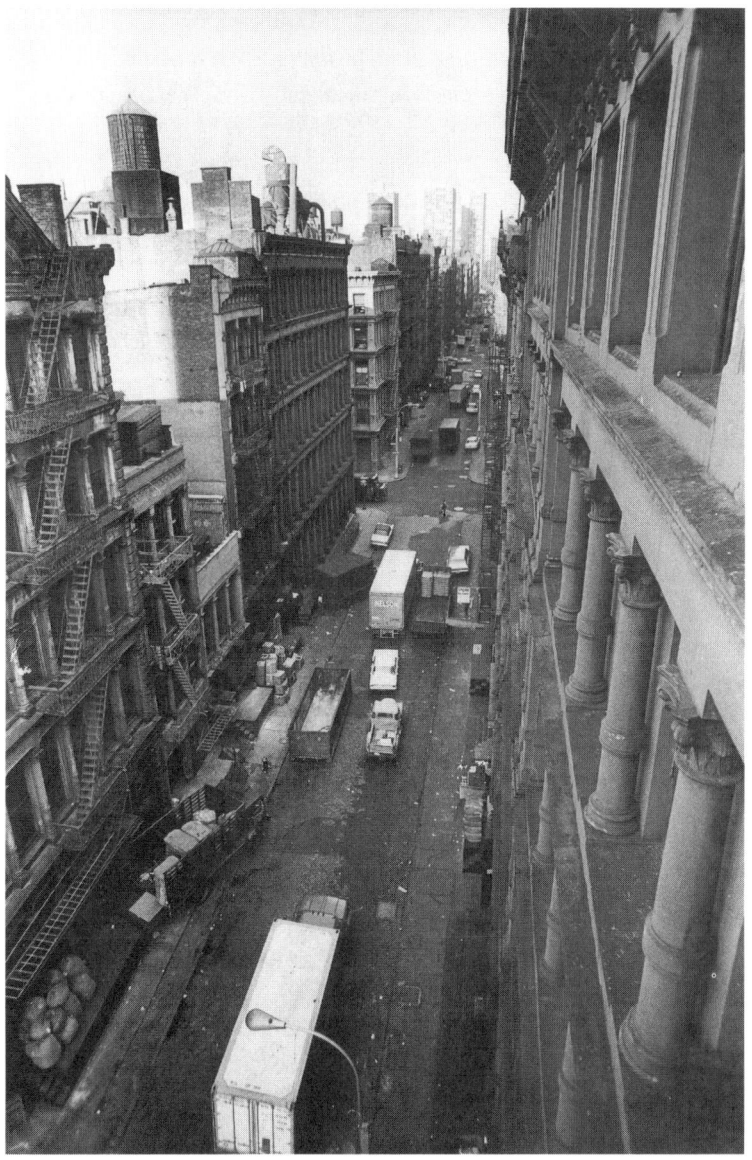

Looking north on Greene Street, clogged with trucks and factory debris, October 1974. Copyright Fred W. McDarrah

times to tune of screeching wheels, sirens, calls on the street. The
bakery workers who load pies all night holler to each other at the
gleeful top of their lungs, crashing metal carts into each other. At
three comes the garbage truck, louder and louder." To avoid interruptions from the street like these when I moved to SoHo, I put my bedroom in the back of my loft, overlooking an alley.

I didn't at first like ceilings higher than usual, sometimes as often
as 14 feet high, compared to 8 feet in a normal apartment. I didn't
like exposing my interior to windows so large that a row of them literally filled an entire wall (except for the vertical casings between
them), incidentally making the earlier suburban ideal of a "picture
window" seem rather modest. Those who preferred living on two or
more floors, as in a brownstone, dividing functions within a house by
ceilings, resisted the idea of living and working on a single level, often
in an open space separated only by partitions that cut off sight but not
sound. (Eventually, I came to like 11-foot ceilings and to feel that
standard 8-foot ceilings were claustrophobic, especially with many
other people in the same room; but I never did like either immense
windows or stairs.) People unaccustomed to noise and physical incon-
venience were scared away from SoHo; the persistence of industrial
trash on the streets was, along with irregular sidewalks meeting metal
plates extending out from the buildings' edges (covering the vaults
extending out from the basements), severely cracked pavement, and
garish graffiti on the walls, also discouraging to most while implicitly
comforting to some. Streets clogged with traffic didn't reassure either.
A guidebook published in 1978, the year before costs escalated pre-
cipitously, estimated that 8,000 people resided in SoHo: 5,000 of
them were artists (and the rest were thus lovers, spouses, and sometimes children).

In one crucial respect, SoHo resembled European cities such as
Berlin, where I lived in the early 1980s, in that its streets were named
in clusters reflecting a similar origin. Thus, Goethestrasse was near
Schillerstrasse, as well as other streets named after nineteenth-century
German writers. Likewise, Kantstrasse crossed Leibnitzstrasse, both
named after other German philosophers. SoHo was one of the few
New York City places whose streets were named on a similar princi-

ple, in this case American generals from the Revolutionary War: Lafayette, Crosby, Greene, Wooster, along with Thompson, Sullivan, and MacDougal, whose names grace streets to the west of SoHo. The current exception, West Broadway, was originally named Laurens Street after Henry Laurens (1724–1792), a president of the Continental Congress. Any sophisticated Berliner could have told him that a street named after General David Wooster (1711–1777) must be near one name after the Marquis de Lafayette (1757–1834). (The names of SoHo's cross streets have other origins.)

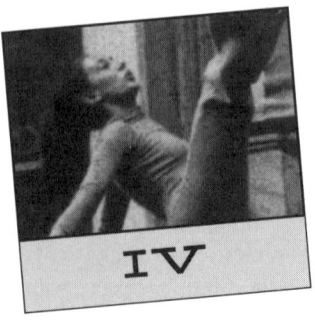

IV

Yes, it is a SoHo heresy: Space, open space, is the whole
thing: the reason people suffer the broken boilers and pour
vast amounts of money into leaky roofs and rotting lintels;
the reason to put up with the tourists who displace locals in
the old neighborhood haunts. Space. And the atmosphere
created by people who needed it to work and who rescued a
neighborhood only to find that they're beginning to need
even more space to breathe.

—Ellen Bilgore, "SoHo," *Town & Country*
(September 1977)

O NLY WHEN I discovered a building whose floors were
concrete, and whose spaces were both quiet and warm
around the clock, did I relocate to SoHo from the East Village. In
1974, Amy Taubin, then an actress, more recently a film critic, whom
I'd known since high school, told me about a co-op into which she
had just moved. On Wooster Street, just south of Houston Street, it
housed factories that were closing. George Maciunas had purchased
the entire building under the witty corporate title of the Good Deal
Realty Corp. The space they had in mind for me, the back portion of
a former jewelry factory, was used by Richard Foreman earlier that
year for one of his theatrical productions, leaving behind good karma.
Another positive factor was close proximity to various subways, in
contrast, say, to the far East Village or certain sections of Brooklyn,
which requires a hefty hike or a bus ride to the nearest subway
station. As this loft had smaller windows that looked out not upon a

street but a West Broadway garage roof, mine cost less than others in
the building. After purchasing 1,850 square feet for roughly $6.00 per
square foot, I spent nearly as much on a renovation of this fairly "raw
space." My design included several partitions that ran from floor to
ceiling, creating spaces behind closed doors that would elsewhere be
called "rooms." The monthly maintenance was $160 per month,
which was slightly less than I'd been paying for rent in the East
Village. By the beginning of October, just three months after I
purchased and commissioned a renovation, a new love and I had
moved in. Immediately above us was a pajama factory that stayed for
several years, its Sephardic owners employing an Italian-American
foreman and Portuguese immigrant seamstresses; on the top floor was
a manufacturer of living-room drapes. On the sixth floor was a hat
factory that, along with the drapesmen, soon moved out.

   Behind the creation of Artists' SoHo were several unique factors.
The first, noted before, was the availability of empty commercial/
industrial space that was comparatively cheap initially because
nobody else wanted it and then because the city forbade nonartists
from moving in. Some artists purchased or rented more than they
needed, sometimes dividing their space to get an adjacent space that
would be rented or sublet. A few purchased as much as 10,000 square
feet entirely for themselves; Nancy Graves for one, reportedly divided
her block-long single-floor into sculpture for one area, painting for a
second, filmmaking for a third, and a personal residence for yet a
fourth. The second factor was the relaxation of restrictive building
codes, thus permitting people to reside in buildings that lacked the
legal prerequisite of a Certificate of Occupancy. (Such leniency continues to this day in SoHo and is perhaps an underacknowledged pre-
condition for all urban renewal by individuals anywhere.) A third fact
behind the creation of Artists' SoHo was that nearly all people living
there were artists and artist-lovers. In this "gentrification," unlike too
many others, no prior residents were displaced, although factories
were closed when their leases expired (and workers presumably laid
off). A fourth factor was the arrival of galleries exhibiting art, which
meant that fortunate artists could not only live and work but also sell
in the same neighborhood. (When a dealer wanted to send a prospec-

tive collector to the artist's studio, the walk was short.) Next came the development of performance spaces, not for dance and music but for mixed-media theater. Watering holes were hospitable for artists to meet and exchange intelligence into the night, after the more remunerative evening customers went home. SoHo became a one-industry town embedded in a larger city, and that industry was the production of contemporary art.

One cultural ritual was the Saturday afternoon stroll. Since the remaining factories were largely shut for the weekend, the streets on Saturdays were free of the trucks that would otherwise clog its sidewalks. People serious about art—collectors, curators, professors, itinerant lecturers, artists, art-lovers, artist-lovers—would walk among the galleries and in the course of greeting friends would incidentally recommend current shows to one another, sometimes even giving new work its initial definition, not to mention meaning and value. Since such advice constituted word-of-mouth merchandising at its truest, reputations could be established on Saturday afternoons, especially for artists exhibiting for the first time, all without the intervention of advertisers or reviewers. The SoHo art strollers were tough, to be sure, especially on an artist whose work wasn't as good as it used to be; but critical discriminations shared among them were honest.

By the late 1970s, you could distinguish between galleries contributing to SoHo and those exploiting its growing reputation with those who didn't live here. The latter were open not only on Saturdays but also on Sundays to attract people who came in cars that they would safely leave on streets whose "no parking" signs were restricted to the industrial hours of 8 A.M. to 6 P.M. weekdays. Already we SoHo natives dubbed these people the "B&T crowd," slighting that fact that, unlike us, they had to go through a bridge or a tunnel to get to SoHo. Since B&T people could also find parking spaces in the evening, new restaurants began in 1975 to attract not natives but interlopers. The first one noticed by me was a Chinese eatery with the witty moniker Oh-Ho-So. Many others have come since, such as the world-class Chanterelle (which has since moved into Tribeca, perhaps for a privacy no longer available in SoHo). I never ate at either, because, not unlike other SoHo veterans (and inveterate counter-

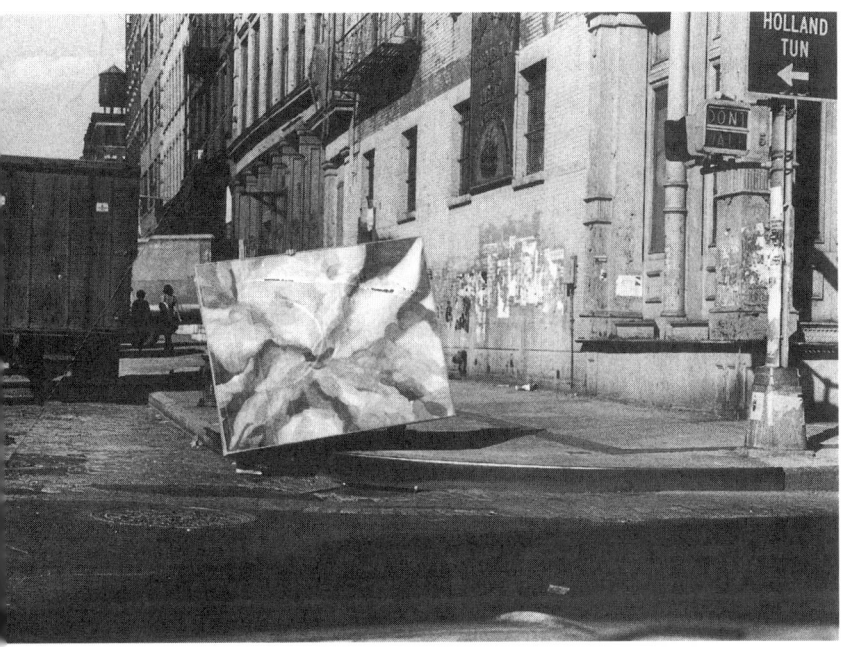

Artist walking his or her painting across West Broadway at Broome Street, April 1974. Copyright Fred W. McDarrah

snobs), I preferred then as now to go to Chinatown or Little Italy for dinner.

When I first moved to SoHo, I could convince my mother, living a few blocks north of Houston Street, that my new neighborhood with its trucks and trash-filled streets was too dangerous for her. Believing me, she never knocked on my door, thankfully. What she didn't notice was that from the time I got here the neighborhood began increasingly to resemble the Greenwich Village where she lived to the north. The first sign of change in my memory was the arrival of a gourmet food store called Dean & DeLuca, which succeeded a modest sandwich shop initially around the corner from me. Somewhat resembling a physically smaller emporium named Balducci's well north of Houston, D&D attracted limousines that would be parked on the streets just outside, their chauffeurs keeping their motors running—"standing," it is called—to evade the 8–to-6 "no parking" signs while waiting for owners who apparently wouldn't dare enter the neighborhood on foot. (The busier streets around Balducci's lacked such standing opportunities.) Dean & DeLuca inspired the most ecstactic description in *SoHo: The Essential Guide to Art and Life in Lower Manhattan* (1979):

> A tour of the shop begins with a collection of flowering plants in clay pots—including poppies, columbine, and orchids—at the right as one enters. Heaping baskets of fruit and vegetables stand before the two cash registers. Along the right-hand wall the lustrous wire shelf system carries stocks of imported tinned sweets, cornichones, mustards, olive oils and dried spices. The rear of the store houses a selection of cookware selected by Joel Dean that has something even the most well-stocked kitchen craves: cookie cutters, Vollrath collanders, tan English mixing bowls, Henkel knives, every kind of glassware for cooking and dining, Pyrex, stainless steel and aluminum pots and pans. There are also cookie jars, jams, jellies, and a glass-fronted refrigerator packed with butters, yogurts, spring waters, Italian fruit drinks, exotic brands of beer and ordinary milk.

It goes on. Need I quote more to demonstrate how impressive Dean & DeLuca seemed at that time; perhaps in a much larger location nearby, some 10,000 square feet, it still is, to some.

When limos began to appear parked outside stores other than the galleries, I began to think that the principal product of SoHo might not be art but something else—the accoutrements of conspicuous high-class taste, not only in food but eventually in clothing and furniture.

Our SoHo co-op was similar to others in most respects but different in others. Like many neighbors, we earned a tax abatement, called a J-51, for economically enhancing a blighted neighborhood, as indeed we did. Like others, we initially lacked the Certificate of Occupancy that is required in New York City before a newly constructed space, even a renovation, can be occupied. Only in 1977 did we fulfill all the picayune requirements necessary to make our residency fully legal. Although this alchemical paper didn't change our living conditions one whit, it was theoretically advantageous whenever we wanted to sell our lofts, which none of us did, at least not for several years. Another SoHo veteran remembered, "All the occupants of the lofts in our building met with a 'fixer.' The 'fixer' introduced himself by showing us a page from the Village Voice listing the 100 most evil men in New York City.' His picture and name were among them. 'That should tell you that I am the man who can help you,' he assured us. It did! We pungled up $4,000.00 and in a short time, we had the C of O. At the time we believed that the city hall was so corrupt that only by using a 'fixer' could we get the C of O." Perhaps my co-op hired a "fixer" as well, though my co-op partners didn't tell me, as I would have been opposed to doing so (and what I didn't know wouldn't hurt me, they might have thought). Indeed, I opposed getting the C of O at all, on the grounds we didn't need one, only to be overrruled. (Perhaps ashamed of themselves, my partners haven't told me since if indeed a "fixer" had been retained.) Some SoHo co-ops still haven't obtained a C of O, it should be noted; yet, no one has been evicted. Indeed, had we been held to the letter of the law—had evictions from otherwise habitable space occurred or had we been forbidden to occupy reno-vated spaces—the urban renewal represented by Artists' SoHo, to repeat, probably wouldn't have happened at all.

With perhaps a dozen partners, all of whom served on the board of directors, we managed ourselves for the initial decade. Then we hired a painter renting here to act as a kind of superintendent, collecting rents, handling minor repairs, and paying bills. When he moved out, we then hired someone not living here but incidentally familiar with the building as an employee of one of the partners. Finally, in the late 1990s, we hired a management company based only a few blocks away. Maciunas's original financial concept was that the co-op would own the ground floor whose rental income would contribute to defraying the communal operational expenses of taxes, insurance, maintenance of common spaces, and the elevator. That structure was a good idea, discarded when we sold our ground floor to pay off a second mortgage, to our misfortune. In another co-op nearby, likewise founded by Maciunas, the partners still pay only a negligible monthly maintenance because the ground-floor stores provide sufficient rental income to pay off all the monthly expenses including interest on the co-op's loan for the entire building.

Whereas most SoHo buildings were commonly identified by their most famous occupant, ours wasn't, as we had several lesser celebrities, one of whom might be more prominent with one or another constituency, none of whom were generally celebrated. Artistic differences among us were never an issue of dispute, though one is an abstract painter, another prefers to paint scenes of her Kansas youth, two are playwrights, one is a filmmaker who became a film critic, two are architects, and one is a literary media artist (me). As most of us were single (actually divorced), we became a kind of family contractually tied to each other, much as a nuclear family is, but in our case through our shares in the same corporation. We were at the end of the 1970s one of perhaps 120 SoHo co-ops. By 2003, as I was relocating, most of the dozen or so pre-1985 partners remained. Only one of the divorcés remarried. Two partners had children in the 1990s. Nearly three decades into our life together, only one partner no longer lives among us, though he continues to rent the space purchased long ago. Another recently purchased a space on a higher floor in our building. Every one of us is a paper millionaire, at least for the value of our lofts, even if our incomes remain negligible. Rather than continue to do office work, one of my partners arranged with her alma mater to receive a reasonable monthly annuity in exchange for donating her principal property in her will. Classier than most, her alma mater also gave her work the largest retrospective it ever had.

One reason why SoHo resembled a college campus is that most of the people residing here belonged to a single community. We shopped in the same few stores and regularly exchanged intelligence about local merchants. Faces seen day after day, year after year, became familiar, even if their names were unknown. Paula Cooper, whose final SoHo gallery was down the street from my home, once at a gathering elsewhere in the 1990s asked someone to identify a face (mine) that she had seen for years but not connected to a name. Because members of a SoHo co-op knew each other in ways that renters in an apartment building did not, SoHo was no more hospitable to secret romances than suburbia, say. If someone sexually credible were seen entering your building more than twice in a week, your immediate neighbors would wonder who she or he was visiting.

Indeed, they might ask the stranger directly if paths crossed in the lobby or the elevator. Because everyone knew about one another, if not one another, people across the street might ask questions as well. If the new frequent visitor was also the local equivalent of a BMOC (Big Man or Woman on Campus) or even a smaller MOC, rumors would be generated. Although marriages broke up, I'm not aware of any wife-swapping of the sort more typical in the suburbs, though I can think of someone who left a co-op with his wife only to return a dozen years later as the companion of another partner in his old co-op. Nor do I know of the SoHo equivalents of Elaine de Kooning and Lee Krasner who, according to Harold Rosenberg, disseminated a new abstract expressionist esthetic by moving from artist lover to artist lover during the 1940s, though comparable carriers might have func-tioned similarly but below the community's radar, a generally more permissive sexual atmosphere notwithstanding. In discouraging secret sex, SoHo resembled a small town more than an urban neighborhood with apartment houses. Conversely, co-op members also knew which neighbors never had guests. (The only partner avoided by us all had been involved in surreptitious consulting while briefly serving as our president.) Those of us who were unattached preferred to date within the community, much as only a few years before we preferred to date classmates within a residential college campus. Only when neighbor-hood options expired did we look elsewhere. When a fire in the spring of 1975 decimated the telephone exchange servicing SoHo north of Prince Street (my turf), disrupting calls for more than a few weeks, I needed only to go out on the street each Saturday afternoon to see my neighbors and get perhaps half my messages for the week.

Most of the people moving here in the late 1960s and 1970s were in their late twenties and early thirties at the time. They already knew enough about New York to understand why a kind of residence gener-ally unavailable elsewhere—an open loft—was residentially feasible. They arrived because, like myself, they knew someone else who had preceded them in making the transition from residing in an apart-ment. Believe me, it wasn't as obvious at the time as it seems now. Though the presence of artists made SoHo loft living seem romantic, especially to publicists who lived elsewhere, lofts posed problems unknown in, say, residential apartment buildings or even brownstone duplexes. SoHo scared off people above a certain age—perhaps fifty in the 1960s, sixty in the 1970s. I remember when the prominent Swiss playwright Max Frisch moved into SoHo in the late 1970s, when he was approaching seventy. Lord knows what happened to him, but I noticed at the time that he didn't stay long. Even now, the only octogenarians residing here are artists who came long ago and overcame the mostly physical obstacles that would have defeated them had they arrived anew at a late age. For instance, we still haven't figured out a graceful way to handle garbage, which is customarily put out on the sidewalk on certain nights. (The design of most new apartment houses, by contrast, includes a place to hide trash.) Cars parked on the street overnight are still vulnerable to break-ins, while the neighborhood still lacks a garage or even a parking lot with attendants who stay overnight.

While restricting occupancy to people like us initially seemed advantageous to us co-opers—keeping out nonartists—it turned out to be disadvantageous, implicitly disqualifying purchase of our spaces by people who could pay a bit more. Somewhere in the 1990s, the city housing authorities implicitly forgot about this restriction, thankfully enabling me, among others, to sell my principal asset (by far) to the highest bidder without any fear of disqualification.

By the mid-1970s, in a real estate market generally remembered as depressed, lofts in other sections of Manhattan were being renovated, with new apartments open to nonartists as well as artists: areas south of Canal Street and west of Broadway previously called Washington Market and later rechristened "Tribeca"; the flat-iron district around Fifth Avenue and 23rd Street; and between University Place and Broadway between 13th Street and 10th Street, among other places. The urban sociologist Sharon Zukin estimated that by the early 1980s perhaps 50,000 people resided (and sometimes worked) in renovated lofts. Even later, loft buildings in yet other areas would be renovated: the West Side in the 1950s, the farthest western precincts of Greenwich Village, West Harlem, and Willamsburg and Dumbo in Brooklyn, and so forth.

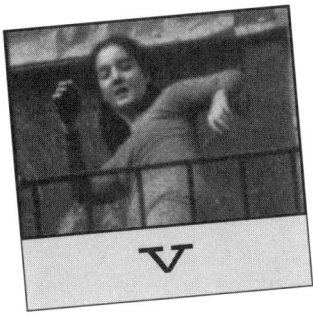

V

Although the creation of a single work of art may be an individual effort, artists have often clustered together to share ideas, offer mutual support, and provide a sympathetic audience for one another. The dynamics of rapid change in artistic styles over the past forty years have required that artists who want to remain current with the latest developments in art be close to the important galleries as well as accessible to others working in their particular field.

—James R. Hudson, *The Unanticipated City* (1987)

W HAT I EXPERIENCED in SoHo was a cultural hothouse unlike anything anywhere else or any community before in American life. I'd already known about "artist colonies," to be sure, but this was an urban oasis created by hundreds of artists, if not more, acting independently. Most knew only a few others already in SoHo before settling there themselves. Eventually most of us got to know everyone in our buildings as well as many neighbors, as SoHo came to feel more like a residential university campus than a typical urban neighborhood. Most of us worked most of the time at our art(s) and never needed to explain to our neighbors that nothing should get in the way of our art-working.

As an artists' colony, SoHo became an educational arena where people were inadvertently teaching one another all the time. Living there, at least at the beginning, was an educational experience, simply from going to openings, walking through galleries, and listening to my neighbors talk. In my observation, visual artists more than poets or composers, say, need a professional social center to learn what cannot be taught in art academies or learned from journalism about art. That accounts for why visual artists rarely acknowledge teachers in their professional biographies, in contrast, say, to poets and especially composers, who nearly always do. Painters and sculptors need to exchange esthetic intelligence and see important new works at first hand, at least at crucial points in their creative lives. For the same reason that, say, Diego Rivera needed to go to Paris before World War I prior to returning to his native Mexico, so ambitious artists from around the world made their way to SoHo in the 1970s. Painters and sculptors teaching in provincial colleges often rented SoHo lofts for the summertime, New York's notoriously humid heat notwithstanding, simply to assimilate what could not be learned back home. (Conversely, aspiring artists who don't participate in this kind of art-center educational experience will forever reveal in their art, as well as their talk about art, an absence of esthetic moxie. Simply, they didn't learn what surely not to do.) As a de facto anarchist community, the university that was SoHo had no hierarchy, no tests, and no degrees; it had scant connection as well with the accredited university (NYU) just on the other side of Houston Street.

Another sign of SoHo's de facto anarchy was the fact that no one planned that it become an artists' enclave. City officials certainly didn't. Nor did any arts institution or artists' conglomerate. Nor did the galleries or major real estate developers. This urban frontier became an art town thanks, I repeat, to the initiative of thousands of independent individuals, seizing a unique opportunity, some of them settling in outright violation of city law, as self-defined anarchists are predisposed to do, often against the advice of their lawyers. (I subsequently met more than one aspiring artist whose lawyers advised against purchasing in an area illegal for living. "You could lose everything," they advised at the time, looking dumber and dumber in the years since. As artistic aspirations were more likely to enervate outside SoHo, more than once I later thanked my lawyer father's junior partner, a few years younger than I and then married to a painter, for approving a purchase that might have frightened a more conservative counselor.) Though artists forged alliances within the community, no one was ever dubbed the "mayor of SoHo," at least not for more than a minute for someone's amusement. Though artists are frequently described as predisposed to rabid radicalism, especially by conservative polemicists with fanciful imaginations, most of my neighbors were registered Democrats, not unlike most other New Yorkers, especially if they owned real estate through their co-ops.

Subtly perhaps, SoHo represented the culture of the 1960s without its radical politics. Everyone qualifying for an artist's variance could live in its co-ops regardless of age, race, gender, political affiliation, sexual orientation, ethnicity, or any other category of discrimination popular in the larger world. No one would have proposed any blanket exclusions, in part because they knew damn well they would be unacceptable. (Nor was "affirmative action" necessary). Women owned nearly as often as men, and they renovated by themselves as well. In my own co-op, from the beginning at least one-third of the partners have been divorced, unattached women. Approximately one-third of the residents are gay. Why African American artists were so few in SoHo remains a mystery to me. Though some landlords with spaces to rent might have discouraged African Americans or Asians, the distinguished visual artist Romare Bearden (1914–1989) lived at 357 Canal Street from 1956 until his death three decades later. However, he was barely visible in Artists' SoHo, because from the mid-1960s he kept his working studio in Long Island City and exhibited uptown. A legendary jazzman kept his loft in an early SoHo co-op through the 1970s even though he refused to pay his monthly maintenance, claiming that he had already paid enough money to purchase his space. Eventually, his co-op partners lost patience with subsidizing his share of current expenses and, after a court battle, took over his property.

Early in the history of my co-op, say around 1975, we had to fill out some form that asked for our annual income. I recall noticing at the time that everyone had independently written $10,000. Even though some might have earned more, he or she didn't want to invite unnecessary envy. Cooperation counted more among us than competition, at least at Good Deal Realty, in part because loft space was plentiful, at least until the late 1970s, and artists were pleased to dis-

cover in SoHo an agreeable alternative to the tradition of their isolation and alienation in America. Many of my neighbors were indeed
scraping by financially (and have continued scraping to this day).
When artist couples split, it was not uncommon for them to divide in
half their principal asset, their SoHo loft, one living on one side of a
new wall that went to the ceiling and the other on the other side.
Their kids, if they had any, would simply run down the hall to fulfill
their legal obligations. (And when one divorcé moved elsewhere, the
adjacent space was sometimes sold to the ex-spouse.) Indicatively,
only one of my co-op partners, the least active artist, had the aca-
demic-bourgeois amenity of a country house until the late 1990s,
when a second partner purchased one. My own sense is that, in the
hidden history of New York City, the subsequent boom in Manhattan
and then Brooklyn real estate from the 1980s to the present originated
in Artists' Soho in 1979; but since the development wasn't planned by
any prominent agency, no publicity-making entity could claim credit
for turning the market for New York City real estate around.

As years passed, the principal division within SoHo itself, and
within individual co-ops, was between the old residents and the newer
people, especially after 1979–1980, when prices escalated precipi-
tously. On my north-south street, co-ops between Prince and Houston
were established by artists between 1970 and 1976. Those on the west
side of the next block, between Spring and Prince, were established
by a commercial developer a few years afterward, costing at least three
times as much per square foot than we paid, if not more. To this day,
I don't know anybody living in those buildings and have never been
to a party there. Who lives there, you ask me, more than twenty years
later? I don't know, I reply. New people, I guess.

Within co-ops, this division between veterans and newcomers
played out in persistent conflicts, as the latter often purchased their
spaces from original residents who moved elsewhere or who smartly
purchased more than one space when the co-op began. Inevitably
wealthier, the newcomers paid more, often much more, for their
properties and were thus more predisposed to advocate expensive renovations, such as burnishing the lobby or replacing the hand-operated
freight elevator with a spiffy automatic passenger elevator more typical

of uptown apartment houses. We once heard a proposal to hire a doorman. (No, no, no, us oldtimers felt; anything but that.)

Indeed, I remember thinking, in visiting certain artists' buildings for the first time, that a sleek new elevator indicated that newcomers must dominate this co-op, unlike mine, which always had an old, slow passenger elevator in addition to a larger decrepit one for freight. Instead, one of our newer people, an architect by profession, persuaded us to commission him to renovate a lobby that for years looked grossly unfinished. (I opposed this proposal but lost to the majority. The new lobby, all austerely gray, reminded one guest of a prison, where he had actually spent some time.) In a co-op dominated by newcomers, a friend pays more than twice as much monthly maintenance than I for an equivalent amount of space.

Few streets in New York, let alone the world, separate one culture from another as deeply as Houston Street between West Broadway on the west and Broadway on the east. On the north side is New York University; on the south side is SoHo. Both are cultural institutions: one formal, the other informal. On the north side are fairly tall apartment houses with doormen; university classrooms and research laboratories; a mammoth library; an athletic complex, all with security men at their doors. On the south side are none of those amenities, as the nineteenth-century buildings of an industrial slum were transformed into artist's lofts in the late 1960s, art galleries in the 1970s through the 1990s, and then spacious stores for expensive merchandise beginning in the 1980s. The two worlds have become so different that no one deposited anywhere on one side of Houston Street could possibly mistake it for the other.

Culturally, they are different as well, rarely intersecting, as professors were in life as in culture slow to follow artists. Margaret Smith-Burke, an NYU professor of educational psychology, bought into our co-op in 1975 with her husband, the visual artist Michael Burke, and stayed after he left. Annette Michelson, a professor of film, rented here in 1976; her colleague in film history, Robert Sklar, bought elsewhere in SoHo a year later. However, both of them belonged to the NYU arts college called Tisch. SoHo had less appeal to professors in the college of arts and sciences. (Two New School urban sociologists moved here in 1977—Arthur Vidich and Stanford Lyman.)

The only NYU faculty other than Richard Schechner, discussed later, ever to have a presence in SoHo art was Michael Kirby (1931–1997), likewise a professor of performance studies and Schechner's successor in editing the periodical *TDR*. The author of the pioneering book *Happenings* (1965), Kirby mounted a series of more modest productions, mostly in undefined SoHo spaces, that explored alternative structures in the articulation of speech. I attended several. Predisposed to Kirby, anthologizing him more than once, I always wanted his plays to be stronger than they were.

At the end of 2001, I met for the first time Professor Perry Meisel who has taught English literature at NYU for nearly as many years as I've lived in SoHo, who likewise spent his high school years in a Westchester suburb, whose writings I've read for many years as he has read mine; but he was a professor residing on the other side of Houston Street. Though we have lived only 100 yards apart—the length of a regulation football field—we'd never met before; and as we talked over dinner, we realized that we scarcely knew in common anyone who might have introduced us. Indicatively, the circumstance bringing us together was a sort of cross-cultural event: a Cornell professor's lecture in a SoHo gallery.

Although NYU was forever purchasing real estate to the east and west of its Washington Square campus, sometimes evicting entrenched tenants, it didn't expand to the south, probably because SoHo's zoning for light manufacturing or its designation as an historic district posed problems for NYU real estate development, such as NYU's preference for replacing existing buildings with larger ones. Though NYU hosted a party for the book *Greenwich Village: Culture and Counterculture* (1993, ed. Rick Beard and Leslie Cohen Berlowitz) to celebrate its proximity, SoHo, nearly as close, NYU scarcely noticed. The cultural difference between the two adjacent neighborhoods perhaps explains why SoHo remained oblivious to certain recent academic fashions, such as political correctness or the inordinate attentiveness paid by some to people above themselves in a hierarchy as distinct from those below. Blindness toward its south perhaps accounts for why SoHo celebrities, notwithstanding their cultural credibility, were not recruited for its faculty.

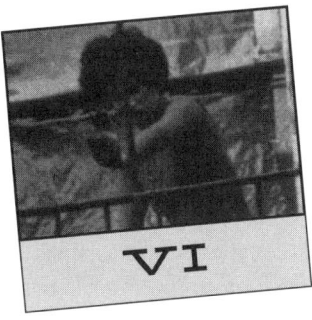

VI

Once these were called "Hell's Hundred Acres" because of the many fires in overcrowded, untended warehouses filled with flammables. Now given over in large part to artists' (and would-be artists') studios and housing, the once-empty streets and buildings are a lively, urbane place, much tended and loved, and hence no longer a potential lonely inferno.

—Norval White and Elliot Willensky, *AIA Guide to New York City* (revised edition, 1978)

OF THE INDIVIDUALS who primarily established artists' SoHo, I knew best George Maciunas, an oddly charismatic figure— oddly I say, because his slight and underdressed physical presence along with his eccentric mannerisms were more disaffecting than reassuring, even to other artists. Born Jurgis Maciunas in Lithuania in 1931, he came to the United States after World War II, studied architecture at Cooper Union and Carnegie Institute of Technology, graduating from the latter in 1954. Returning to New York, he spent several years working toward a doctorate in art history at NYU's Institute of Fine Arts, by common consent the most prestigious graduate school in the field. He worked in commercial design and product development before establishing in 1961 not only an uptown art gallery, A.G. Gallery, whose life was short, but an art group that he named Fluxus. He also changed his first name from Jurgis to George after the board of directors of the Lithuanian Society of New York denied him use of their auditorium for rehearsals. When he returned again to New York in 1963 from Fluxus activities in Europe, George rented a rickety loft on Canal Street and later an apartment in a residential building on the east side (or SoHo side) of West Broadway. In 1967, at 80 Wooster Street, in a building purchased from the Miller Paper Company that had occupied it for thirty-five years before, he established Fluxhouse Cooperative II.

Maciunas spoke emphatically, if not loudly, with an indefinite foreign accent, typically confusing verb tenses and dropping his articles ("the," "an," etc.), much as Russians audibly do when speaking English. He was forever writing letters on his IBM compositor that, because it could do proportional spacing in the age of typewriters, looked like professionally printed communications. When I purchased space from him, my girlfriend, herself born abroad, thought him "an eternal immigrant." Nonetheless, he made things happen that wouldn't otherwise occur because he knew how to make otherwise skeptical people accept his leadership, first with Fluxus that he formed, split apart, and later kept alive in the art world's memory. The second achievement, likewise depending upon his genuine charisma, was SoHo housing cooperatives that he not only sponsored and organized but also renovated for individual purchasers' needs. In the mid-1970s, SoHo dinner-table conversation could be wholly devoted to stories of his audacious activities, even though few would ever think of inviting him into their homes.

In September 1967, the month after he established at 80 Wooster Street the Fluxhouse Cooperative II, he solicited deposits for shares in three buildings at Grand and Wooster Streets at price ranging from $2,200 to $5,000, or roughly $1.00 a square foot. Once he had the $50,000 necessary for a down payment on the real estate, he went to contract, as is said in New York City, which means that he paid a deposit, customarily 10 percent of the final price, that gave him the exclusive option on purchasing the building at a predetermined sum within a certain amount of days, which was generally several months. (The risk was that, if he failed to deliver the remaining money due, he would lose his deposit.) Maciunas customarily persuaded the departing owner to take a "purchase mortage," as it was called, for a good deal of the final price. As Charles R. Simpson recalls, "Maciunas moved from

FLUXHOUSES were formed in 1966 as cooperatives consisting solely of artists, film-makers, musicians, dancers, designers, etc. seeking adequate combined work and living space. Its aim is to purchase, renovate and maintain suitable buildings for artist occupancy. A comprehensive survey led FLUXHOUSE to select the area of Manhattan between Houston and Canal as most suitable because of economy, structural soundness of buildings located there and accessibility from them to subway transportation. 8 buildings have already been purchased, grouped in 3 cooperatives and renovation work commenced or nearing completion. The buildings already purchased are at: 80 Wooster street (also housing *Film-Makers' Cinematheque*), 16-18 Greene st. (which will house various cooperative workshops, dark-rooms, studios, food distribution center and a theatre to be called *18 Greene street precinct*; 64-70 Grand and 33 Wooster st. and 131 Prince st. Buildings may be formed into independent cooperative corporations or grouped with an existing cooperative. Each member becomes a shareholder with shares proportional to the square footage he owns. Since Fluxhouse Cooperatives are not receiving any assistance from any foundations or government agencies, members must purchase buildings with own money and finance own renovation costs. All buildings to be purchased will have the ground floor owned by all members of the cooperative and leased for profit, thereby reducing for all the monthly carrying charges. This scheme requires members to put up cash of about $2 per square foot to purchase the building with a monthly charge of about 3 cents per sq. ft. per month to carry mortgage interest, amortization, realty tax, insurance premiums, heating and elevator maintenance. Cash payment for the purchase of the building also includes legal fees, organizational commission, brokerage or finders fees (if any). Not included are: renovation costs (extent of which is determined by the members), architectural fees which are determined from cost of renovation), further legal fees, (residence permits, proprietary leases etc.). Renovation costs amount to the following: 2x4 stud partition with 5/8" gypsum board, both sides - 30 cents per sq. ft. without labor, 60 c. with labor; electric system within floor (conduits, fixtures, outlets, switches) about 15 cents per sq. ft.; new plumbing system (brass water pipes, bathroom fixtures and kitchen sink) $1000 per bathroom; carpentry and ceramic tile work - $300 to $500 per bathroom, tile alone - $1.30 per sq. ft. labor & mtls. Labor costs: unskilled (demolition, hauling etc.) $1.50 per hour; skilled (carpentry, masonry, minor electrical etc.) $2.50 to $3.00 per hour.
All these buildings are located in M1-5 (manufacturing) zone and prior to its legal use for residences and studios, it will be necessary to obtain appropriate permits either (1) by ammendment of sec. 276 of N.Y.State Multiple Dwelling Law, or (2) by reclassification of artists residence-studio by the City Zoning Commission, or (3) by obtaining zoning variances from the Board of Standards & Appeals.

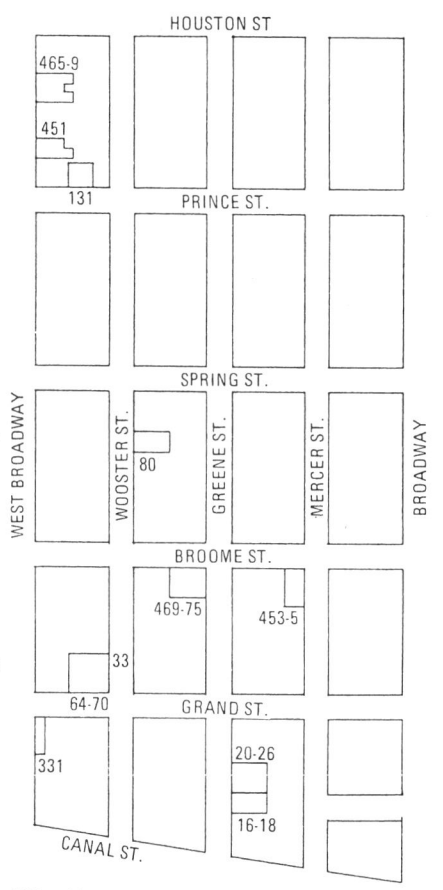

All inquiries should be directed to GEORGE MACIUNAS 349 West Broadway, apt.11, tel: 925-0274, president of Fluxhouse Cooperative, Inc., who is performing all organizational work: forming cooperatives, purchasing buildings, obtaining mortgages, legal and architectural services, conducting work as general contractor for all renovation and building management (if so desired by the members). Checks should be made out to: Fluxhouse Cooperative, Inc. Meetings and tours of buildings for prospective members start weekly at 80 Wooster st. ground floor, every Thursday 3 P.M. Buildings can be also visited by appointment. This bulletin is not an offer. Inquiries will be accepted.

Fluxhouse Cooperatives informational leaflet, circa 1967, designed and written by George Maciunas. Courtesy of the Gilbert and Lila Silverman Collection, Detroit

block to block throughout SoHo, tracking down owners who were closing their businesses and anxious to sell their buildings. His method was to hold buildings with deposits, then to line up shareholders to provide the down payments. Maciunas balanced his increasingly complex financial arrangements with a continuous flow of new cash deposits. By June of 1968, he had sponsored cooperatives on Prince Street, Broome Street, and along West Broadway, a total of eleven cooperative units involving seventeen buildings." This was no small achivement for an immigrant operating without assistance or family money, while also conducting an art career.

Disrespectful of legalities, Maciunas took money collected from one co-op to support the development of another—"comingling" this legal infraction is called. As a result, his lesser partners sometimes discovered suddenly that their money had gone elsewhere—not into Maciunas's pocket, to be sure, but into some other building's account. "When a particular cooperative is in danger of losing a building to foreclosure or lien," he explained in one of his periodic Fluxhouse newsletters, "every effort—all the funds, go to the rescue." Failing to register his co-ops appropriately with the New York State attorney general, he was enjoined from dealing in real estate around 1969. He nonetheless persisted, using other artists as his up-front partners. Because of a warrant out for his arrest, he didn't leave his basement apartment until 5 P.M., after the city sheriffs with their limited sense of human activity went home, as he gleefully boasted. Once arrested outside his basement apartment, he asked to pick up some sundries, rapidly closing his door behind the sheriffs (who no doubt expected to collect a bounty) and then escaping as they smashed through his apartment door. He later installed a floor-to-ceiling pipe immediately behind the door and bolted to the door perpendicularly protuberant blades (that, because they couldn't be feasibly removed, remain to this day, covered over with a protective board). He also built a tunnel leading to the upper floor of the building. One of his original partners in Fluxhouse II, Charles Ross, recalls Maciunas chasing away a city building inspector with a samurai sword. When Susan Inglett's Wooster Street gallery mounted an exhibition on Maciunas's real estate endeavors in 1999, the announcement reprinted a summons from the New York State attorney general to testify "in regard to matters relating to practices of Good Deal Reality Corp.," which is to say our co-op.

Seriously thrifty, Maciunas would purchase large quantities of whatever happened to be on sale in the local grocery and store it. He would make periodic shopping trips to lower Manhattan surplus stores, particularly favoring one named Job Lot. From a local baker, Maciunas purchased not one but two large batter mixers, each several feet in diameter, using one as his personal bathtub, parking the other outside directly on Wooster Street chained to a tree until he could sell it (or it was taken away—I can't remember which). Earlier this tree and its companion were rescued by Maciunas from the sidewalk of a nearby parking lot and planted in violation of New York City law. Jonas Mekas remembers that when some city officials demanded that the trees be removed, Mekas, on Maciunas's instruction, told them, "No, George is not going to do it. He says you have to do it. And he wants me to take some pictures when you do it." Dissuaded, they went away, never to return again, though they did not know that Maciunas, ever ingenious, used the trees to cover his tap into the Con Edison electricity lines buried under the street. Indeed, the trees still standing perhaps 30 feet high outside 80 Wooster Street have become nature's measure of how long SoHo has been a residential community.

Scholarly as well, Maciunas would read encyclopedias and thick books about architecture. He knew enough New York architectural history to tell the historian James R. Hudson that New York City artists inhabited midtown lofts during World War II. In the early 1970s, Maciunas called himself a Communist of the Soviet persuasion, in contrast to the Maoism more fashionable then, scarcely recognizing that a few of his neighbors—artists, not poltical radicals, after all—cared nothing about the distinction. At signage he was especially witty. On the wall outside his basement apartment was a supergraphic of large sans-serif letters reading repeatedly in a geometric array: "Nosmo/king." In the basement lavatory for his workers were three piles of paper: "For your face, not your hands or your ass"; "For your hands, not your face or your ass"; etc. Just as he was skilled at organizing co-ops, he was also a master at organizing others into artistic activities—performances, editions, exploratory walks. Whatever he did was

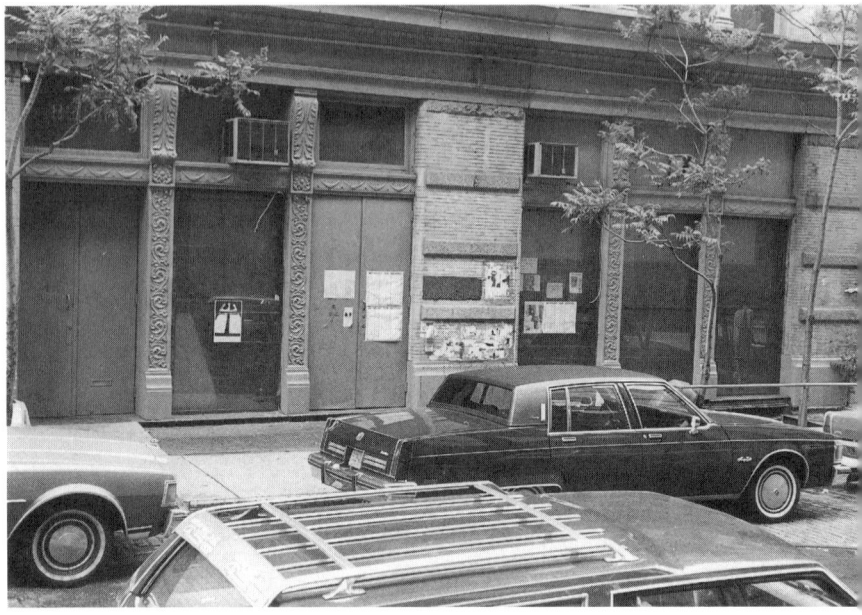

Trees planted in front of 80 Wooster, home of George Maciunas's first co-op and the Film-Makers' Cinematheque. Photo by Robert Haller, 1981, courtesy of Anthology Film Archives

unforgettable. Only later did we discover that he liked to dress himself in women's clothing. When he decided to marry, to the surprise of everyone who knew him, he and his bride cross-dressed for the ceremony. Soon afterward, he died young from cancer of the pancreas (itself caused by taking too much cortisone for his chronic asthma). Disaffecting though he surely was, many missed him (and still do).

Because the IRS instituted a minor judgment against Maciunas and he had no more respect for federal officials than state ones, he refused to open a bank account that would be vulnerable to government confiscation, instead doing business mostly with third-party checks and cash. To our co-op around 1979, he extended a second mortgage of $135,000 with a pile of monetary notes gathered from various sources. (Anne Tardos documented this impressive show on videotape.) He wittily named his mortgage company Carp's Corpse

Corp. I heard, back in 1975, that he had purchased a corporate papers kit in the name of our Wooster Street building, but used that corporation to purchase a Broadway building that had suddenly become available (and thus had a corporate moniker named for another address), rather than spend something like $125 to purchase another corporate kit for them. That accounted for why our co-op had the unforgettable generic name of Good Deal Realty.

Maciunas offered incomparable bargains, reducing the prices of loft spaces for those artists he liked or who were, like myself, recommended by those he liked. His charges for renovations could not be beat. When the Film-Makers' Cinematheque solicited bids to construct a theater in the building where he also lived, he quoted $40,000 against the next bid of a sum for more than twice as much. The bargain was meant to be a favor to the Cinematheque founding director, his friend (and fellow Lithuanian immigrant) Jonas Mekas. The initial charge for renovating my empty space in 1974 was $7,000.

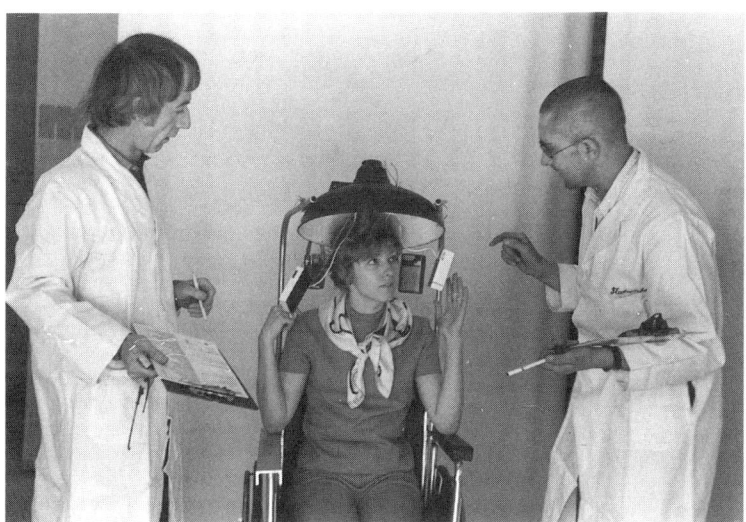

George Maciunas (r) with Robert Watts (l) performing a FluxClinic experiment on Jane Barret (c), part of Hi Red Center Hotel Event, at the Waldorf Astoria, June 11, 1966. Copyright Fred W. McDarrah

Soliciting a competitive bid, I got this reply, "He can't charge so little; that's the price of the materials. He's cheating somewhere." He wasn't cheating as much as working frugally, employing as construction workers foreigners who lacked American working permits; young black men recruited mostly in Washington Square, whom he allowed to camp out at nights in spaces undergoing renovation; and a crew of young lesbians, all paid, as I recall, at the puny rate of $3.00 an hour. When Maciunas in 1974 declared to me that he had "five men working on your place," no enlightened soul at the time of early feminism could complain that those industrious girls weren't exactly men. Nonetheless, he invariably underestimated real costs, creating needless problems not only for his customers but also for himself.

Plumbing he assigned to Yoshimasa Wada, a musician who came to use broad pipes as his performing instrument of choice. Wada's assistants in 1974 included young Rhys Chatham, a New Yorker who has since become a prominent avant-garde musician working mostly in Europe. (Philip Glass also did a lot of plumbing for SoHo renovations through the 1970s.) His Communist politics notwithstanding, Maciunas had no use for unions or for licensed tradesmen, getting some of the latter to sign for plumbing or whatever done by his unlicensed laborers.

What were his motives in dispensing such bargains? My sense at the time was that as a contractor for renovations (and as an artist) he wanted people to remember him. Offering bargains and yet withholding on promises became an eccentric immigrant's way of feeling himself popular. As he customarily left work somewhat unfinished, you would need to call him and beg him to get it done. If you offended him, he would postpone completion, threatening to ignore it forever. Richard Foreman warned me in advance that working with Maciunas was a kind of a perverse spiritual test. Some were cheated, no doubt; others sued him, sometimes taking possession of his shares in a co-op, when he refused adequately to defend himself against their appropriation. However, because his prices were so low to begin with, few in the end lost money on his promises.

What I could never understand is where his money went. For my own building, which was among his last SoHo ventures, he paid a

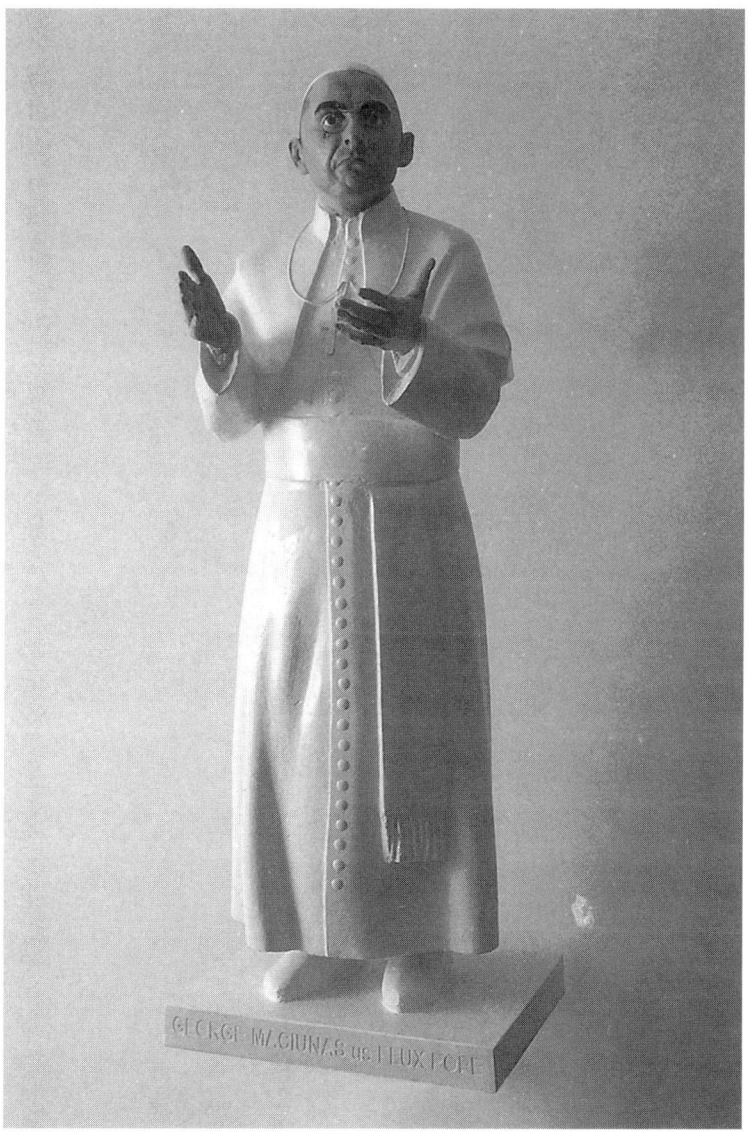

Flux Pope George Maciunas, 2000, height 1000 mm, at Ciurlionis Museum in
Kaunas, Lithuania. By Redas Diržys, Kęsrtutis Grigaliūnas, Arūnas Kulikauskas.
Photo courtesy of Arūnas Kulikauskas

certain amount along with partners to purchase spaces that became his share. He sold those spaces for sums well in excess of what he paid. Nonetheless, when he died in 1978, there was no money. My old friend Donald Porter, a partner in an early Maciunas co-op, swears that he once saw ledger books in Maciunas's hands. Because these were never recovered (and he couldn't take them with him when he died), where did they go?

Maciunas also made remarkable art, usually in small editions; so that in the traveling Fluxus show initiated by the Walker Art Center in Minneapolis before it came to New York's Whitney Museum, his pieces were the strongest. My own favorites are his elaborate charts of art history. Lacking customers for his marvelous productions, he also gave a loft purchaser at the time, a genuine fan of his art, Fluxus objects and publications that she later sold to a dealer who sold them in turn to a museum in France. As I said, no one in SoHo really lost money from dealing with George Maciunas. Once he died, no one replaced him in organizing so many artists' co-ops.

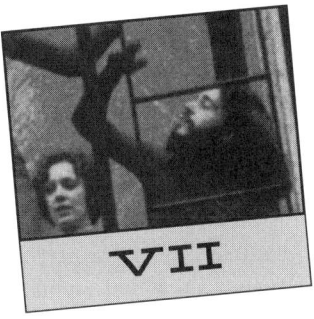

VII

Other magazines fought in the same cause, but the [Saturday Evening] Post was persistent and powerful enough to be regarded as chief of the aggressor nations. It published stories about the Villagers, editorial and articles against them, grave or flippant serials dealing with their customs in a mood of disparagement or alarm, humorous pieces done to order by its staff writers, cartoons in which the Villagers were depicted as long-haired men and short-haired women with ridiculous horn-rimmed spectacles—in all, a long campaign of invective.

—Malcolm Cowley, *Exile's Return* (1951)

I F EARLIER AMERICAN bohemias were portrayed as rebelling against bourgeois America, the denizens of early SoHo were likewise differentiating themselves culturally, if not so pointedly. The key word in defining their culture was "downtown," which was meant to distinguish the SoHo world from "uptown," which was everything north of Houston Street to some or 14th Street or 23rd Street to others. From big things to small, downtown was different. Even certain words were used differently downtown. Early on, Stephen Koch noticed that when a SoHo artist spoke of "work," he meant his art. A "job" is what he or she did for money, usually uptown, if not farther elsewhere. "How is your work going?" was for many years a cordial greeting, referring exclusively to one's art. It was also a blanket invitation to someone else to educate me, not only about themselves but art in general. As a single gent, I learned early not to date uptown "professional" women who would invariably boast about their money, much of it wasted profligately, avoiding them out of a fear of acquiring contagious bad habits I couldn't afford (although other artists succumb to them, to their regret).

Even today, many SoHo artists survive on incomes below every measure of "poverty"—a condition that no other SoHo veteran holds against them. A Columbia University informal survey made in the mid-1990s discovered that many SoHo residents had annual incomes scarcely above the official poverty level. Sometime in the mid-1980s a SoHo artist was invited to an expensive midtown restaurant by an uptown professor who liked, shall we say, to cruise SoHo on Saturdays. When they finished eating, the professor said that he expected the artist to share the extravagant bill. So offended was the artist that he excused himself to the lavatory and then exited directly to the street, leaving the professor behind to pay the entire check and then later warning his downtown colleagues about this professor's insensitivities. I don't recall this uptowner ever appearing in SoHo again; he must have eventually known he did something egregiously wrong. Whatever artists lack in wealth and power they compensate with pride, often to the surprise of people who measure only in wealth and power. To us, people disrespectful of financial limitations are, in a single word, boorish.

Downtown culture didn't regard itself as at war with uptown as much as blissfully unaware of it. When I first moved to SoHo, one thing I noticed was how few of my neighbors read the *New York Times* or any other newspaper for that matter, not because they disliked it or disputed its persistently obtuse art reviewers (until Roberta Smith) but because they felt it wasn't necessary for their culture. And indeed it wasn't meant for them, aimed instead at uptown readers and suburbanites. Veteran SoHo gallerists and other cultural producers felt their shows neglected, they thought because they failed to advertise in its pages. Some can still remember their efforts to get Hilton Kramer, then the *Times*'s chief arts critic, to come downtown. In *The Art Dealers* (1986), the successful gallery owner Ivan Karp attributed this neglect to the reluctance of SoHo exhibitors to take ads in the *Times*, a negative bias in the arts coverage thus duplicating a pattern noted by me in examining the *Times Book Review* in the early 1970s, when publishers received attention proportionate to their advertising.

Indicatively, book reviews weren't read either, beholden as they are to the purveyors of commecial culture. As newsstands around SoHo were always scarce and forever closing down, SoHoites needed to hike several blocks to get a newspaper. Morning delivery could be problematic, given the absence of doormen. As the neighborhood lacked a bookstore carrying bestsellers until Rizzoli established a shop on West Broadway for B&T folk in the 1980s (since closed), books of that sort were rarely found on SoHo shelves or coffee tables.

Reviews in art magazines were rarely read, mostly because they usually appeared after the exhibition closed and were likewise aimed not for us but at readers outside New York. (Actually, if university courses in art history were a parade not of real pictures but slide reproductions, courses in contemporary art were based again not on work seen at first hand but on articles in art magazines.) People serious about art customarily trusted the recommendations of one another over those from reviewers they didn't personally know. That's what colleagues are for, we'd think, although a few bad tips could jeopardize a friendship. (This is true in any one-industry town situated apart from the visible media.) SoHo artists patronized the uptown art museums but rarely the uptown galleries; the opera sometimes but rarely the Broadway theater. I doubt if many set foot in the 92nd Street Y, whose large auditorium has forever seemed a publicity platform for uptown promotions. Discriminations both negative and positive, even if unconscious, inevitably reflected serious taste.

The epithet "downtown" identified distinctly alternative styles not only in visual art but also in theater, performance art, dance, and even literary writing. Downtown dance was not only less slick but more collaborative, for instance, epitomized by a group calling itself the Grand Union, which had a changing membership over its history, in contrast to the more formal, hierarchical companies favored by uptown choreographers. (Oddly, Merce Cunningham, so important an esthetic influence on downtown dance, ran his professional life in an uptown way.) SoHo theater artists, beginning with the Performance Group and Richard Foreman, tended to build their own theaters within spaces whose uses were previously industrial, installing seats in various alternative configurations with their stages on the same level as the seats, rather than petitioning uptown producers and directors to appear in their proscenium theaters, or even renting a space with a raised stage. (Similarly, in the late 1960s the downtown composers Phillip Glass and Steve Reich formed their own instrumental groups to perform their own music, rather than courting independent musicians.) These SoHo spaces came in sizes odd for theatrical presentations, either too square or too skinny. Creating a theater from scratch was the equivalent of self-publishing in literature, with individuals who had sufficient respect for their work taking initiative, instead of waiting patiently (if not eternally) for the authorities to approve. Inhabiting a different country, the denizens of SoHo didn't play cultural games by uptown rules, declaring independence by simply living where they did.

One of the few direct downtown challenges to uptown icons was a biannual series of artist-organized exhibitions occurring in the springs of 1977, 1979, and 1981, directly in response to the Whitney Biennial, a survey of recent activity that has always had a dubious reputation, continue though it still does. The Whitney Counterweight, as it was wittily called, was a series of group exhibitions and performances in the smaller SoHo galleries located mostly on Grand Street, rather than on the West Broadway of Leo Castelli and O.K. Harris. The organizers published a "catalog" that was really a gathering of pages contributed by the participants. The catalog for the third exhibition has the subtitle "the cutting edge," which was an early use of an epithet that became popular in downtown artists' critical conversation for the next decades. The immediate historical model for the Counterweight was a 1951 exhibition at 60 East 9th Street, in which ninty local artists selected work of their own to be displayed for three weeks, most of them carrying their contributions on their own shoulders from their studios nearby. Bruce Altschuler recalls in his book *The Avant-Garde in Exhibition* (1994) that when Alfred Barr, the director of MoMA, "came down to the opening of the Ninth Street Show with MoMA's chief curator Dorothy Miller, Barr was shocked that he knew so few of the artists. He asked Leo Castelli, who assisted with the show's organization [before he became a dealer], about all of those artists whose work he had never seen, and they retreated to the Cedar Street Tavern around the corner. There Castelli marked the back of a photograph with the names of the artists whose work was pictured." Altschuler continues: "It was a revelation to Barr, and to the uptown deadlers and collectors who made their way to East 9th Street that spring, just how large and accomplished the downtown art world had become." To make sure that the works were seen, the gallery stayed open past 9 P.M. A brief mention of the show appeared in the *New York Times* at the end of a longer notice of an Alfred Stieglitz show at MoMA, the reviewer acknowledging work of the more prominent artists, identified by names, as "interspersed in a highly democratic manner among those of the newcomers to the exhibition field." (Curiously, I was attending elementary school only a few blocks away at the time, but I missed this. So did classmates whom I still know.)

Underfunded at less than $1,000.00 and undercurated by "an artists' consensual process to arrive at the strongest immediately emerging work," to quote again from the third catalog, these SoHo Counterweights tended to be rich gatherings varying radically in style and quality. On second thought, the same judgment about unevenness could probably be made about the overcurated uptown Biennial. One difference between the two shows was the level of publicity. Whereas uptown media recognized the Whitney exhibitions, only downtown media noticed the Counterweights. The exception was Grace Glueck, who had regularly recognized SoHo in the *Times*'s art columns, not as an official critic, of course, but as a conscientious cultural reporter. In Elliott Barowitz's shrewd judgment, "While artist-initiated exhibitions were widespread in Europe and indeed in the U.S. early in the twentieth century, such exhibitions were frowned upon by the uptown dominated art establishments, even in the heyday of SoHo. Critics frequently said that downtown art was no good, though one wonders how they know since they were rarely there. The exceptions were Thomas Hess and Lawrence Alloway." It was not for nothing that even in the early 1980s the uptown culture guardians feared the challenge of downtown.

The Counterweight differed from the heavyweight in including musicians and poets along with visual artists. Among those participating were the cellist Fred Sherry, later to head the Chamber Orchestra of Lincoln Center; the poet Sharon Olds, later to become a prominent writing professor at New York University; and the video artist John Sanborn, later to be a senior executive at the Comedy Channel.

Counterweight opportunities could be unique. On the evening of Saturday February 14, 1981, I recruited spontaneously from the audience at a gallery on 96 Grand Street sixteen male performers to recite without rehearsal a theatrical text titled "Seductions," interweaving sixteen different narratives one line at a time. What made this performance particularly memorable to me even now is the fact that the text was never done again. Conceptually, the Counterweights also echoed the more recent example of the New York Musicians' Festival, which was a 1972 response to the exclusion of downtown loft jazz musicians from the Newport Jazz Festival that came to New York that year. The difference in effect was that in the following year the loft jazz musicians were incorporated into the Newport Festival. Whether the Whitney Biennials ever included any of the Counterweight participants is not clear to me. Remembering how marvelous the Counterweights' parties were, I wish they had continued, if only as expressions of the belief that downtown represented a radically alternative art world. Perhaps their death could be considered, in retrospect, an early sign of the demise of Artists' SoHo.

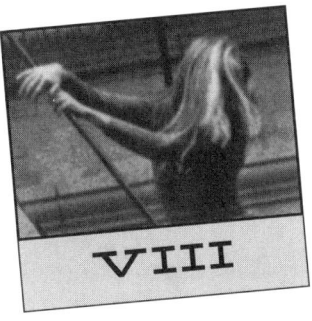

VIII

From all over the world, critics, artists, dealers, museum professionals, and art-interested people converge on this factory district in order to see the most innovative works of the day.

—Helene Zucker Seeman and Alanna Siegfried, *SoHo*
(1978)

SoHo GALLERIES WERE small and large, new and old. Some filled ground floor spaces, welcoming strangers off the street; others were upstairs, catering more exclusively to those who knew in advance where art was publicly exhibited. Some of the galleries were physically large enough to exhibit two or more artists at the same time. At the final location of Ivan Karp's O.K. Harris, which has nearly 11,000 square feet, the front of three rooms worked best with large sculptures; the second, proceeding into the interior, was appropriate for large paintings; the third space, more modest, was more appropriate for smaller art. Sometimes the work of yet a fourth artist would be mounted on the corridor walls. In the rear space, essentially offices (opening to Wooster Street), were displayed works by gallery artists not currently featured. I remember that when I first thought about exhibiting in SoHo, I realized that most of my artwork wasn't large enough physically to fill the spaces. That's one reason why I showed my art on neighborhood turf only in group shows.

The weightiest building of all, artwise, was 420 West Broadway, a former paper warehouse that ran back 200 feet to Thompson Street, with perhaps 10,000 square feet of space to a floor for exhibitions and

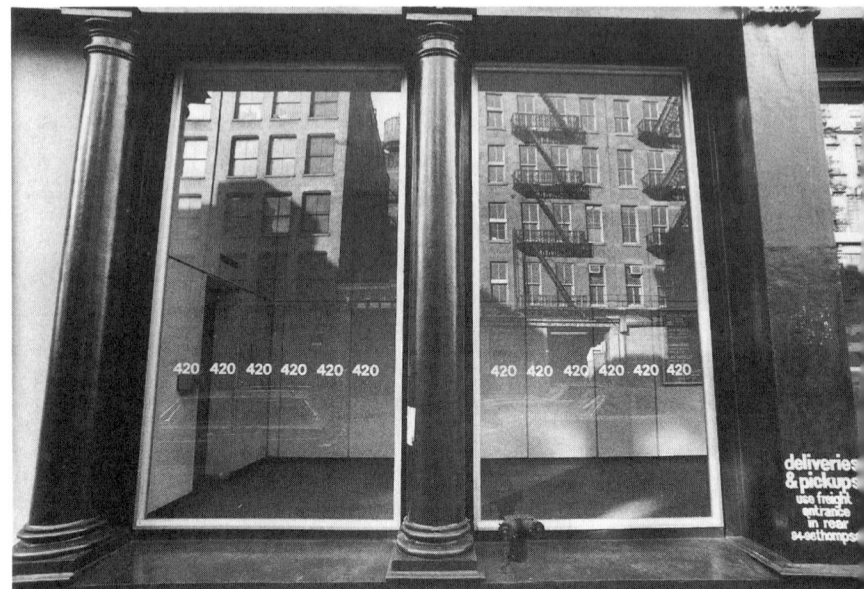

Front view of 420 West Broadway, former location of Castelli and Sonnabend
Galleries, April 1974, now all condos. Copyright Fred W. McDarrah

support offices. After 1972, on its second floor was Leo Castelli, who
had already established himself uptown, whose previous gallery was
the floor of an Upper East Side brownstone with only a fraction of the
square footage. Having represented James Rosenquist, whose work
approached outdoor billboards in size and scale, he knew he needed
a larger exhibition space for his artists. By the late 1970s, when he was
in his mid-seventies, Castelli was representing a multitude of stars:
Lee Bontecou, John Chamberlain, Hanne Darboven, Dan Flavin,
Jasper Johns, Donald Judd, Ellsworth Kelly, Roy Lichtenstein, Robert
Morris, Bruce Nauman, Kenneth Noland, Claes Oldenberg, Robert
Rasuchenberg, Edward Ruscha, Richard Serra, Frank Stella, Cy
Twombly, Andy Warhol, Lawrence Weiner, and Mia Westerlund. (No
other downtown gallery housed half, or even a quarter, as many mete-
ors.) On the third floor of 420, as we called it, was his ex-wife Ileana
Sonnabend, whose Romanian family's fortune had financed Castelli's

initial forays as an art middleman in post–World War II America. Though she had spent the previous decade as an art dealer in Paris, the opportunity presented by SoHo persuaded her to return, even renting a loft on Crosby Street where her favorite artists from outside New York often stayed and worked. For several years, another floor of 420 belonged to John Weber, a dealer predisposed to minimal art. When he moved to a smaller space at another address, the fourth floor was rented by the Canadian government to showcase Canadian artists, natch. Andre Emmerich, another uptown veteran, had for a while the top floor that was later rented to the gallerist Charles Cowles, previously the publisher of the periodical *Artforum*. Over a generation younger than Castelli and Sonnabend, Cowles actually resided in SoHo as well. The ground floor at 420 was divided into two exhibition spaces that had a succession of tenants, including in 1978, Mary Boone, a young woman whose career prospered initially across the street on West Broadway and later elsewhere.

420 West Broadway had such a strong presence that I can remember a provincial art gallery chief telling me of traveling exhibitions that came to his museum from New York. Considering his choices, I realized that all of these exhibitions originated from galleries within the same building. My image was that, once in SoHo, this backwoods artsman never left 420. Also, I can still remember two guys, dressed to suggest they didn't live in SoHo, with a guidebook in their hands, shaking their heads dubiously as they failed to connect the recommendation in its pages to art they apparently didn't understand. After the galleries left, around 2000, the former paper warehouse at 420 West Broadway became another luxury residential condominium whose elevator opened to the street, rather than an interior lobby, as before; for the latest renovation lacked any sign recalling the building's artistic distinction only a few years before.

Around 1975, galleries originating in Germany opened SoHo outlets: Heiner Friedrich from Munich, and René Block and Reinhard Onnasch, both from Berlin. That coup gave the new neighborhood credibility in the international art world, even though the last two soon closed their doors while Friedrich became a coconspirator in the Dia Foundation that was based on French-Texas money.

The German gallerists showed mostly artists they had already exhibited in Europe, including certain Americans who were then less recognized at home, such as Walter de Maria or Edward Kienholz. Among the most memorable shows was Joseph Beuys living with a rented coyote at René Block's for an entire week. "*I like America and America likes Me* (sometimes referred to as *Coyote*)," is remembered by Robert C. Morgan as beginning "at Kennedy airport where [Beuys] was wrapped in a felt blanket and put into an ambulance, then taken from the ambulance to the René Block Gallery, where he was carried inside on a stretcher and placed in an area partitioned from the rest of the gallery by a cyclone fence and containing a live coyote." I paid a visit to Block's upstairs space, as did many other curiosity-vultures. At the time, Ivan Karp, always quotable, told a magazine reporter, "Their own galleries in Germany usually are empty. They see crowds here so they assume there's lots of action. They don't know that my crowds are all students and artists, with an occasional bus excursion lost on its way back from the Secret Mysteries Temple in Chinatown."

By 1977 or so, it became clear that cheap space available in SoHo permitted a proliferation of retail art galleries, compared to 57th Street or the Upper East Side. Many of these were on the street level, again in contrast to those uptown that were mostly upstairs. The 1978 SoHo guidebook claimed that the neighborhood had 85 galleries with a new one opening every month (and older ones closing nearly as often, needless to say). They ranged in size from the mammoth emporia already acknowledged to 3 Mercer Street, a modest storefront just north of Canal Street, run by Stefan Eins, an Austrian whose specialty was "low-cost art—no painting, no sculpture, only found objects, performance and collage." From small to large these art retailers depended upon the fact that SoHo was zoned for industrial parking, which meant that only vehicles with commercial license plates could stand on the street weekdays between 8 A.M. and 6 P.M. Exemptions were necessarily made for limousines whose chauffeurs, mentioned before, stayed in their cars and kept their engines running. No one watching the street could miss the arrival of a well-heeled collector amid the delivery trucks. To honor the artists they were exhibiting, as well as attract a larger crowd, SoHo galleries had openings, customarily after 6 P.M., at which wine and sometimes small edibles would be served. The exhibiting artists could invite friends and relatives they wouldn't see otherwise. These gallerists' gifts to SoHo also became the occasions at which socializing artists renewed acquaintances and new friendships were sometimes made. If an artist friend wanted to meet, a future opening would be an appropriate venue. Then and there you could decide if you wanted to eat together afterward or see each other later. Going to several SoHo openings during a single evening was also an efficient way to do a lot of professional networking.

Some commercial galleries lasted longer than others; some were more successful at launching new artists than others. In the second respect, Ileana Sonnabend, for instance, was more consequential than her ex-husband, as she sponsored the American debuts of the British performance artists Gilbert and George and some of the strongest performance installations by Vito Acconci, then a poet with an M.F.A. writing degree, nowadays working mostly as an architect. Surviving is crucial in the contemporary art world, as one rough rule is that a good dealer will have twice as many devoted collectors as the number of years they have been in business.

What is not commonly understood is that art dealers are fundamentally retailers who know their principal customers, much as, say, a restauranteur or newsstand operator does, in contrast, say, to book publishers, who are wholesalers. Thus, if considering the artwork of a new supplicant, an art dealer should necessarily think if he or she can sell the candidate's work to James and Suzanna, Wolfgang and Roxanne, who have already purchased art from the dealer and are thus already predisposed to accept his or her recommendations. "Quality," later to be determined, is necessarily a secondary issue. Neither book publishers nor gallerists have perfect records in identifying excellence subsequently acknowledged, but they fail differently, book publishers because their sense of a possible audience is limited, gallerists because they are limited by the preferences of their immediate customers. If art "sells," the customers might be no more than a dozen; for a book to "sell well," it must have a million buyers.

Expensive work from new artists is thus primarily sold from dealer to collector. A secondary channel is from collector to collector, which is to say that one collector seeing the work of a new artist in another collector's house asks where he or she can get this artist's work for himself. This channel depends upon the fact that collectors customarily like to show their collections, especially to fellow collectors. A third channel is from artist to collector, where a collector not only purchases from an artist befriended (in a retail transaction), especially if the artist is skilled at "smoozing," but the collector also asks an artist already in her or his collection for advice about other artists. That's why colleagial networking—making professional allies—is more crucial in visual art than, say, in literature. (Networking also helps visual artists get residencies and other part-time jobs, but not grants or recognition in the critical histories.)

One point of sketching this hierarchy is establishing that reviews and advertising, which are so important in wholesaling culture, barely count in art retailing. Indeed, since strangers coming off the street rarely buy, I've always questioned why galleries should be open to the public at all. The only good reasons are that gallerists like showing work they like (much as collectors do) and that public exhibitions can create within the art community a foundation of positive gossip that eventually persuades genuine collectors to purchase. Favorable reviews become more influential when a museum curator needs to justify an acquisition to a boss or a board, otherwise ignorant, who is necessarily impressed by a printed recommendation. Since the amounts of money passing from collectors to dealers are customarily kept secret, monetary value is necessarily established in secondary markets, such as auction houses specializing in contemporary art. Even when a work of art is donated to a museum, the amount of the taxable deduction (and thus even the museum's interest) is determined not by the reputation of the artist, critical reviews, or collegial respect but, simply, by prices known to have been previously fetched.

Since new visual art is so hard to sell, even paintings and sculptures subsequently acknowledged as good, it is scarcely surprising a new gallery can sell nothing—NOTHING—even though it sponsors celebratory openings and stays open more than thirty hours a week. I was part of one that struck out in a trial year even though it printed stylish announcements (not on paper but plywood) and exhibited not newcomers but artists who had exhibited and sold before. No wonder many new galleries are supported by another resource, in this case an adjacent retail store, but at times framing, work from the gallerist's personal collection, subsidies by exhibiting artists (if not in the primary gallery then in a secondary gallery), or lord knows what. So secret might this source of income be that the young person sitting out front—the gallery's receptionist—might not even know what the other business is. Given these realities, there are practical reasons for aspiring artists wanting to establish a reputation to exchange work with colleagues before even trying to exhibit.

Because the number of passable painters and sculptors is so great, the turnover in visible practitioners is quick and, alas, usually final. Look at art magazines from the 1960s, pre-SoHo, and the first thing you notice is that most of the painters featured are just no longer prominent. The truth is not that they are less prominent but that nearly all of them have disappeared. Likewise many of the galleries visible decades ago are forgotten. These two developments are complementary. One reason is that nearly all artists who have shown with a gallery that goes out of business have trouble connecting to another one. A second, more pervasive reason is the general sense that a new artist who fails to have a knock-out debut may not have a second show, not only with the gallery initially exhibiting him or her but any other gallery, so competitive is the art world. In both cases, the swiftly churning turnover depends upon the continued influx of "promising" newcomers. Second shows for aspiring artists are less common than, say, second novels from aspiring writers.

One truth to remember is that visual art is more competitive than literature or music or almost anything else in our society. Numerically, there are more people competing for remarkably few outlets. If you graduated from medical school, the chances are nearly 100 percent that you would be earning a living from medicine a decade later. If you graduated from law school, perhaps 90 percent. By contrast, of all the graduates with an M.F.A. from even the most prestgious art school, perhaps 1 per cent will be living off the receipts of his or her work a decade hence. Given how many aspire, the fact of simply surviving off one's work for more than two decades is comparable to becoming the president of a corporation, a general in the military, or a big-league ballplayer.

Nonetheless, one benefit of the SoHo real estate situation has been permitting once-successful artists to live among other artists, most of them likewise once more prominent, still in SoHo simply because they owned their lofts or had a legally protected rental. Into the 1990s, they could tour the galleries in their own neighborhood, greeting colleagues who remembered their earlier successes, going to receptions that would be densely packed with colleagues. Whereas nearly all failed artists in previous generations would have disappeared from other artists' view, many SoHo artists discovered they would be remembered as long as they stayed in SoHo. (Once they went to teach and thus live in the provinces, they were as good as gone.) If Greenwich Village declined when literary residents moved out, SoHo declined when its principal distinctive business vacated: the art galleries. The artists staying in SoHo in the twenty-first century could (and should) have created new galleries, probably co-ops, in their own lofts, were they not already filled with the acquisitions of decades.

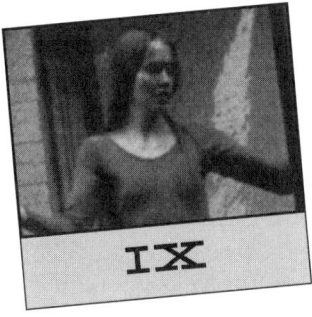

IX

I F SoHo ARTISTS had patrons offering a regular allowance, they didn't say. I doubt if any did, because private support of talented individuals was no longer important to very wealthy people — no longer was patronage per se something about which they could significantly boast. (The last example known to me of an artist to receive support for several years from a single person is a poet born in 1929.) Some artists had parents who purchased SoHo property, especially after they had given up on their dream of children pursuing bourgeois lives. Some inherited trust funds that were established before they became artists. In my observation, not until a later generation, say those born after 1960, did wealthy parents gladly give money to their children to become full-time artists or writers. (The exceptions, not surprisingly, were those from patrician backgrounds, such as Robert Motherwell [1914–1991] and George Plimpton [b. 1926].) A few of my neighbors have spouses earning enough income to support an artist, such as Ann Fallert, whose husband Whitman Knapp was a prominent federal judge. Some ex-spouses or ex-lovers were sugar daddies, continuing to invest in a genius who had once given them personal pleasure. Whenever one of these artists had a retrospective exhibition, someone would inevitably notice that most of the works were lent by a single collector.

Perhaps because of their antipathy to the uptown world, or at least their unconscious reluctance to engage it, many SoHo veterans discovered ways of making a living previously less known among artists. In my own co-op, two partners who live together have prepared packages of slides of new artists' works, mostly obtained in publicity packets from galleries, for sales to university art departments. Another partner had the foresight in 1974 to purchase more than one residential space at the time her father had closed his business, thus subsidizing her meager professional income with rentals in-house. One partner was a playwright who would disappear for long periods of times in exotic places, such as northern Canada, while he sublet his SoHo space for a sum considerably greater than his monthly maintenance to the co-op. Once he returned home, he had from both his job and the rental enough savings to tide him over until the next job. Yet another partner operated a jewelry store around the corner while cultivating his ambitions to become a rock musician. And so on.

Many SoHo part-time chefs at one time or another sold their home-cooked specialty foods to Dean & DiLuca, among other local gourmet retailers. Another colleague from time to time sold art that had been given to her decades ago by artists who had subsequently become successful, including her ex-husband. Indeed, at selling off one's "collection" she was scarcely alone. When applying for a real estate loan from a national bank with a branch in SoHo, I was surprised and disappointed to learn that the bank's lending authorities would not accept such art as legitimate collateral, as it was a real asset whose value was as solid as, say, gold jewelry's. I also sold copies of old books authored or edited by me, at least until the used bookstores around the world organized their wares through such websites as the Advanced Book Exchange. In response, I became an online bookstore myself (as Archae Editions). Upstairs in another residential SoHo loft is the more literary stock of another book retailer who's mostly online, Harry Nudel, although he also sells on weekend afternoons directly on Spring Street for much of the year.

While some SoHo visual artists sold work steadily, most did not, some instead having a windfall now and then, usually from an exhibition or commission out of town. Remarkably few had full-time teaching positions, though many taught part-time in and around New York and others accepted visiting institutional positions around the country (and sometimes even in Europe) for a few months at a stretch. Some visual artists who had once exhibited in SoHo (but weren't exhibiting any longer) created large-scale works for shopping centers, train terminals, and other public places, such "public art," as it was called, compensating them far better than individual paintings and sculptures could. The problems with such commissions were a dispiriting amount of paperwork and the creation of art seen by very few SoHo colleagues. (Sometimes I was invited to a local party designed to show colleagues' work, or at least a scale model, that would never been seen again.) As many SoHo artists found inventive ways to earn a living, so most discovered that they would sooner be self-employed than, say, work in an office, inevitably uptown, becoming small businesses rather than employees.

What was economically more important in the end was the collegial custom among SoHo artists of patronizing one another, giving one's art as presents or exchanging work. Decades later, more than one of us had a surprising pleasure of discovering that something coming free could be sold for princely sums sometimes in excess of a year's income.

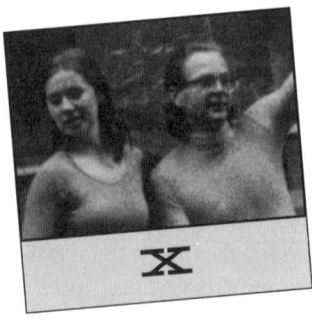

Recognition for artists by artists has been considered significant. Artists' self-grouping and self-generating has been the norm and not the exception.

— Preface to "Whitney Counterweight 3" (1981)

T HE FIRST IMPORTANT theater within SoHo proper was the Performing Garage at 33 Wooster Street. Thirty-six feet wide, perhaps 50 feet deep, and at least 20 feet high in its ground floor, with a large door fronting directly on the street, it was indeed a garage similar to other street-level garages in the neighborhood (some of which later became art galleries and restaurants) originally built to house large trucks. Shares in the co-op including the garage were purchased for $72,000 by a nonprofit entity called the Wooster Group, Inc., founded by Richard Schechner, an NYU professor who had recently come to New York University from Tulane in New Orleans, where he had edited the *Tulane Drama Review* (*TDR*) that, once in New York, became *The Drama Review* (likewise *TDR* to the cognoscenti). Having already covered alternative theater in his magazine, he recognized unique opportunities in building a performance venue within undefined space.

The first of Schechner's productions there, *Dionysus in '69* (1968), was the most famous. Its impact on SoHo artists—and beyond—was great; I myself was awed by it, seeing it four times, although I found it less compelling each time I returned. A combination of audience participation, improvised scenes, and Euripides' *The Bacchae*, the production influenced other downtown performance art.

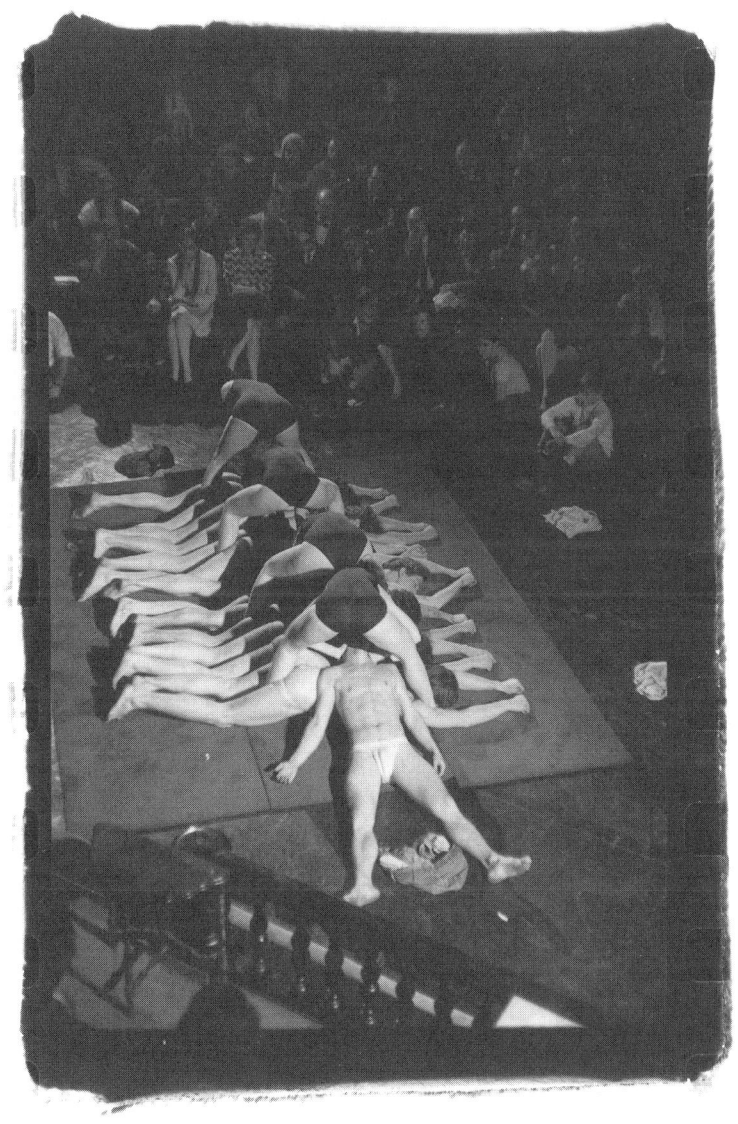

Birth scene from *Dionysus in '69* by Richard Schechner's Performance Group, 1968. Copyright Fred W. McDarrah

As members of the audience entered a theater that lacked seats, they were asked to sit wherever they could, among two extended platforms and rafters, while members of the "Performance Group" did various exercises in the middle of the floor. The play began officially with an exchange of lines between Patrick McDermott and a woman in street clothes. For the remainder of the evening, the characters moved in and out of Euripides' lines and characters. At times, they shifted into contemporary language, as well as using one another's real names. Since behavior on stage became rather extreme, there was a constant argument over the nature of theatrical artifice.

Several scenes in the original production were memorable. A dance sequence occurred early in the play in which the audience was invited to participate. There was also a stunning birth portrayal in which a male body clad only in a jockstrap is passed over a carpet of similarly clothed male bodies that lie, face down, in sequential alternation with five parallel pairs of female legs spread wide apart. (Photographs of *Dionysus* usually emphasize this remarkable scene.) Then there was a group therapy sequence in which every question must challenge another company member, as well as include a risk to the questioner. The final major sequence was a frenzy in which the players crawl all over one another and even pull two male members of the audience into their melee. At times past, I gather, more, if not most, spectators joined. One night, the situation got so messy that the production never reached its false coda (which Schechner reportedly inserted against the objections of the group), in which Finlay declares, "A vote for William Finlay in '68 brings Dionysus in '69," and one of the women passes out campaign buttons reading "Dionysus in '69." Finlay concludes, "Some of the things you thought would happen here tonight have not and for that you should be grateful."

When the play was revived in December 1969, the main change was the addition of total nudity. In addition, Richard Schechner, as the group's chief, cut out the opportunities for audience participation, both in the ecstatic dance sequence and the Dionysian revel. Third, since Election Day was behind us, he cut the political dimension of a "Vote for William Finlay in '68 brings Dionysus in '69," which considerably muted the earlier theme of advocating Dionysian, as opposed to Apollonian, politics. Fourth, the group therapy sequence, so terrifying the first time I saw it, was eliminated. What was most effective was the intimacy and frankness of the nudity, not only because the performers displayed themselves in all positions and from all angles but also because the audience was only a few feet away.

Although I returned to the Performing Garage many times since, especially for performances by the successor company, The Wooster Group directed by Elizabeth Le Compte, nothing there impressed me as much as *Dionysus in '69* in the beginning. Indicatively, for many years now, the Garage has had a row of seats banked upward, as in a conventional theater, directing the audience's attention to the space in front of them. For a while, the adjacent space, previously an envelope factory and thus called the Envelope, became a smaller theater for more modest productions. I remember seeing one by a young man named Terry Curtis Fox, whom I thought bright. A production of his realistic play *Cops* (1978) included such future stars of uptown as well as downtown as Spalding Gray, Willem Dafoe, and Elizabeth LeCompte. Not unlike too many other young people once prominent in downtown theater, Fox, however, disappeared from the scene, illustrating the truth, so often forgotten, that avant-garde art is cruelly competitive, sending even the most ambitious into other work.

Spalding Gray, meanwhile, became the American master of a performance genre based upon monologues purportedly about oneself, especially one's neuroses and sensitivities, though perhaps fictionalized; allegedly spontaneous, though surely rehearsed down to the smallest physical detail. Some of these Gray "autoperformances," as Michael Kirby called them, have been done at the Performing Garage; others were done uptown, customarily on nights when a theater's principal show was resting. They have also appeared on films and in books. Admiring them though I do, influential though they are, I can't figure out how they might resemble other art indigenous to SoHo.

In the wake of *Dionysus in '69*, SoHo became a hothouse for performance art, which has become an inclusive term for live presentations, often in nontheatrical spaces, minimizing text among other theatrical strategies, sometimes from people whose reputations were first established in arts other than theater.

Some of the best SoHo events were those that featured groups of individual performers. In November 1974, Jean Dupuy put together an anthology of very brief events at The Kitchen called Soup & Tart, some of which were quite stunning. Philip Glass performed an abstract vocal; Jon Gibson played a composition of his own on the soprano saxophone; Joanne Akalaitis, who with David Warrilow (exploiting his arrested alcoholism) provided a stunning frame for the evening; Hannah Wilke let the art world again see her renowned breasts as she went through a number of poses (some of which resembled Jesus on the cross); and the filmmaker Deedee Hallek recorded Jean Dupuy's narration of how to make apple tarts against a film of the recipe played backward. Some of the performers were silly (Charles Atlas, Brendan Atkinson) or irrelevant (Yvonne Rainer). What struck me was how few literary people were in the audience, even though this sequence of individual presentations resembled a poetry marathon, and then how it would be impossible to produce a comparable anthology with poets, because every participant would take too long before retiring to the eaves. As most of these artists were, by contrast, interested in making a concise statement, they felt no need to hog the stage for an unjustifiably long spell.

In March 1975, the father of SoHo co-ops, George Maciunas, presented a Flux Harpsichord Recital at Anthology Film Archives, 80 Wooster Street. It was a spectacular joy—a Fluxus production at its best. The opening act was Beth Anderson playing La Monte Young's Composition 1960, No. 13, which turns out to be terribly straight baroque music, at least in Anderson's interpretation. (What kind of open instructions allowed that to happen?) Next was Maciunas's No. 14 (1975), in which a beach toy is inflated in the bed of a piano. In Toshi Ichiyanagi's No. 5 (1961), three performers bang the wooden outsides of a single harpsichord, in response to a score. Nam June Paik's Lesson consists of a lecture in his inimitable pidgin English on the most appropriate way to place one's feet in order to arise and then bow before a nobleman. To perform George Brecht's Incidental Music (1960), Paik, now an interpreter, piled children's blocks on a harpsichord's strings until the blocks fell down, and then he taped down a few of the harpsichord's keys. In Dick Higgins's *Constellation No. 4* (1960), several performers made one sound apiece whenever Larry Miller hit his top hat. In George Brecht's *Center* (1962), three performers put a board on a basketball and then a harpsichord turned sideways on the board, which, to no surprise, they help balance. In Joe Jones's *Flux Harpsichord* (1975), eight little motors are suspended over the harpsichord bed, some of them occasionally striking the strings. Yasunao Tone's *Geodesy for Harpsichord* (1963) is a long, somewhat boring piece about climbing a ladder and then dropping on the harpsichord things that don't make noise. Robert Watts's *Trace for Harpsichord* (1975) invites the audience to aim ping-pong balls at the bed of the harp while the performers throw the balls back at the audience for more attempts. Tone's *Harpsichord Piece for Sixteen Fingers* (1975) has eight performers tap only two of their fingers apiece on the top of a closed harpsichord. Alison Knowles's *Twenty-Eight Pole Limas* involves tossing lima beans over a harp bed covered with a piece of paper and then picking them up with tweezers. For George Brecht's *Symphony No. 3*, Yoshimasa Wada [chief plumber in the renovation of my loft] falls off a chair in the course of approaching the harpsichord. For Tomas Schmit's *Keyboard Piece No. 1* (1962), Larry Miller piles pieces of wood into a precarious construction and then tilts the top of the piano, so that all the blocks fall off. For his own *66* (1975), Miller cuts the shape of a harpsichord out of a large piece of paper and then passes the harpsichord through the hole. The theme of the evening was, of course, using the harpsichord for everything except that for which it was initially intended. A good time was had by all.

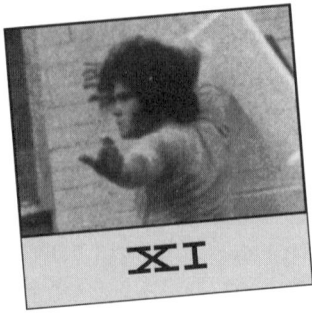

XI

The look [of SoHo dance] was either formal, neutral,
spiritedly engaged in compositional problems, and based in
more or less ordinary movement behavior, or ritualistic and
theatrical but likewise performatively neutral and
nonvirtuosic.

—Marcia B. Siegel, *The Tail of the Dragon* (1991)

T HE FIRST CENTER for modern dance in SoHo was a pair of adjacent buildings on Broadway, just north of Spring, that George Maciunas, always sensitive to the particular needs of his fellow artists, had, in 1974, purchased, organized, and renovated with dancers in mind. Wider than the standard 25 feet, the buildings, first, had no interior pillars, making them ideal for dance spaces. Second, their floors were made entirely of wood, rather than wood directly over concrete, as, say, in my own building, which meant that dancers would not jeopardize their legs and feet with their jumps. Into the northern building moved Lucinda Childs on one floor and David Gordon and Valda Setterfield, longtime husband and wife, both choreographers as well as dancers, on another. While Childs is best remembered for a spectacular repetitive solo on a diagonal line for nearly an hour in Glass and Wilson's *Einstein on the Beach* (1974), Setterfield had danced with Merce Cunningham, as did Meg Harper and Douglas Dunn, who took separate spaces in the northern building. Another space went to Trisha Brown, who had lived in an earlier Maciunas building on Wooster Street. Whereas New York dancers of a previous generation customarily lived in modest apartments distant from their studios, SoHo gave them the opportunity to live in the same spaces where they did their daily exercises and sometimes performed.

Several of these dancers participated in the Grand Union, which was a collaborative performance group organized in 1970 by Yvonne Rainer, then a prominent downtown choreographer, not yet a filmmaker. The concept, reflective of the times in general and SoHo in particular, was that several dancer-choreographers would perform together, with minimal preparation, much as a collection of prominent jazz performers had been doing for decades. Among the principals were Gordon, Setterfield, Dunn, Trisha Brown, Barbara Dilley (who had as Barbara Lloyd performed with Cunningham), Steve Paxton, Nancy Lewis, and Becky Arnold. Enjoying what they did, I also found the work limited, much as improvised music can be, and so was not surprised when the Grand Union disbanded in 1976. An early history of the group appears in Sally Banes's *Terpsichore in Sneakers* (1980). Indeed, most of the dancers featured in individual chapters of that pioneering book lived in SoHo, though they didn't necessarily perform there as well.

The southern building, sharing with its northern companion a magnificent interior courtyard with cast-iron architecture, became more visibly a SoHo-sized theater for dance, because two of the partners opened their spaces to concerts and classes. On the penultimate floor was a dancer older than the others, already in her fifties when she moved into SoHo, Frances Alenikoff. "Massive renovations were required," she once wrote, "and the floor was an obstacle course, with gaps and lurking splinters that necessitated nightly applications of gaffer tape to spare trauma to dancers' feet and body parts. In 1978, I received a donation of a wonderfully silky new floor." Alenikoff not only used the well-lit front space for her own performances but she also rented it to others under the name Eden's Expressway throughout the year — "countless numbers of dancers, choreographers, theater artists in various media, and teachers of assorted movement. So many energetic and imaginative people have enhanced the space with their own vitality and vision, and many of whom have become friends and an inspiration in my own life and work." Into the 1990s, Eden's

Expressway was the home base for Maggie Newman's regular Tai Chi classes; in 2000, a dance entity called Movement Research took over the public space for its classes and workshop. In the back remained Alenikoff's residential space.

On the floor above was Elaine Summers, who had performed in a loft on Canal and Wooster as far back as 1952. She had established the Experimental Intermedia Foundation, which was committed to incorporating dance with other arts. Her husband Davidson Gigliotti was an early video artist; their colleague in the foundation was Phill Niblock, living a few blocks away, distinguished as both a composer and a filmmaker (and filmmaking professor). Summers also conducted popular classes in dance and movement until she and Gigliotti decided to exploit the increased value of their loft and retired to Florida in 1989 only to return to a different SoHo in the twenty-first century.

The initial defining mark of modern dance in SoHo was the use of spaces not initially intended for performance; for much as the Performance Group had created their venue within a former factory, so choreographers used open lofts that left spectators to stand or sit as well as they could. A related move typical of the time was performing in outdoor spaces, as Twyla Tharp did in Central Park in 1969 or in SoHo itself. For the 1972 SoHo Arts Festival, choreographer Marilyn Wood used fire escapes fronting on the street for her "stage" in her *SoHo Fire Escape Dance*. The classic work in this last respect was Trisha Brown's afternoon *Roof Piece* (1973) in which the spectators atop 64 Wooster Street and 35 White Street watched six dancers performing on the roofs of 420 West Broadway, 476 Broome, 83 Wooster, and 173 Spring Street. "In *Roof Piece*," she wrote, "the emphasis was on immediate and exact duplication of the observed dance and the silent passing of this dance to a series of performers on down the line. The intuitive and kinesthetic systems were impaired by the distance between buildings." Indicatively, for the first major exhibition of SoHo art, a photograph of this Trisha Brown work, rather than, say, a painting, graced the catalog's cover.

No one remembers any ballet in SoHo. It remains an uptown art. Whether any ballet dancers ever lived in SoHo, no one knows; probably not.

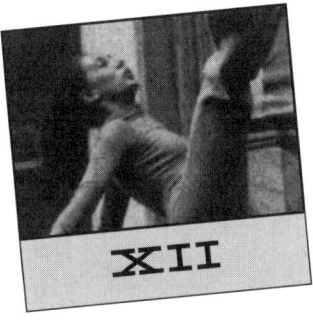

XII

*If it lie within your desire to promote the arts you must not
only subsidize the man with work still in him, but you must
gather such dynamic particles together, you must set them
where they will interact and stimulate each other.*

—Ezra Pound, "Patria Mia" (1912)

B ORN IN HOLLAND in 1942, the bookseller Jaap Reitman
came to America in the 1960s and worked in the store of
George Wittenborn (1908–1974), the most sophisticated Manhattan
retailer of art books for decades after World War II. Located uptown
at 1018 Madison Avenue, just below 79th Street, Wittenborn
complimented the galleries that were also in his Upper East Side
neighborhood. Quite simply, he stocked art books, especially from
Europe, that no one else had. Realizing in the early 1970s that SoHo
needed a comparable resource, Reitman opened his eponymous
store, originally located on the street level at the northeast corner of
West Broadway and Spring Street, literally at the intersection of the
neighborhood's two main streets. Reitman established reliable
relationships with galleries and museums around the world to get
enough copies of their latest catalogs. An attentive retailer, he got to
know his customers as well, regularly telling them as they walked into
his store if a title new to his stock should interest them. Such
thoughtful retailing resulted in shaping the community's literacy, for
instance giving downtown artists a greater access to European
"theory" than would otherwise be possible. Certain kinds of books,
such as those from a Seattle small press called Bay, he sold better

than anyone else. He profited enough to take a taxi daily to his family's apartment on the Upper East Side.

No longer needing street-level visibility, Reitman moved his store upstairs on Spring Street, first west of West Broadway in the early 1980s and then east of SoHo's main drag by the late 1980s. Other bookshops opened in the neighborhood, one initially owned by the magazine *High Times*; another was part of the Rizzoli chain. A third, Spring Street Books, offered a more literary line of trade paperbacks. Around 1995, Reitman's store suddenly had fewer customers, even on Saturday afternoons; I never understood why. Someone at the time attributed it to a decline of interest in French theory, but that explanation was insufficient. He closed, not to be replaced. The Spring Street Bookstore closed a few years later; Rizzoli's in 2001. The closest surviving semblances are a basement shop in the New Museum on Broadway and a much smaller street-level store, called Untitled, located not in SoHo proper but on Prince Street west of West Broadway. Owned for three decades by the art-photographer Bevan Davies, a veteran SoHo resident, it sells art postcards on one side of his narrow space and artbooks on the other. He told me early in 2002 that he had to stop stocking criticism books for lack of sales, so profoundly had tastes of his street customers changed. Every cultural hothouse needs a good bookstore (though not necessarily a moviehouse or even a newspaper stand). When the influential bookstore dies, much else goes as well.

An art collector based in Connecticut, formerly a successful clothing designer, Larry Aldrich (1906–2001) did two favors for early SoHo that were essentially selfless, if short-lived. In 1973, he established on Prince Street a ground-floor alternative exhibition space called the SoHo Center for Visual Artists explicitly to show young unaffiliated artists. Although his museum in Connecticut was emblazoned with his own name, this was not. Indeed, for the outer eastern wall of this building a local beautification outfit named City Walls had commissioned Richard Haas in 1975 to paint a marvelous trompe l'oeil mural that resembles a typical SoHo cast-iron building until, looking closely, you see that only two of the many windows are real. The rest are painted to look like loft windows—and still do, a quarter century later.

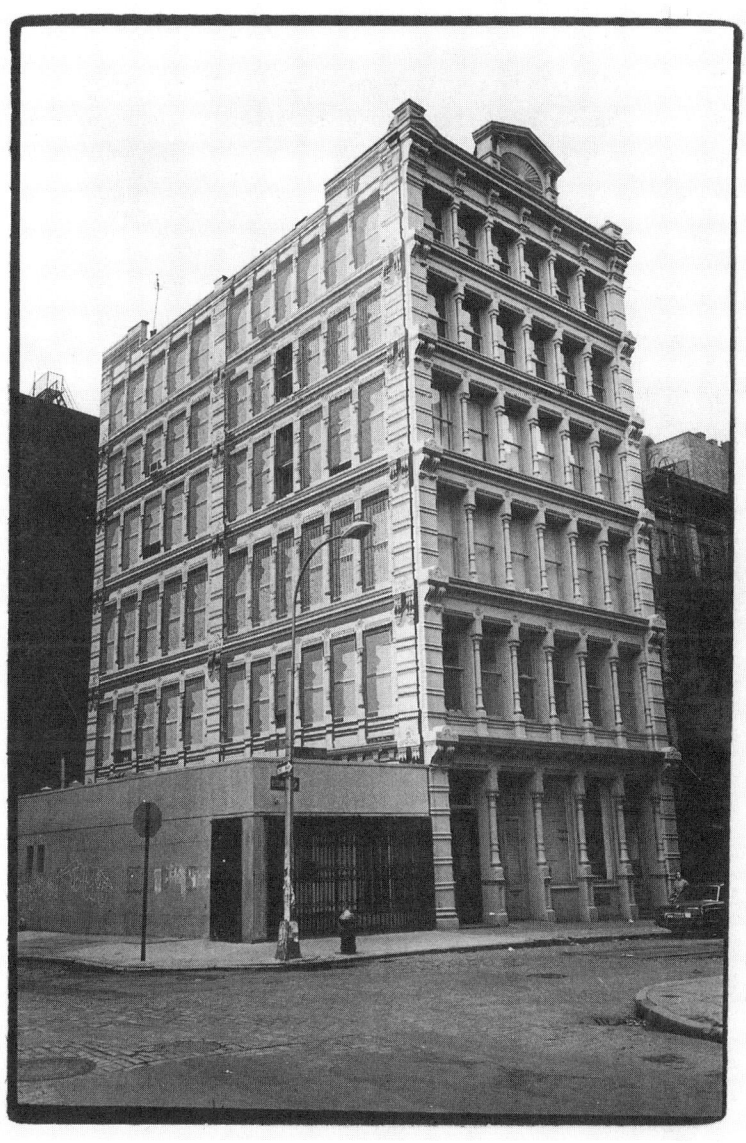

On the left façade is Richard Haas's *trompe l'oeil* painted to appear as if it were cast-iron, Greene and Prince Streets, February 1976. Copyright Fred W. McDarrah

Whether the SoHo Center had any important shows I can't honestly recall, but what I do remember, quite vividly, is that next door, in a single-story building, fomerly a pizza parlor, Aldrich established a reference library exclusively for visual artists. Once I had a pass with my name on it, I guess based upon my residing in SoHo, with which admission was free. I went there more than once to read art journals from around the world, use reference books, and try to pick up attractive bookish young women. With no more fanfare than went into their founding, Aldrich abandoned both institutions during the 1980s. Whereas the exhibition space became a private gallery, the single-story library building with its ceiling too low for exhibiting art became a retail store. The books, reportedly numbering 10,000, were donated to the New Museum, which opened on Broadway south of Houston in the 1980s, serving not the community but exploiting its address, much as the pioneering high-priced neighborhood retailers did at that time. I recall in the late 1980s consulting in its basement some books marked to acknowledge Aldrich's SoHo Center Library. Once the New Museum had a problem with mold in its basement, the books disappeared. They are purportedly kept on its SoHo premises in boxes that cannot be accessed.

Other casualties of SoHo development were specialty stores huge for Manhattan, almost warehouses, with an abundance of certain materials cheaply priced. When the loft of an NYU professor was featured (in that same article as mine) in the *New York Times* Thursday Home section, she revealed that she purchased her steel bookshelves from B-Z on Greene Street, which had a huge stock of them "used," mostly gleaned from office closings. I purchased them too because, unlike wooden bookshelves, these could be easily assembled at home with just nuts and bolts and then later reassembled when you wanted to change the heights of individual shelves. Another useful store nearby was Zelf, which rented fairly sophisticated construction equipment to self-renovators. Outside was a sign with a happy face next to a rocket proclaiming, "I made it myself at Zelf." Those of us working on paper, especially in Book-Art, remember Gem Paper on Broadway, just below Houston, which had not only a complete floor, perhaps 10,000 square feet, but also a basement nearly equal in size filled with odd lots of esoteric papers, obtained Lord knows where. It was owned by two brothers differing radically in personality and appearance. Over time, you necessarily learned to look for the smaller, friendlier one if you needed considerate assistance. From the other brother, you purchased only what you knew, as he was never helpful. Both these popular specialty stores were gone by the 1990s. Likewise gone were the well-stocked hardware stores on which all our renovations necessarily depended.

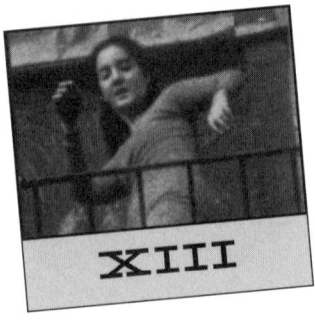

XIII

Work and residence, which had become separated as the industrial system became more complex, were reunited in SoHo, which became a community unifying work, residence, and ideology. Among SoHo residents, personal relations were directed at unification through mutual support. . . . Artistic ideas were shared, enhancing the feeling that it was here that what was important was "happening." Nonthreatening criticism was offered and accepted. The testy relationships of the more competitive New York milieux were muted, if not absent. Soon organizations for improving and defending the community grew alongside organizations for solving the marketing problems of artists.

—James R. Hudson, *The Unanticipated City* (1987)

THOUGH THE COMMERCIAL galleries made SoHo the center of the art world in the 1970s, the neighborhood also became the center for noncommercial art. The key institutions here were the Cooperative Gallery and the Alternative Space, both of which were established primarily to exhibit artists who were not currently represented and, in the second case, to give them opportunities to do what could not be done in their normal venues.

Co-op galleries were invariably founded and run by artists, who paid all expenses for both their exhibitions and the gallery's operations, beginning with the rental of semi-permanent space. Once a cooperative has been established, its members can vote on accepting new members, who are customarily required to pay an initiation fee running a few hundred dollars in addition to a monthly membership fee likewise in the low three figures. When a member artist's work is exhibited, he or she is customarily required to design, print, and mail the announcements, to hang or install the work, and to contact reviewers. Once the show begins, the member artists are obliged as well to staff the gallery during its open hours or hire someone who would. Sometimes the members of a co-op gallery agree to employ a full-time administrator mostly to art-sit for them. When work is sold, the artist usually receives all the proceeds, rather than, as is customary in a commercial gallery, splitting them with an art dealer. While attractive conceptually, no co-op gallery ever gained the authority of a successful art dealer, such as Leo Castelli, who is necessarily an alchemist in persuading collectors to pay a sum of money that is much, much more than the cost of producing a work. Indeed, Irving Sandler, later a distinguished art historian, reported that during the three years in the 1950s that he directed the Tanager, a 10th Street co-op still remembered, he made only one sale.

Scarcely new to SoHo, cooperative galleries existed in New York during the 1950s, if not before, giving early exhibitions to artists who later pursued commercial careers. In this last sense, perhaps the most successful co-op galleries were 55 Mercer Street, founded in December 1969 and still located in SoHo on the fourth floor of that address, and A.I.R., which was founded in SoHo in 1972 and was at last report still on lower Wooster Street. If the former was open to all kinds of art and artists, the latter restricted membership to women and also sponsored ancillary feminist activities, such as panels devoted to the discussion of feminism and art. Among the prominent alumni of 55 Mercer are Janet Fish and Ursula von Rydingsvard, who subsequently showed at commercial galleries and had museum retrospectives; among those previously showing at A.I.R. were Nancy Spero and Dottie Attie. Some of the later co-op galleries had more particular esthetic designs, confining their roster, say, only to representational painters, some of these forming a Figurative Art Alliance. The 1978 SoHo guidebook identifies seventeen co-op galleries among a total of eighty-five in the neighborhood at that time.

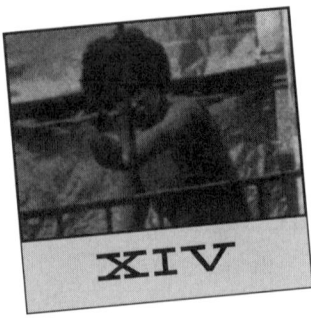

XIV

True to its word, Artists Space provides "alternatives"; they constantly bring to our attention things that for one reason or another are being missed. They remind us that there are other things going on then what is presented by more established institutions.

— Roberta Smith, quoted in 5000 *Artists Return to Artists Space: 25 Years* (1998)

THE ALTERNATIVE SPACE, by contrast, was a nonprofit institution formed to serve groups of artists or genres of art that were not adequately included in the commercial galleries. The pioneer for SoHo was the 112 Workshop, commonly called 112 Greene Street after its street address. Founded by Jeffrey Lew, who had purchased the building previously housing a rag-salvaging business, the 112 Workshop was a ground floor 33 feet wide, 110 feet long, and 16 feet high, with several Corinthian columns within the space and large windows in both the front and the back. Lew simply made it available, initially to his friend Gordon Matta-Clark (1943–1978), the American son of the Chilean-Parisian painter Roberto Matta, who stayed here during World War II. As Robyn Brentano remembered, "Matta-Clark used 112 as a laboratory, activating the structure on every level. He uncovered its subterranean recesses, grew things in impossible places, and brought sunlight downward through a matrix of glass bottles. His love of cooking found strange permutations in the agar brew he concocted from molds and the furnace he built to melt down the glass he had

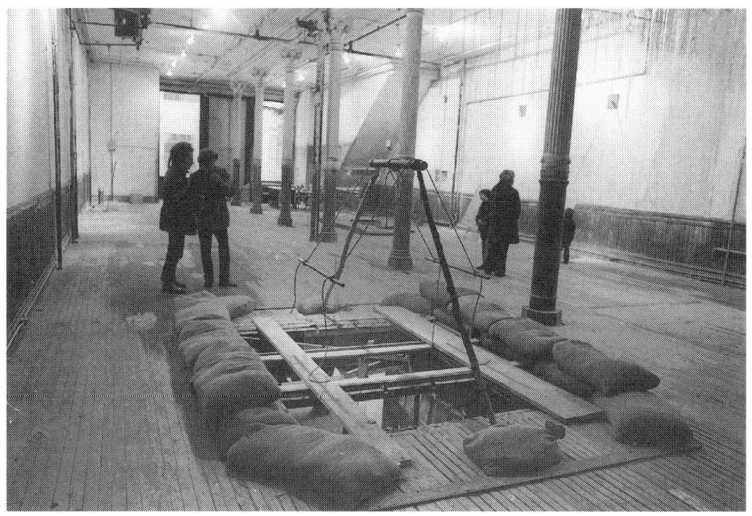

Interior view of 112 Greene Street Gallery with George Trakas's *Floor Piece*, January 23, 1971. Copyright Fred W. McDarrah

collected. Once, with the classic humor of a court jester, Matta-Clark dragged a baby carriage full of junk off the street and installed it in a group show, signing the piece George Smudge. He papered walls with the images of the walls in gutted buildings and plastered an enormous photograph of a subway train across the airshaft wall facing the rear windows of 112, forcing the viewer to traverse the rear of the space as if in a subway station. The impression one has of him is that of a magician who performed with the matter-of-fact manner of a day laborer." In addition, he put on the street an industrial dumpster into which artists were invited to put things as well as take. Aside from his own activities, Matta-Clark established an ambience for 112 that informed subsequent activities that were documented in a rich eponymous book appearing in 1981, soon after his premature passing. More artists subsequently important worked here than anywhere else in SoHo, including the composers Phillip Glass and Jon Gibson, the dancers associated with the Grand Union, even the Hollywood filmmaker Kathryn Bigelow, among others. Once Jeffrey Lew took back his space in 1976, the nonprofit entity moved to the storefront of a truck terminal way west on Spring Street and was renamed White Columns, which still exists at yet another Manhattan address.

Out of the 112 regulars, particularly Matta-Clark, Richard Landry, and Tina Girouard, came the favorite SoHo artists' restaurant called simply Food, located on the northwest corner of Prince and Houston Streets. The designers Milton Glaser and Jerome Snyder, who wrote "The Underground Gourmet" for *New York* magazine praised it soon after it opened ("no phone yet") for epitomizing "a new trend in the food ethic. In seeking to provide an alternative to typical restaurant fare and ambience, the young owners of these establishments are offering wholesome, satisfying, imaginatively prepared food, served unpretentiously, for a modest price." (The rest of the review, which I clipped and kept, made me cry with nostalgia.) Organized as a SoHo-style co-op, Food employed neighborhood artists for its staff and survived well into the 1980s, which is to say longer than the 112 Workshop. The space has since housed a boutique.

If the 112 Worship was selective, or at least self-selective, in intimidating those who were less ambitious, an institution like Artists Space became everybody's galley in offering to keep on hand slides from anyone who would submit, purportedly making the images available to curators and collectors, much as commercial galleries do for their artists. This was a free service; the only limitation was that the Artists Space artist could not be represented by a commercial gallery. Most of those depositing their slides lived outside New York and thus were geographically disadvantaged in making contacts prerequisite for exhibitions. By the early 1990s, over 3,000 artists around the world were included in the Artists Space registry. In 1996, it put some of these images on its website (artistspace.org) and accepted new digital images for inclusion there. For a while, from the Artists File its curators selected new images each month for a "virtual exhibition" on its website.

From its initial venue as an entire floor at 155 Wooster Street, upstairs from the Paula Cooper Gallery, Artists Space also sponsored individual exhibitions of unaffiliated artists, customarily chosen by

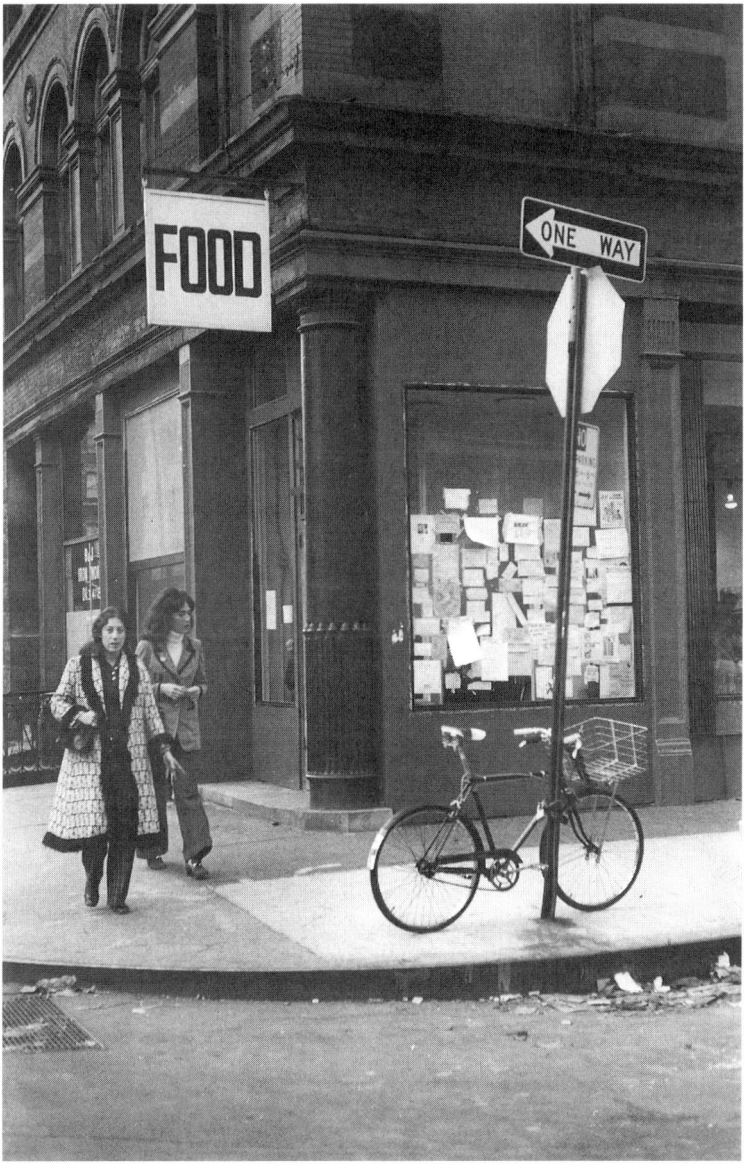

Best soup in SoHo was served in Food, a restaurant at 127 Prince, October 1972. Copyright Fred W. McDarrah

more established figures, usually three at a time in its large space, later in Tribeca at Hudson Street, then on lower West Broadway, and finally on Greene Street. The Committee for the Visual Arts, Inc., as it was formally known—its language reflecting a desire to be helpful—had group shows with various themes, always with a majority of unfamiliar names. Here as well were the initial year-end readings aloud continuously of the complete text of Gertrude Stein's mammoth classic *The Making of Americans*, which customarily takes at least two full days around the clock. When Artists Space left SoHo for Tribeca, these were done at the street-level space below—the Paula Cooper Gallery—later in biannual alternation with James Joyce's *Finnegans Wake*, which a squad of enthusiasts can read continuously aloud in half the time.

Thanks to a favored relation to the New York State Council on the Arts, which collaborated in its creation, Artists Space also had, from 1976 to 1991, an Independent Exhibitions Program that became the conduit for modest grants, customarily in the middle three figures, for displays in unconventional venues, such as spaces temporarily available for art, street events, and collections of open studios. Likewise from 1972 to 1991, which was a watershed year, it also administered the Emergency Materials Fund for artists already scheduled to exhibit at alternative venues, including universities, libraries, or galleries. "These grants of $75 to $150 each were intended to cover the basic presentation costs associated with the exhibition that would not be absorbed by the host venue. By covering a portion of the costs, the EMF grants enabled a significant number of artists to improve the quality of presentation for exhibition of their work," according to an impressively thick retrospective book published in 1998 that has the title *5000 Artists Return to Artists Space: 25 Years*, its title boasting explicitly of serving aspiring professionals at the rate of roughly 200 per year. Of the many who exhibited, only a few sold anything. Notwithstanding such democratic virtue, Artists Space sponsored early exhibitions of some who subsequently had visible careers, such as Laurie Anderson, Jonathan Borofsky, and Cindy Sherman. Few exhibitions in alternative spaces were as influential as Architectural Manifestoes, curated in 1978 by

Bernard Tschumi, who later became dean of the architectural school at Columbia University. In *5000 Artists*, he remembers it as perhaps "the first show of architectural drawings in a gallery or a public space." In this respect, the Tschumi exhibition established a viable precedent for a later alternative space in the 1990s. Just east of SoHo on Kenmare Street, in a triangular wedge-like space with an abundance of windows, the Storefront for Art and Architecture has specialized in exhibiting hypothetical architecture.

In 1971 Alana Heiss, then married to a sculptor, founded the Institute for Art and Urban Resources, Inc., located initially under a clocktower on Leonard Street, just south of SoHo. Her skill was finding large empty spaces downtown, usually owned by the city itself, and persuading either landlords or city officials to make them available to her organization to use: if spacious, for art exhibitions and concerts or, if smaller, for individual artists' production studios. For short periods of time, her nonprofit corporation controlled large empty spaces on Bleecker Street and Reade Street, all in close proximity to SoHo, sometimes in buildings that were soon demolished or sold. I remember walking with her through lower Manhattan one evening around 1973 as she pointed to various buildings whose unused spaces, often whole floors, she had discovered, wondering how she could make them available to artists. Her passion for wanting to help was as impressive as her research.

In the late 1970s, she persuaded the city to lease to her nonprofit the largest abandoned public school, P.S. 1, not in SoHo but in Long Island City, just across the East River from midtown Manhattan. Here she had classrooms that could be rented as nonresident studios to New York artists at a nominal fee and later to artists from around the world, their expenses often paid by their own countries. The larger spaces at P.S. 1 have housed exhibitions and performances, as eventually did the courtyards. I had an exhibition of my Book Art there in late 1978 in a ground floor corner room that I knew must have previously been the school principal's office, because it still contained on one wall a box controlling the interior ringing bells. Very much in the spirit of SoHo for its first two decades, P.S. 1 became something else by the year 2000: not only a social institution attracting on weekends young people from all over Queens, especially to its summer court-yard mixers, but an affiliate, no joke, of the Museum of Modern Art. When the main branch of the MoMA closed for renovations in 2002, the principal site for exhibitions became a former factory in a Queens industrial district. If not for the success of P.S. 1, based in turn upon the example of SoHo, I doubt if MoMA would have relocated where it did in the twenty-first century.

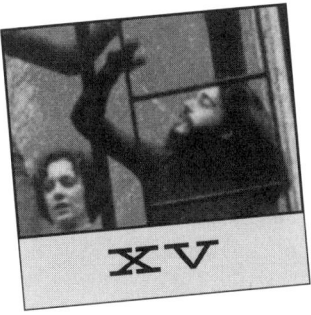

XV

*Collaboration not only meant that the artists got their work
done with the help of their friends, it also brought many
disciplines together under one roof. Distinctions between
art forms naturally began to break down. Sculptors and
painters gave performances with their work.*

—Robyn Brentano, *112 Workshop* (1982)

S OME OF THE alternative spaces served kinds of art that were
not being adequately serviced by the commercial spaces. For
the increasingly influential genres of video art (as distinct from
television) and of performance art (as distinct from dramatic theater),
there was the Kitchen on the second floor of a magnificent building
on the northwest corner of Broome and Wooster Streets. Indeed, not
only did the Kitchen present video screenings, but it established an
archive with nearly two hundred tapes that could be viewed on the
premises in a room made especially for that purpose. Eventually, the
Kitchen issued a catalog of its videotape archive. As Seeman and
Siegfried wrote in their 1978 guidebook, "the Kitchen maintains that
one of its prime functions is to serve the needs of the SoHo
community. Therefore, an open policy has been established that gives
many artists the opportunity to perform that they may not have found
elsewhere." Here I also saw concerts of dance and music, particularly
remembering one by Richard (aka R.I.P.) Hayman that asked
spectators to stay all night, hypothetically integrating his mellow
sounds, as I recall, into their dreams. I had done so, delightfully, until
awakened by large trucks that typically begin to rumble down Broome

Street, only a floor below, around 5 in the morning. When my anthology of North American Sound Poetry appeared, *Text-Sound Texts* (1980), it was the Kitchen, no place else, that sponsored not only a publication party but also a concert. While the Kitchen has moved elsewhere, the percussive sounds of Broome Street trucking continue to resound through lower SoHo.

Printed Matter, then on Lispenard Street, one block below Canal and parallel, later at 77 Wooster Street, became not only a retailer for book-art but, more important perhaps, a kind of research library simply through the volume of its stock (much as Barnes & Noble bookstores did many years later). Franklin Furnance, initially a few blocks south and likewise parallel to Canal on Franklin Street, became the archive for this new genre between literature and visual art.

Many alternative spaces in SoHo and elsewhere arose in response to the availability of public funding. As Robyn Brentano remembered in her book about 112 Workshop, Brian O'Doherty, an Irishman who became the most savvy and effective official of any American public arts agency ever, then directing the visual arts program of the National Endowment for the Arts, "recognized the importance of government support for the new alternative spaces," again not only in New York but also elsewhere in the United States, implicitly extending certain SoHo concepts to artists' neighborhoods far away. One practice common to nonprofits was requiring artists to handle their own publicity. Mailing lists of critics, collectors, and VIPs were kept and exchanged. Small gatherings were held in artists' lofts to address and stuff envelopes, or paste address labels on, say, picture postcards. I sponsored a few of these parties, participated in them, and remember walking in on one while exclaiming, "This must be SoHo," as indeed it was. If advance notice was insufficient, as it always was, the artist had only him or herself to blame.

Conceptually more substantial, Exit Art began in 1982 as a nonprofit entity "dedicated to transcultural explorations of contemporary art," to quote from its own history. "Conceived as a cultural laboratory, Exit Art presented exhibitions, multi-media projects, film and video series, and performances, as well as instituting a publishing program." Its founders were Jeanette Ingberman and Papo Colo, initially a curator and an artist, respectively, lovers who eventually married. Originally at 225 Lafayette Street and then in a building that housed other galleries, both commercial and noncommercial, where they mounted one-person shows that are remembered of David Hammons, Ursula von Rydingsvard, Antonio Muntadas, and Tehching Hsieh— eccentrics all—Exit Art moved in 1992 to the entire second floor of 548 Broadway, a block-long building that had no other public spaces. Within a total of 17,000 square feet, it has two huge exhibition areas and a performance theater, in addition to a café and a store. Its specialty is genres previously unexhibited, such as a mammoth collection of art gallery announcements (that most of us throw away, impressive as design though they often are) and an even grander show of record covers from the LP era (most of them disappeared along with their discs in the new CD era). In the wake of the destruction in 2001 of the World Trade Center it mounted an exhibition open to everyone wanting to contribute, suspending their sheets of tasteful clear mountings hung from the ceiling, collectively reflecting the esthetic temper of a large community. By the twenty-first century, it, too, left SoHo.

If Artists Space and even Exit Art served a large number of artists, the Dia Foundation, by contrast, favored only a few—indeed, a very select few—mostly extending the collecting designs of a French-Texan family named DeMenil (whose fortune is based upon the oil-services company Schlumberger). If most alternative spaces show artists otherwise unavailable elsewhere, Dia favors larger and most ambitious works unavailable elsewhere mostly by familiar artists. On West Broadway, Dia purchased at 393 a large ground-floor space solely to house permanently Walter de Maria's *The Broken Kilometer*, which has gold bars aligned in parallel rows from one end of the space to the other. In a second-floor space at 141 Wooster Street that it assumed from the Heiner Friedrich Gallery, Dia installed in 1977 the third replica of de Maria's *Earth Room*, where the artist filled much of a gallery with earth 21 inches deep. Previously exhibited in Cologne and Munich, the *New York Earth Room*, as it is called, is customarily open to the public from noon to 6 P.M., Wednesday through Saturday, except during the summer months, its attendant conscientiously counting everyone entering the space, which was featured near the end of Robert Hughes's mid-

1990s public television survey of American art. I can remember in 1977 that the man delivering bags of choice earth to 141 Wooster Street asked, "Now that you have all the dirt, what are you going to do with it?" Little did he or anyone else think that more than two decades later more than twenty tons of his earth would still fill much of the second floor at that address. Neither de Maria work is for sale, not that anyone less than the Sheik of Arabie would want to buy.

Another limited gallery in SoHo was established by Donald Judd (1928–1994) on the ground flood of his own classic cast-iron building (1870, Nicholas Whyte, architect) at 101 Spring Street on the corner of Greene. With usually large and tall windows fronting two SoHo streets giving it a nearly continuous expanse of glass, it has been an ideal showroom for attracting the attention of passersby. For years before and after his death, the space exhibited his own work; other times, I've seen first-rank art from his own collection, including the brilliant fluorescent sculptures of Dan Flavin. (Now belonging to the Cianti Foundation established by Judd, the 101 Spring Street building received a top grant from the National Trust for Historic Preservation in 2001.) Just on the other side of Houston Street, as West Broadway is renamed La Guardia Place, is another one-person museum, this devoted exclusively to the work of Chaim Gross (1904–1991), established in his former studio not by an independent foundation but the late artist himself, subsequently administered by his widow, recently in her nineties, very much as a Manhattan parallel to the one-person museum in Queens established by the sculptor Isamu Noguchi (1904–1988) in his former studio there.

In 1985, the Dia Foundation assumed control of a former firehouse at 155 Mercer Street. Here, for nearly a dozen years, it showcased emerging choreographers, in addition to offering rehearsal space at bargain rates to dozens of local dance companies. Upstairs was a Sufi mosque directed by Tosun Bayrak, whose earlier career as a SoHo artist is remembered by some. In 1996, the sometime firehouse was acquired by the Joyce Theater, a dance showcase based in Chelsea, which has used it as a testing venue.

No memoir of SoHo museums should forget the downtown branch of the very uptown Guggenheim that opened in 1992 on the northwest corner of Prince Street and Broadway only to close a decade later, its premises replaced by the classiest of high-class retailers, Prada, whose renovations reportedly cost $40 million, making art of another kind, while the Guggenheim left behind upstairs offices for certain staff curators better located downtown.

The ultimate alternative space was one's own studio, where one could exhibit one's own art, inviting a colleague, a dealer, or even a collector for a "studio visit." From time to time, several artists in and around SoHo combined to open their studios at a certain time, usually a Saturday afternoon, and issued a collective invitation under a banner like "10 Downtown." The annual rosters of these artists, reprinted as an appendix to the 112 Workshop book, acknowledges Leon Golub and William Creston in 1968; Rudolf Baranik and Elliott Barowitz in 1969; and Georges Noel and May Stevens in 1970, in an impressive succession. More than one collector, or potential collector, remembers 10 Downtown not only for the art but also for glimpses of not one but several artists' studios, incidentally educating them about possibilities of interior design.

Some SoHo artists opened their studios regularly for prospective shoppers, especially female artists for suburban women in the late 1970s, customarily on weekdays. I can remember in my own building a unique cackle emanating from the elevator shaft on occasional Wednesday afternoons. It came from a busload of women, never quiet, visiting the studio of one of my co-op partners. Thank God they don't live here, I recall saying to myself. (Eventually, my co-op partner decided this studio display wasn't worth doing, while the suburban women later discovered the many boutiques that were capitalizing on SoHo's reputation for advanced taste.)

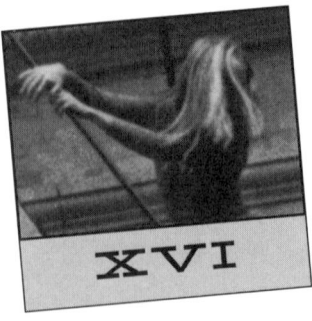

XVI

*To accommodate others, [Allen Daugherty] created the Red
Spot Outdoor Slide Show Theater, Inc., which allowed any
philosophy, point of view of aesthetic as long as it fit into
the slide tray or could be performed on the roof at 535
Broadway or on the street below, or could be heard on the
FM radio station 98.6.*

—Clayton Patterson, in "Downtown" (August 14, 1991)

RECOGNIZING IN THE early seventies that SoHo itself was
an art gallery, a Turk named Tosun Bayrak, scarcely young
at the time, did radical performance pieces—"actions" they could be
called—whose audacity remains unrivaled. When his wife was
evicted from a West Broadway building that was sold to a new owner,
Bayrak embedded bags of bovine blood and entrails in the walls and
ceiling of her loft and replastered them. Inviting people into the loft
one Saturday afternoon, he chopped at the walls with an ax to "free"
the gore, so to speak. White pigeons, very much a symbol of peace at
the time, were released from beneath the floorboards. This piece he
called *The Living Loft*.

For an earlier piece, titled *Love America and Live*, Bayrak purchased perhaps a dozen white rats each several inches long from a laboratory and then colored them black to resemble common New York
City street vermin. Obtaining permission in advance from the NYC
police, he worked outdoors on a SoHo street closed from traffic.
Covering the pavement with paper, he allowed the rats to run along the
sides of the paper, near the street gutters. Meanwhile, a penis appeared

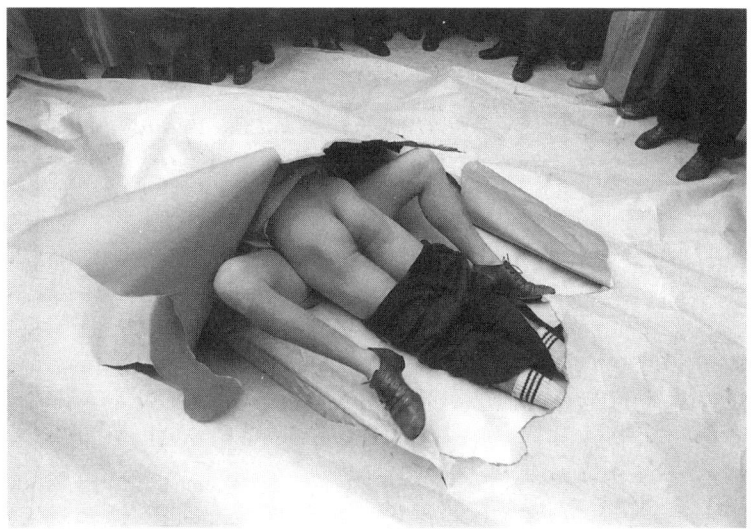

From Tosun Bayrak's performance *Love America or Live* on Prince at Mercer, November 7, 1971. Copyright Fred W. McDarrah

and a woman rubbed it, pretending to take its sperm and put it into a vagina that also appeared through the paper. Later, under the paper a naked couple copulated, their activity recognized by passersby and the cops, who stood by, necessarily respecting official clearance. Gallons of bovine blood poured down from nearby upper floors, all to the sound of a John Phillip Sousa march. Most of the rats were retrieved later.

Another time, Bayrak and a few coconspirators, in the middle of the night, celebrated May Day by covering SoHo's street signs with the names of Lenin, Karl Marx, and Leon Trotsky. So neatly did his alternative signage resemble the originals underneath that the cops reportedly tore down the entire street signs. On another Saturday afternoon he took from a baby carriage dollar bills topped with urine and excrement and simply placed them on the street in front of galleries. Another time he got Ivan Karp, always generous toward artists, to give him permission to use the street in front of his gallery as well as the lot next door; but as the piece was evolving, Karp got angry enough to renege and call the police.

For the birthday of his very young daughter, Bayrak, dressed as a harlequin, had a sexually ambiguous human painted white emerge from a birthday cake in front of 55 Mercer Street while he gave away enormous bullfrogs. From there the procession walked a full mile to Washington Square, several people carrying on their backs crosses with the names of Americans fallen in the Vietnam War. Elliott Barowitz remembers, "We planted the crosses on the north side of Washington Square Park. Ed Koch, then my neighbor on Washington Place and a congressman [and later the city's mayor], joined us and came back to my house as we got cleaned up."

A more provocative display in a basement gallery on Spring Street had a sheep carcass enclosed in an aquarium with leeches. Titling this work *Requiem for a War Hero*, who was his father (in World War I), Bayrak also cooked chicken legs, onto which he put a paste mixed from cooked chicken liver and human sperm. Typically announcing what it was, he offered it to people, with an audacity that was at once obnoxious and awesome. Only in SoHo at that time, with its cultivated tolerance of extreme art, were such "actions" possible.

Earning a Guggenheim fellowship in 1965, Bayrak became a professor at Fairleigh Dickinson University in suburban New Jersey, where he taught until he retired in the late 1980s. Meanwhile, he accepted the tutelage of a holy man prominent in his native Istanbul and, exercising his persuasive powers in another realm, became a Sufi Sheikh (pronounced sheyk, not sheek), working during the 1980s in an upstairs space at the former Mercer Street firehouse, then owned by the Dia Foundation, and later at a retreat in upstate New York. Under the name Tosun Bayrak Al Jarrahi, he has published books with such titles as *The Name & the Named: The Divine Attributes of God* (2001), which promises, among other things, "the 201 traditional names of qualities of the Prophet Muhammad." The biographical note on the back of this volume mentions numerous other works "interpreted and compiled by Sheikh Tosun Bayrak." Though acknowledgment of his art has been rare in print, it is remembered, in part because no one ever quite equaled him at provocative public interventions.

A later, younger SoHo artist with his own alternative exhibition venue was Rene Moncada, a Venezuelan born in 1943, who in 1977

rented a ground floor on upper Wooster Street. Here he established a
modest street-level gallery, living behind and above it with his wife who
worked uptown in finance. Indeed, he constructed a sleeping loft in
full defiance of the city's M1–5 rules against residing in ground-floor
spaces. Naming his gallery after only his first name, Rene showed
mostly his own work, much of it devoted to glorifying women, sometimes whittling wood carvings and sculptures as he sat inside or outside
the front door of his emporium. I can recall that on weekends this
space would sometimes be rented out in the evenings to yuppies having
a private party, apparently getting SoHo space cheap for a few hours.

Moncada's principal achievement, however, was not small works
but large ones, murals actually, that he painted in the tradition of
urban grafitti, but always with permission of the property owners, on
spare walls throughout SoHo, most of them carrying in large letters
the inscription, "I Am The Best Artist," against a simple background,
sometimes abbreviated as "IATBA," and signed with only his first
name, "Rene." Essentially, he took an unadorned wall containing
nothing and added something that was uniquely his. Working in the
great SoHo tradition of playwrights who built their own theaters, he
found his own walls. Once he established his unique way of exhibiting himself, no one dared imitate him. The most prominent Rene
mural, near the corner of Broome Street and West Broadway, measured 10 feet by 50. Those who didn't know better might consider him
SoHo's most visible artist; but since his murals lacked an address, they
didn't necessarily know where to find him. "The art establishment
wouldn't even acknowledge that I existed. So I decided it was up to
me to make myself known," he told an interviewer. "If you want to
advertise something, you have to create an image, so I came up with
'I Am The Best Artist.' Now I can safely claim that everybody knows
me, because if you have not seen that sign, you have nothing to do
with art or you've never been to SoHo." Much as Alanna Heiss found
empty spaces within industrial buildings, so with his painting of otherwise empty walls Rene successfully transformed SoHo itself into his
alternative exhibition venue.

Moncada once proposed to our co-op to artify an open wall,
fronting on a parking lot. I thought that it was a good idea at the time,

when all of us were still on the board of directors. However, a majority of my partners refused his offer, one of them adding a mural would be acceptable to him if it didn't have Rene's name—a bit of attempted artistic censorship I found objectionable. Instead, Moncada painted the attendants' house in the parking lot, getting permission from its owner. When the building opposite his Wooster Street mural became a fancy restaurant, I congratulated him on getting attention from a better class of people. Responding to the abundance of limousines parked on our street, he and I (who resemble one another enough to look like brothers) planned to spend our summer evenings drinking beer and playing loud Latin music on his doorstep in the great tradition of SoHo street protests, but the restaurant closed before we opened, so to speak. When he was finally evicted from his ground-floor residence in 2001, I felt that SoHo had lost something unique. Thankfully, his murals remain.

Allen Daugherty resembled Rene (Moncada) in realizing that the walls of SoHo buildings could provide an exhibition arena for art; but whereas Rene painted permanent murals emblazoned not only with his name but also with self-aggrandizing slogans, Daugherty worked anonymously, initially behind the pseudonym Red Spot, with transient images and sounds. His taken name came from a poster of a red circle he had plastered all over SoHo, where the scruffy walls of industrial buildings welcomed posters—not just single images but often whole rows of the same picture. Near the bottom right corner was the inscription "Area Hello" with white type on a small black square. His close collaborator, the artist Anna Lascari, remembers, "He told me once that he had named the theater Red Spot after the red spot of the poster."

Temperamentally shy, Daugherty/Red Spot created an alternative venue for successfully making friends and serving his artist neighbors generously. From his rented loft on Broadway just north of Spring Street, he projected westward onto a neighboring wall at night images as large as 40 feet square every Friday and Saturday night through the 1980s. The Red Spot Outdoor Slide Theater, as he called it, was thus visible from Broadway just south of Spring Street. He also projected perpendicularly onto a translucent screen that was suspended across the southern edge of the roof of his building, which had only a lower building between it and Spring Street, so that another set of images could be seen from points to the south. As most of these pictures were painted directly onto slides 2.25 inches square and put in powerful Hasselblad projectors equipped with long-range lenses, these were clearly visible from a distance.

Generous in his tastes, Red Spot accepted all sorts of art, claiming that "the only criterion for acceptance is image visibility." His nonprofit "Inc." even published a full-page ad in Artforum containing instructions for hand-preparing slides. From me he solicited transparencies entirely of words that, once projected, friends incidentally on the street at that time recognized as mine, so different were my images from what everyone else in his screening was doing. Because names weren't attached to images on the wall, this medium-without-crediting-tags advantaged work that had a unique "look."

Daugherty also put together a lower-power FM radio station, literally a sublegal operation, that was audible only for a block or two. (Residing four blocks away, I couldn't get it.) From 1981 to his death in 1991, he broadcast five nights a week from sundown into the night. The poet Charles Doria, still on the board of the directors of the Red Spot foundation, remembers hearing "mostly Hank Williams, Carter Sisters, Gene Autry & Riders of the Purple Sage, with many station identifications: 'You are listening to 98.6 on your dial, etc.' Dreamy, sentimental Texas. I lent him some harder edge stuff: tapes and discs like Bob Wills & Texas Playboys, Michael Murphy (Cosmic Cowboy), Doug Sahm, (Texas Tornado & Austin) Kinky Friedman and Texas Jewboys (Ballad of Charles Whitman), Mother Earth, Freddy King, and so on. Usually he or one or more of the assistants would go downstairs with one or two portable radios and strategically position them on the street or stand around holding them, so there was always a soft carpet of 98.6 sounds and words." Oh yes, the sounds too were Red Spot's anonymous gift to SoHo.

Like Tosun Bayrak more than a decade before him, Red Spot also closed off Spring Street one June night in 1986 to make it a performance stage, paving the street with white paper. For this Product Sacrifice Show, as he called it, participants were invited to bring

actual products that were steamrolled. Needless to say, the announcement in the *Village Voice* noted, below a photo of a sledgehammer
decimating a microwave, that the event was "free."

As the video master Clayton Patterson wrote, "The major thinking behind Red Spot's shows was artistic cooperation, lack of competition, inclusion of 'every-one,' no matter what color, body type,
gender, sexual orientation, or age, and included an openness of others,
sharing methods and information about the making of your slides for
the Red Spot Shows," implicitly reminding everyone involved that the
major theme of SoHo was not the selling of art but its creation and
dissemination. The result was an unsung institution that was taken for
granted until its absence was felt when he died too soon. "After Allen
passed away," Charles Doria remembers, "there was a scene in his loft
like the one in *Zorba the Greek* after Lila Kedrova died—people came
in and stripped the place down to sheetrock. Get a chunk of a genuine artist loft before they're all history." The last time I looked, the
ground floor of this building was the sleek local outlet of a national
jewelry chain named Zale's. The Red Spot Outdoor Slide Show
Theater, Inc., survives nonetheless, currently headed by Anna Lascari.
It has in storage 80,000 slides along with two powerful projectors,
someday to be revived, to be sure, but probably, given how SoHo has
since changed (Zale's!), in another place, perhaps even, heaven for-
bid, alongside other monuments of American art history in a university museum.

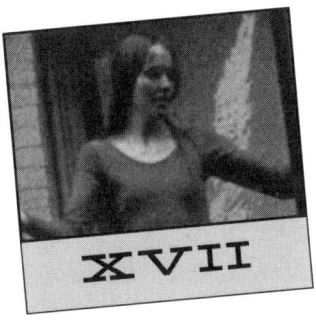

XVII

A place like SoHo epitomizes what cities are all about: people really work there; the life of the community and the lives of the people flow together; and those who live, work, and visit there are active participants in its social life.

—James R. Hudson, *The Unanticipated City* (1987)

T HE SCALE OF SoHo's loft spaces made them appropriate for music designed for audiences smaller than those in the standard musical concert venues of New York. When Robert Buecher in the 1970s founded the SoHo Baroque Opera Co. in his own upstairs loft-gallery on West Broadway, his initial mission was presenting forgotten operatic works from the late eighteenth century, drawing upon scores that Buecher unearthed himself. Among the operas he revived were J. Philippe Rameau's *Les Indes Galantes* (1735), G. Philipp Telemann's *Der geduldige Sokrates* (1721), Domenico Cimarosa's *La Astuzie Femminili* (1794), and Baldassare Galuppi's *Il Filosofo de Campagna* (1754), most of them as new to New York as to SoHo. In this labor of operatic love, his regular musicians included the flutist Andrew Bolotowsky, the harpsichordist Elaine Camparone, and the countertenor Daniel Collins. "Buecher sent people back to the baroque opera," the poet Michael Andre remembers. "I found Dittersdorf, later publishing W. H. Auden's translation of the Goldoni/Dittersdorf *Arcifanfaro* in the last issue of my magazine *Unmuzzled Ox*. He also commissioned new music. The best by far is Elodie Lauten's *Deus Ex Machina Cycle*."

In later years, Buecker sponsored free concerts of both baroque and contemporary music for a select list of invited friends, usually on Monday evenings, which is customarily the night off for uptown pit musicians receptive to doing higher-class work. I can recall other Monday classical and avant-garde chamber-sized concerts upstairs in private downtown lofts. One of Tom Johnson's first reviews for the *Village Voice* in 1973 praised a Charlemagne Palestine solo "presented at a Greene Street loft by Acme Productions." The loft belonged to Jim Burton, who had in the previous summer of 1972 presented concerts on his building's roof, which was the sort of venue one could use for music in a neighborhood officially designated as nonresidential. If summertime parties uptown were on penthouse porches typically with designed floors, those in SoHo were held on flat industrial roofs furnished with an array of shipping skids taken from the street or, at best, plain wooden platforms.

For more avant-garde musics, the crucial venue was the Kitchen, the classic downtown alternative space originating literally as a part of the Mercer Arts Center in the bowels of the Broadway Central Hotel between Bleecker and Third. When that venerable building collapsed from excess water on its roof, the Kitchen relocated in 1973 to a more attractive, larger space, perhaps 5,000 square feet, upstairs on the northwest corner of Broome and Wooster. Here, on the second floor, with large windows looking out upon the principal truck route from east lower Manhattan to the Holland Tunnel, its presentations would always be threatened by crunching street noises. Created primarily to show the new medium of video, the Kitchen, under the official name Haleakala, Inc., also had a music program, originally entrusted to Jim Burton, also a painter, whose earliest allegiances were to "downtown" (i.e., nonacademic) Manhattan music in the tradition of John Cage.

The first music program at the new address, 13 December 1973, was a rich presentation of Cage's music, including some of his more esoteric works: *26"1.1499" for String Player* (1955), whose score was based upon random specks in his manuscript paper, played by the double bassist Jon Deak, long a veteran of the New York Philharmonic; Cage's very early, rarely performed *Sonata for Clarinet* (1933); *Water Walk* (1959), in which many physical actions are rapidly performed; *Water Music* (1952), played on the piano by Don Gillespie, just beginning his career as Cage's editor for music publishing; *Speech* (1955), in which two speakers read news clippings against a background of five randomly tuned radios; and *WBAI*, which this time was a four-channel recording of Cage reading a favorite lecture.

Within the next six weeks, the Kitchen presented concerts by Yoshimasa Wada and Palestine, both of whom made music in radically different ways. Whereas the former got an original sound by attaching a mouthpiece like that used for playing a tuba to humongous plumbing pipes, Palestine at his strongest simply pounded several keys of a Bösendorfer grand piano as rapidly as possible for 20 to 30 minutes, generating rich combinations of overtones previously unheard. The title of his program, "Spectral Continuum for Piano," was at once pretentious and accurate. As Tom Johnson wrote at the time, "Most of the time Palestine sits eyes closed, his head turning to one side, listening intently to the overtones. And the strange activity of these overtones is essential to the music. Like all overtones, they are elusive, hard to pick out, and pure as gold when you can bring them into focus. But unlike most overtones, they seem to fluctuate in rational ways." As a musician-performer who also exhibited his visual art, Palestine epitomized the kind of SoHo artist that the Kitchen aimed to support.

Soon afterward the Kitchen music program was run by Rhys Chatham, barely out of his teens. Fully two generations younger than Cage, Chatham soon opened the Kitchen to other kinds of music, sponsoring mostly jazz and, later, electronic rock. Chatham recalled that his immediate successor as music director, Garrett List, in 1975–1976, "caused a sensation when he opened the Kitchen's doors to improvisers such as the Art Ensemble of Chicago, Don Cherry, and Cecil Taylor." When Chatham returned to his position late in 1977, the Kitchen became the New York outpost for an international synthesis of rock with electronics developed by the avant-garde: Laurie Anderson, Peter Gordon, and Brian Eno, who reportedly emigrated from England to settle for a while on Broome Street (which is incidentally a rich fount of ambient noise). Featuring avant-garde rock in his programming, Chatham felt "an uproar from both the art and jazz communities. But by the middle eighties, there was no longer this feeling of transgression. It had become the norm, to the point where music producers at alternative art spaces and festivals [around the world] appeared to be putting on variety shows rather than concerts of serious music." As noted before, the Kitchen fulfilled its cross-disciplinary mission by presenting concerts by people not initially established in music, such as the first retrospective of my own electroacoustic compositions in 1975. Several reviews of important SoHo performances are reprinted in Tom Johnson's indispensible *The Voice of New Music* (1989).

The Dia Foundation presented avant-garde music in its second-story space at 141 Wooster Street, before it was filled with Walter de Maria's earth. Sponsoring only a select few, as is its style, it offered, in 1974, a Terry Riley concert and, in 1975, La Monte Young playing his lush but interminable Well-Tuned Piano live in concerts classic enough to be recorded (and available decades later on several CDs) before installing Young in his own facility from 1979 to 1985 on Harrison Street in Tribeca.

Another key address for avant-garde classical music was 112 Greene Street, discussed earlier as an alternative space for visual art, it also sponsored concerts in its ground-floor venue and a 24-track recording studio in its basement. Nearly everyone involved in downtown avant-garde music used the latter, initially for mixing capabilities unavailable elsewhere in the city. On its premises in 1977 I advanced my own electroacoustic music with *Praying to the Lord* that electronically multiplied my own voice reciting familiar prayers into a chorus of 256 voices. Technologically advanced at the time, this studio became obsolete as computer-editing of sound developed during the 1990s.

Otherwise, SoHo was receptive to "loft jazz" in small ensembles likewise too intimate for a concert hall but for audiences more respectful than those in a club serving alcohol. When Ornette Coleman resided on Prince Street in the mid-1970s, he had concerts in his ground-floor loft. The 1978 SoHo guidebook reminds me of Ali's Alley at 77 Greene Street, charging an admission of only three bucks. Ali, a drummer who also composed, established the space in

1974 with only himself and his group performing. After an hiatus during which a liquor license and other permissions were obtained, he reopened at the "new" Ali's Alley that was particularly popular with both European visitors and B&T drivers, who regarded the industrial neighborhood as a free evening parking lot. Among the groups performing there were the Rene McLean Sextet, James "Blood" Ulmer Quintet, Ted Daniel & Energy, and, of course, the Rashied Ali Quintet. On an elevated platform was a visible tape machine recording all performances.

Since jazz is not among my enthusiasms, I also learned in the 1978 guidebook about later, similar venues: Axis in SoHo, housed in the same West Broadway premises as the Marvin Elson Gallery, favored free jazz such as Sun Ra and Paul Bley. Lacking a liquor license, it charged four bucks admission and sold capuccino, juice, and cheesecake. Dennis Michaels opened the Basement at 480 Broome Street in 1977, while Danielle Bellamy founded Motivations on the Fifth Floor of 476 Broome Street, both long gone. On the 11th floor of 476 Broadway was Environ, a cooperative venture connected to a nonprofit called the Environmental Community Arts Corp., which sponsored both jazz musicians and jazz dancers. Among the stars reportedly playing there were Anthony Braxton, Dave Brubeck, Marion Brown, and Steve Lacy. At the end of the LP era, it issued a series of five records called Live at Environ. Another venue remembered by many was the Ballroom, founded on West Broadway in 1976 as essentially a restaurant that presented singers of Broadway show music and related cabaret. On its wall was Marion Pinto's mural portraying many early SoHo celebrities gathered around restaurant tables.

Otherwise, important concerts of avant-garde music happened from time to time in art galleries: not only Charlemagne Palestine singing at a steady pitch through several spaces of the block-long Sonnabend Gallery to discover acoustics indigenous to each space, but David Borden's Mother Mallard's Masterpiece Band and Petr Kotik's SEM Ensemble elegantly performing in the Paula Cooper Gallery. A few times each year, for several years, the latter presented a unique mix of new music in the Cagean tradition, Kotik's own music (including a six-hour performance of his setting of Gertrude Stein's *Many Many Women*), and baroque chamber classics. Once these galleries left SoHo, the kinds of concerts presented in their spaces disappeared as well. Who can play instrumental music in a space devoted to peddling clothing or furniture?

The critic Peter Frank, who reviewed this scene at the time for the SoHo News, remembers concerts at 530 Canal Street, 10 Beach Street, and 325 Spring Street, all on the fringes of SoHo proper. "Don't forget Byrd Hoffman's School of Byrds was [upstairs] on Spring St in the earlier '70s," he wrote me recently. "I heard Phil Glass' *Another Look at Harmony* and beginnings of *Einstein on the Beach* during Spring in '75, and I think I heard Ingram Marshall there too."

In his own more spacious loft beyond the southeastern edge of SoHo, the composer and filmmaker Phill Niblock has presented for many years under the banner of the Experimental Intermedia Foundation nightly concerts around the equinox milestones, often introducing European avant-garde musicians who wouldn't (couldn't) perform anywhere else in New York City. In Tribeca, beyond SoHo's southwestern edge, Jim Staley's Roulette has presented concerts for audiences no more numerous than fifty, mostly of electronic music, in sporadic seasons for over two decades now, including many New Yorkers who don't otherwise perform downtown, such as my own second solo concert in 1981 (after a first one at The Kitchen). Way west of SoHo, on Spring Street near the Hudson River, is the Ear Inn, ostensibly a watering hole, which has presented intimate concerts and later poetry readings from the 1980s into the twenty-first century.

Just as SoHo had bookstores at once reflecting and influencing the tastes of the community, so were there sophisticated record stores. The most visible was the SoHo Music Gallery on the southwest corner of Grand and Wooster in the mid-1970s. Among its junior clerks was the composer-to-be John Zorn, incidentally an avid record collector. When it closed in 1985, its stock was purchased by Manny Maris, who opened a store called Lunch for Your Ears on Prince Street near Mulberry just east of Broadway. (When it closed in 1991, much of its highly selective stock went to the Downtown Music Gallery, which survives into the twenty-first century on East 5th Street, just east of the Bowery, essentially extending the taste at once eclectic and selective of the SoHo Music Gallery.)

Upstairs on Broadway north of Grand was New Music Distribution, a nonprofit founded by Carla Bley and Michael Mantler, essentially avant-garde jazz musicians. Initially carrying music they personally preferred, NMDS, as it was called, expanded its outlook to include avant-garde classical and comparable rock. In the memory of Tony Coulter, recently New York's most distinguished radio presenter of late modernist music, "One of the best things about NMDS was the catalog they published, which reviewed almost every record in stock in a thoughtful, non-hype-driven way. I cherish those catalogs to this day, and am still looking for many records they listed that I neglected to pick up at the time." He paused, pain coming to his face. "The worst thing about NMDS was that, particularly towards the end, they didn't always pay musicians for records sold, most of what they carried was on consignment. When they went out of business with many unpaid invoices, it created a serious ripple effect in the New Music scene as lots of musicians were screwed financially."

Printed Matter carried records, often self-published, by artists who also produced books in its stock. The last SoHo record retailer was Artmarket on Grand Street, where Tony Coulter worked part-time. Once it closed in 1999, aficionados of new music had to venture into East 4th Street in NoHo—not only to a huge Tower outlet but to a more selective shop across 4th Street named Other Music.

By 2002, the principal survivor of SoHo-style musical programming, connecting the avant-garde in classical and jazz and rock, was the Knitting Factory, a presenter that began in the 1980s just east of Lafayette on Houston Street and then skipped over SoHo when it moved downtown to Leonard Street in Tribeca. For all kinds of music, SoHo proper in the twenty-first century was dead.

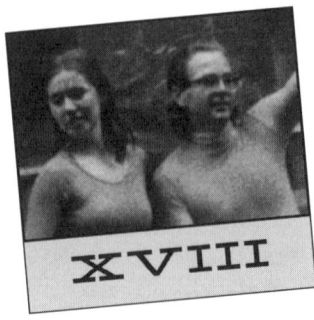

XVIII

I'VE KNOWN Richard Forman since we were teenagers, as he was three years ahead of me first in high school and then in college. Before I entered Brown University, he advised me on which professors were best (and they were); fifteen years later, he encouraged me to move to SoHo where he had already gone. We've remained friendly for over four decades now, though he is notoriously nonsocial, perhaps because we choose not to be competitive (and have had to overcome comparable obstacles in our professional careers). One personal fact not often mentioned is that he was adopted as an infant—a fact I apparently heard well before he did, I guess from gossip in our highly "thoughtful" suburban community where no one told him. The discovery of his alternative parentage prompted a trauma in his mid-thirties. Where this fact is reflected in his highly personal work I'll let others discover.

From the time we first met in the summer of 1955, he established that he wanted to make theater—not film or fiction, in which he later also worked, but live performance. In addition to acting in high-school productions, he designed sets for his teacher's productions with the local community theaters. As a teenager, he went many weekends by himself into the city to see Broadway matinees. His performance as a freshman at Brown as Willie Loman in *Death of a Salesman* is still remembered by those who saw it. Eventually, he studied playwriting, taking an M.F.A. at Yale before moving to New York in the early 1960s and managing a small apartment house on Riverside Drive. For all his love of live performance as a medium, he came by his mid-twenties to disparage conventional theater.

I remember that soon after he moved to Manhattan he showed me scripts, one named "Good-Bennie," that I found impossible to read, assuming the difficulties were not mine alone. He hustled directors, some of whom he knew from Yale, and joined the New Dramatists, which was a collaborative designed to favor those similarly situated. I recall him introducing me to a Yale classmate, Oliver Hailey, who went on to have a prosperous commercial career. In my notes made at the time I find an anecdote that would have otherwise been forgotten: "Around the beginning of 1967, Richard had a slicker comedy under option to some well-known producer; but I don't think this was ever presented." An uptown playwright Foreman was not destined to be. Not for several years would someone else mount his texts.

Rather than knock his head against a wall, Foreman decided to produce and direct his texts himself, drawing upon his experience as a set designer and actor. Reflecting his extensive reading in modern philosophy, he called his theater Ontological-Hysteric. An enthusiast for avant-garde film from his first days in New York, he befriended Jonas Mekas who had founded the Film-Makers' Cinematheque, which was then located in George Maciunas's initial co-op at 80 Wooster Street. On its incompletely renovated ground-floor premises Foreman presented in the spring of 1968 his production of *Angelface*, which remains the initial play in his own published list. Most of his few performers were better known as avant-garde filmmakers, Bob Fleischner, Ernie Gehr, Andrew Noren, Stuart Sherman, and Jim Jennings among them.

According to notes I made at the time, "Only a score of people, at most, attended its premiere. The major innovation consisted of having the characters speak their lines on tape and then repeat them live at a slower, more halting speed; so that taped speeches and live ones occasionally overlapped. As the play's director, Foreman ran the tape from a perch in front of the audience, making sure that the repetitions were completed before the taped words began again." I had trouble following the plot, if there was any, instead remembering stunning images such as "two characters supposedly known as Angels trying to get through passageways but discovering instead that their wings were too broad, memorably pounding against their physical fate." More than three decades later, I can see that by then Foreman had established his use of audiotape for presenting his words, his practice of controlling each production from a perch visible to the audience, and his preference for images over plot. To someone previously unfamiliar with his work, these moves still seem radical.

In March of 1969, I saw in the East Village Foreman's production of *Ida-Eyed* about which I wrote to myself: "The method is abstracted lines that usually have little to do with each other, or the actions of the people; for here, as before, he is striving for abstract sounds on stage all against a background of chugging noises. The stage imagery is equally abstract but to my mind more effective." By 1970, he had moved from an Upper West Side apartment to a loft on the northern edge of SoHo, a few blocks north of the Cinematheque.

A later production likewise presented at the Wooster Street space, *Total Recall* (1971), I found similarly devoid of articulate plot, character interaction, or psychology, among other conventional theatrical qualities. What unified the performance was the abstract style of the dialogue and visual coherence in the setting, costumes, and lighting (which remained bright for the entire performance). Notes made at the time tell me now: "I think the theme is a vision of human behavior, and the key to Foreman's view is that his characters' activities follow their voice on tape, so that they are incapable of doing anything without first hearing what they should do. The vocabulary of their stage activities is very limited. To separate the protagonist's voice from his presence on stage is clearly to disembody him." On this note card dated 15 January 1971, I also find this aside: "He told me that last Wednesday was the first time ever that nobody walked out during a production of one of his plays." Foreman added, as I recall, that it was snowing outside, although since the performance space lacked any windows, no one seated in the audience could see the snow.

In *Hotel China* (1972), likewise at the Film-Makers' Cinematheque, I found other stage devices, including strategic placement of rocks in its first part and the throwing of pebbles in the second. One departure was props that moved mysteriously. "The lines consist mostly of descriptions of the actions the performers are pursuing, all declaimed in straight-forward voices resembling a radio announcer.

The lines were all pre-taped and merely echoed softly by the performers."

With his 1972 productions of *Sophia*, Foreman introduced an annoying buzzer to signal the change of a scene (and perhaps to wake up spectators who might have dozed off), and he has since favored sounds that I find needlessly loud. Other characteristics unique to his theater were a predominantly brown stage, catatonic expressions on the actors (most of whom had previously appeared in his productions), the absence of any change in the lighting, noncentered stage compositions, and memorable tableaus. His characters seemed to represent philosophical positions rather than emotional qualities. Sophia, whose name is Greek for wisdom, is identified as "the guardian of wisdom," and the introduction of erotic material (previously scarce in his work) acknowledges its contribution to the gaining of wisdom. Nobody else's theater, anywhere in the world, looked or sounded like Foreman's.

In *Evidence* (1972), the voice on the tape, clearly Foreman's, repeatedly reiterated that his notebooks for this play consist of what could not be put into the previous play, *Hotel China*. This material was not rejected for its own inadequacy, the voice explained, but because it could not be theatrically developed. Between some of these passages was a loud quacking noise that complimented the intrusive buzzer sound. One new factor was the appearance of Kate Manheim, a beautiful young American raised in Paris, who would become the principal performer of his plays for the coming decade and eventually Foreman's second wife. A second was the action of writing crucial messages on the blackboard, the last of them reading, "To be continued."

The first critical point was that, once staged, the putatively omitted material resembles what was included. Second, this work, like others of Foreman, is esthetically coherent in spite of all the effort to remain inscrutable. Recalling that Foreman had written an early appreciation of Robert Wilson's performance theater, I recognized that his work had come to resemble Wilson's in echoing visually what was conveyed verbally, or vice versa; but whereas Wilson wanted to work with many people in gigantic spaces larger than any found even in SoHo, Foreman's was more appropriate to the scale of his native neighborhood. Whereas Wilson wanted to make bigger than Broadway, Foreman wanted smaller than off-Broadway. A few days after seeing his work, as well as Wilson's, my memory typically retained not lines of his prose, strong though these often were, but images and sounds.

Two new qualities in *Particle Theory* (1973) were a rather rapid tempo, especially in the first part, and more various forms of sound than before, including some refrains from soap-opera music. In *Vertical Mobility* (1974) there was a deafening drum between some country and western music. He also ran strings between the audience and the stage, increasing the alienation effect he earlier admired in Bertolt Brecht. This last device would reappear in his work into the next century.

It became more clear to me that Foreman was presenting mental states and that this play, like its predecessor, was based on the mind of an artist. Much like Gertrude Stein, whose influence he acknowledged, he was working out of expressionistic esthetics to make a theater different from earlier work dubbed with that label. Like Stein, who self-published through her companion Alice B. Toklas, Foreman produced his texts, working with others but shaping every detail to his vision. For all the appearance of anarchy, his was a very authoritarian theater (much as Stein's might have been, had she directed her own plays). By 1974, only a few years after his work was sparsely attended, I noticed his theater filled, often with downtown celebrities, as he had successfully insinuated himself into a SoHo world that had no theater other than the Performing Garage. His programs around this time acknowledged support from the National Endowment for the Arts, NYSCA, and the Rockefeller Foundation. Later programs would identify yet other foundations, as well as private donors. Isolated and underappreciated he no longer was.

In *Pain(t)* (1974), which was presented not at the Anthology but in the SoHo space that became my own loft, I perceived an attempt to produce writing as strong as his images, recording in my notes at the time that the play opened with this declaration: "This play is about making art with a certain kind of energy, which is energy most

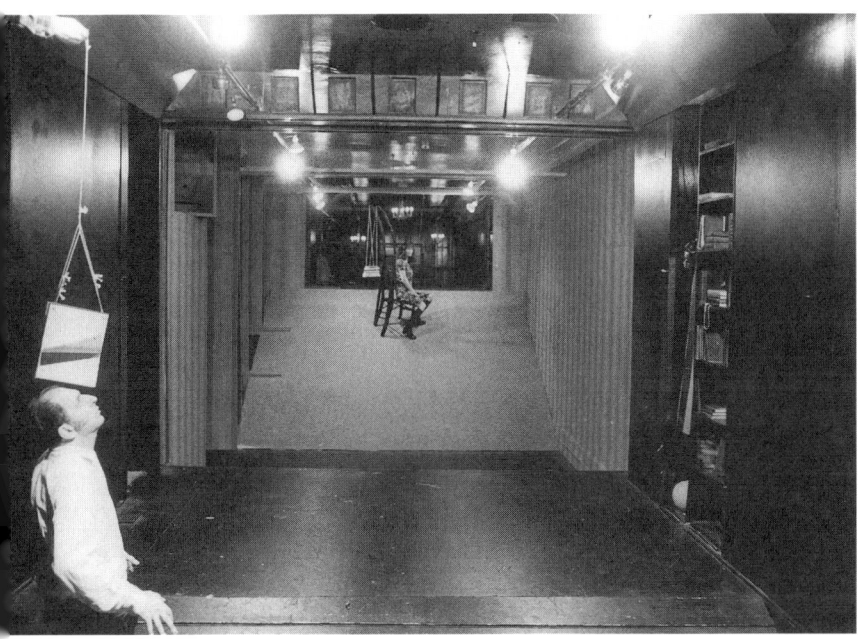

Two planes slanting upward utilize the deep stage fashioned by Richard Foreman at 491 Broadway for his play, *Rhoda in Potatoland*. Photo by Babette Mangolte, courtesy of Richard Foreman

people use most of the time." Later I heard and wrote down: "Higher values are manifest in a physical form." "We each have a different part of the picture we like best. Does that mean it's a good picture or a bad picture?" This time the lines were spoken initially by the players, instead of their repeating speeches previously broadcast on tape. Kate Manheim and her sister Nora appeared nude in this production, as did Mimi Johnson, whose devotion to Foreman's work extended to her also representing him in securing support outside SoHo. One of the most provocative scenes in *Pain(t)* had three men trying to shove the word "painting" up Kate's rectum.

By 1975, Foreman had finally established his own theater in a narrow loft at 491 Broadway, just north of Broome Street. Putting the audience in seven banked rows at one end, he had a stage that was far deeper than its width of 14 feet, in an unusual departure from theatri-cal tradition. Indeed, the stage sloped up from the floor to an initial plane and then dipped before rising to a yet higher plane. With such an abundance of side walls, Foreman frequently pulled props and set-tings out of the sides, rather than dropping them from above. I found the performance of *Rhoda in Potatoland* (1975) more nervous than its predecessors and the audiotape more dense and intricate, if not hys-terical, all these changes perhaps reflecting the influence of Kate Manheim's more active metabolism on Foreman's work. Though Manheim and Bob Fleischer, normally an experimental filmmaker, were given "starring" roles in an unusual departure for Foreman, I found them less predominant than before, not because other perform-ers supplanted them but because the unusual speed of the piece seemed to defeat individuals.

By the mid-1970s as well, Foreman received a fellowship from the Guggenheim Foundation, always attuned to reward recognition accorded elsewhere, and other performers began to use Foreman's texts. Lawrence Kornfield, long a major figure at the Judson Church Theater from the pre-SoHo 1960s, produced and directed *Lines of Vision* (1976), which reflected Foreman's penchants for placing strings across the stage, muted colors, and striking tableaux along with Kornfield's own pronounced enthusiasms for lush costumes and campy songs. This production also took more time than Foreman, normally succinct, would have allowed. By this time as well, Foreman also accepted uptown directing jobs and designed a production of Brecht's *The Threepenny Opera* for the New York Shakespeare Festival in 1976. With a new translation by Kate's father, the translator Ralph Manheim, and the prominent actor Raul Julia as Macheath, this had a healthy run. Foreman collaborated with the composer Stanley Silverman on uptown musicals. He also began to work more often in Europe, where several SoHo artists (including myself for a while) found support unavailable back home.

Consulting notes made back at the time, I see now that I thought *Book of Spendors, Part Two (Book of Levers): Action at a Distance* (1977) disaffecting, as it opens with lights shining at the audience and a crunching sound track. It featured five women, all of whom were nude at least once, perhaps to compensate for a text that was even less accessible than before. On Foreman's own list of productions, 1978 was the first year since 1968 to have nothing.

Reflecting his enthusiasm for philosophy, which he continues to read avidly, much as professional novelists read fiction, Foreman is skilled at high-pitched statements about his purposes, some more persuasive than others. This I've reprinted before for its clarity:

> In 1968, I began to write for the theater that I wanted to see, which was radically different from any style of theater that I had seen. In brief, I imagined a theater which broke down all elements into a kind of atomic structure—and showed those elements of story, action, sound, light, composition, gesture, in terms of the smallest building-block units, the basic cells of the perceived experience of both living and art-making. The scripts themselves read like notations of my own process of imagining a theater piece. They are the evidence of a kind of effort in which the mind's leaps and inventions may be rendered as part of a process not unique to the artist in question (myself) but typical of the building-up which goes on through all modes of coming-into-being (human and non-human). I want to refocus the attention of the spectator on the intervals, gaps, relations, and rhythms which saturate the objects (acts and physical props) which are the 'givens' of any particular play.

This text, as well as other shrewd essays on his purposes, can be found in the books containing collections of his plays.

Penguin Torquet (1981) was the first play-as-play that Foreman presented outside his own turf, and I found it a departure in other ways. It lacked nudity, suggesting that his theater would survive without Manheim's strikingly pinkish body. Here quite pale, her hair dyed blonde, she is terrorized by all sorts of characters, as well as props, at a nearly hysterical pitch. The scenery reminded me of 1920s French films that Foreman liked so much, while the sounds were so atrociously loud I had to stuff my ears with tissue, as I would have done in a rock concert only a few years before. "The lines are the least concrete element in the mix," I noticed at the time. This was the last time I saw Manheim perform, though she continued doing so in French.

In an interview with me published in 1982, Foreman told me how differently he proceeds from other theater artists:

> These days there's a text that is simply a series of lines with no character indicated [much like Gertrude Stein's scripts in this respect]. The first thing I do is to design a set. It's difficult to say how I decide to design a set, how I decide what form the set will take. When the time comes to produce a play, I have many, many texts that I've generated (I prefer to say rather than written) over the past few years. I very casually pick one. I pick them on the basis of a very casual reading of the text, you know, just skimming through it. Then to design the set, I might look at it over the period of a minute and a half, just getting the feel of what some of the scenes are like, some of the pages are like—and then I start to make sketches and just sort of doodle my notion of articulating a kind of space. As the set proceeds, it sort of takes on a life of its own in a certain sense, in a way similar to the way that Cage and Cunningham, the American composer and dancer, work when they're creating dances, where Cage will perform a musical score that Cunningham doesn't listen to while he is creating the choreography.

To which I respond, "Except that you are both the author and the stage designer here," in effect collaborating with himself. His rejoinder:

> I think of myself as a writer. I feel that in all kinds of ways my writing is much more adventurous than my staging, which, I fear, tends to take these rather exploratory texts and turn them into a more classical kind of theater than I'm totally satisfied with.

My sense is that while his stagecraft has had more influence than his writing, someone would need to proceed as he does to reach a comparable end.

Sometime in the 1980s I stopped making notecards about Foreman performances that I saw, possibly because I had nothing new to say about them to myself. From 1979 to 1985, he worked mostly in Paris, Manheim's home city, thanks to funding from the French government, incidentally selling his SoHo theater space. However, patronage from France ended with a change in political administrations. Professionally homeless at home in the late 1980s, he directed plays with the Wooster Group, which inherited the Performing Garage, and the Public Theater. The strongest of the latter was *Film Is Evil, Radio Is Good* (1987) about which a good deal of criticism has been written, some of it reprinted and acknowledged in the anthology *Richard Foreman* (1999) edited by Gerald Rabkin.

In 1991, Foreman was offered exclusive use of an upstairs room at St. Marks Church, located not in SoHo but in the East Village. Previously it had housed Theater Genesis, which was a precursor to the Theater of the Ridiculous, which was a classic off-off-Broadway group. Thirty-six feet square, 15 feet high, this he organized differently, putting the audience in a few sharply banked rows only 15 feet deep along its longest edge. Not horizontal strings but a Plexiglas wall separates the spectators from the stage, the glass incidentally reflecting the spectators' faces back at them. Because the St. Marks Church is an historic building, air-conditioning can't be added, thus limiting performances here to New York's colder months.

Every winter since 1992 Foreman has offered a new production, each rehearsed for a full three months before they are premiered. They tend to resemble the others in my memory, so familiar had his theatrical style become for me, striking differences in titles notwithstanding: *The Mind King* (1992), *Samuel's Major Problems* (1993), *My Head Was a Sledgehammer* (1994), *I've Got the Shakes* (1995), *The Universe* (1996), *Permanent Brain* Damage (1996), *Benita Canova* (1997), *Paradise Hotel* (*Hotel Fuck*) (1998), *Bad Boy Nietzsche* (2000), *Now That Communism Is Dead, My Life Feels Empty* (2001), and *Maria Del Bosco* (2002). Usually, every evening's performance is sold out, sometimes in advance, until he decides to close them in the spring, letting his assistants and interns use the space for their own productions during the summer months.

About *The Universe*, I wrote to myself: "Only a few of several performers speak. Accompanying them is a kind of chorus of idiosyncratically dressed people who move, often transporting props, but rarely speak. Here they are wearing ragged dark suits, white gloves with their fingers torn away, and sneakers, while each carries a white cane. Though the articulate actors are only a few feet away, they speak into microphones, while the audiotape background of music and/or speech is often strident. The lines they speak make sense neither as exposition nor narrative but as discontinuous observations supposedly based upon Foreman's musings at the time the text was written. Sometimes they are aphoristic; others times, funny. There is no attempt to put the most important lines in intrinsically strategic places. What I cannot tell anymore is why one production might be better than another." Perhaps someone else, looking at his work afresh, can identify distinctions so far invisible to me.

In the most recent production, I found not Plexiglas but strings again between the audience and the stage, an audiotape with lines spoken mostly in his own voice, other sounds that were often raucous, three skinny women who repeatedly mimed terror and sexual violation, five silent men dressed approximately the same who tended to crowd the small stage whenever they appeared, an awesomely intricate single set that included printed papers mounted on the walls, memorable theatrical images, and a packed house that included people sitting in the aisles.

Throughout the 1990s, companies other than Foreman's own staged his plays as well—in France, Tokyo, Melbourne, Berlin (where German translations have appeared since the early 1980s), and all over the United States. A theater company located in New York's Lower East Side produced all his scripts over three summers in the late 1990s. "I saw them all," he told me, "each summer one or two were awful, most were not bad, and each year one or two would be really outstanding." In 1995, Foreman received a "genius" grant from the MacArthur Foundation, which also rewarded Elizabeth LeCompte and Meredith Monk in the same round, representing a recognition of SoHo unknown at that granting agency both before and since.

Foreman also developed a website (www.ontological.com) that differs in one crucial respect from anything any previous playwright has done in offering the world "hundreds of pages of unedited texts which Richard Foreman is making available freely for use by theatrical authors directors from which to create plays of their own. The material is offered freely. I ask no royalty. Because of the unique way I generate plays—this may mean I myself will be using from this pool of materials in the future. I invite you to do so also." Not unlike others who see themselves working in a small community, he puts below this blanket invitation not only his home address but also his telephone number. In my experience, except when he's working at his theater, Richard Foreman is nearly always home and he answers his own telephone. Though the words might be free, Foreman's stagecraft is not so easily appropriated by others.

While much in these recent productions is familiar to me, I know that people seeing Foreman for the first time(s) remain impressed by his originality and strength. And they tell others, continuing to spread his reputation mostly by word-of-mouth. As before, Foreman is usually present at his small theater—an unprepossessing, shy (if not grumpy) man supervising the box office and customarily running the audiotape player himself from a visible seat in the theater, reflecting his commitment to live theater that, in the SoHo tradition, an orphan established from scratch. Rather than expanding (or vulgarizing) his operation with his success, he has kept it to a SoHo size he can comfortably control.

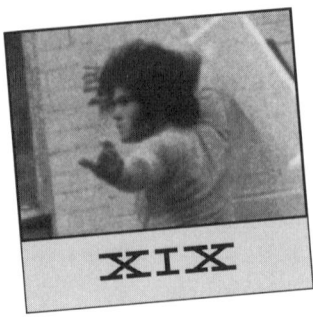

XIX

At that time [in the late 1960s], there was a lot of gear and a lot of technical complexity. I would borrow the projectors and tape records, and my friends would run them in the performance. So things were accomplished in a grass roots kind of way. Then I started doing some big outdoor pieces with about 60 to 100 people. I would make big choral pieces. In those days there were volunteers. Entire families would be in those pieces. Now it's a little more difficult to do something like that because people are so centered on making money because they have to. It's so difficult to survive.

—Meredith Monk, in an interview (2002)

MEREDITH MONK has been a protean polyartist whose career at once precedes SoHo, exploits its opportunities, and yet reflects the hothouse as she has worked in varying success in several media since the mid-1960s. I first knew her as a dancer just out of college, performing in a small theater on St. Marks Place called the Bridge. About her dance *Break* (1964), I wrote to myself, "a moderately creative dance, with marvelously disjointed syntax; but I didn't discern much coherence." (A dance on the same program by Kenneth King, yet younger and likewise just beginning, impressed me more.)

Short and short-legged at the time when George Balanchine established a contrary physique as ideal for American dancers, Monk was the sort of dancer who, unlikely to perform with others, necessarily created pieces for herself. They were middling in quality until she suddenly got better, much better, as sometimes happens with ambitious young artists. The crucial work establishing her greater presence was *16 Millimetre Earrings* (1966), in which she not only performed but also incorporated film footage that she had produced and audiotape likewise of her own creation. Her work has since continued to be on a higher plane. In 1968, she formed a multimedia production company called the House, which provided her with a fairly stable company of performers through the 1970s. Even then, I remember, she conducted herself with a self-confidence based upon genuine achievement.

This mixed-means vein she continued to pursue in several ambitious pieces. *Title* (1969) included the departure of live statues displayed in the theater's lobby, mostly of performers wrapped in corrugated cardboard through which they break before the show's end. *Juice: A Cantata in Three Installments* (1969) was performed successively at the Guggenheim Museum, a second three weeks later at the Minor Latham Playhouse at Barnard College, a third yet another week later in her own loft. The three parts of *Vessel* (1971), roughly about Joan of Arc, were performed in a SoHo loft perhaps her own, in the Performing Garage at 33 Wooster Street, and in the huge parking lot between Wooster and West Broadway, just north of Canal Street. In Sally Banes's succinct summary of the third part: "Not only the scale of the setting, but the cast, colors, and lighting courses magnified as Joan neared her immolation. The eighty performers included pioneers sitting around campfires and dancing with ears of corn; children in court costumes; a kazoo army battling a pennywhistle army with rakes; a Spanish dancer; a Scottish dancer; a motorcycle cavalcade, a VW bus full of 'cuckoos' continually emptying itself; and the House people in their living room, transplanted intact. Finally Joan, in a black derby, skittered away into the sparks of a welder's torch at the far end of the lot." (The last location was, incidentally, just across the street from St. Alphonsus Church, where the German émigré Erwin Piscator had his first New York City Theater. Now it is the site of the plush SoHo Grand Hotel.)

In the early 1970s, Monk mounted versions of a continually developing piece with the fetching title of *Education of a Girlchild* with mostly female performers, customarily presented to a predominantly feminist audience. To quote Banes again, "*Education* is an epic with ambiguous meaning: its strange tribe of women could be goddesses, heroines, ordinary people, or different aspects of one person. The actions of the epic may describe a journey or the landscape of a planet; explain the structure of a family; map a soul. In the first part of the piece, six women dressed in white populate the stage, forming tableaux, traveling, enacting odd rituals. They dig up a colorfully dressed creative, a wide-eyed woman who learns to be one of them, to walk and sing their way. The second section is a solo for Monk; it is a voyage down a white canvas read, down a lifetime; from ancientness to middle-aged womanhood to virgin/saint/ from remembering to knowing to wondering, the changes marked by transformations in voice and movement." I saw the work three times (once in April 1972 at Monk's own space the House on 597 Broadway and again in June and November 1973 at 70 Grand St.), and enjoyed it each time. In its April 1972 performance, the work consisted solely of the Monk's solo; the first part was added in the 1973 performances.

Meanwhile, Monk developed as a solo singer, performing with a unique vocal style that was also effective in records—indeed, more than a dozen discs have appeared. To Kyle Gann, the most thorough critic of recent American avant-garde music, her "vocal techniques include glottal stops, warbly American-Indian-style vibrato, nasal singing, nonsense syllables, and many of the strange voice tones children use in games." In 1978, she formed Meredith Monk and Vocal Ensemble. Not unlike Robert Wilson, with whom she was friendly in the late 1960s, Monk has worked by herself and collaborated with others both more and less prominent than she, with ensembles both large and small, around the world. Kyle Gann considers Monk the pioneering figure of a group of "women composers [who] are far more likely than men to use their own voices and bodies as material for their music; the singing of unusual and virtuosic vocal techniques, or the musical structuring of body movements." Among those women composers working in Monk's wake Gann identifies Laurie Anderson, Diamanda Galàs, Shelly Hirsch, Eve Beglarian, and Christine Baczewska.

While continuing to perform and record, Monk began to make 16 mm. films, the most distinguished being *Ellis Island* (1981) and *Book of Days* (1988), for which she also wrote and performed the music. She mounted a large exhibition of her visual art at the New York Performing Arts Library in 1998. She received a MacArthur "genius" grant in the same round in which Richard Foreman and Elizabeth LeCompte got their awards. Her music has been incorporated into Hollywood films and even into commercials for Mercedes-Benz in Japan. She might be the only artist ever to receive honorary doctorates from both art schools and music conservatories (the San Francisco Art Institute and Juilliard, respectively). Though Monk has written operas that won't make the standard repertory, few have equaled her at adventurously producing major work in more than one traditional genre. What is missing for me is the coherent thread that I find in the greatest polyartists' work in various genres: Constructivist geometry for Moholy-Nagy and noncentered space and time for John Cage. Perhaps there is an overall coherence I've not yet identified.

A free spirit who had been consistently productive, whose career is too often taken for granted because it seems devoid of crisis, Monk has continued to work at the intersection of "music and movement, image and object, light and sound," as her website claims. "I think of my work as a big tree with two main branches. One main branch is the singing, and it started from my solo work, exploring the human voice and all its possibilities. And then the other branch is the composite forms, which could be operas or musical theater pieces, or installations, or films." Though officially residing in Tribeca, she remains one of the stars of polyartistic SoHo. I still make an effort to see, hear, and enjoy everything she does.

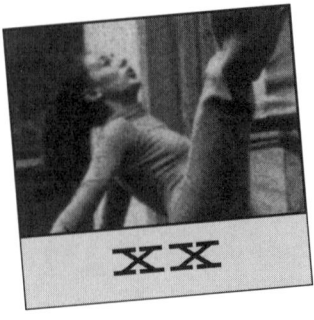

XX

*I hated the theatre in the '60s. . . . What I was doing did
not resemble the Living Theatre, The Open Theatre, or the
Performance Group. I went against everything they were
doing. I loathed the way their theater looked. I had more in
common with nineteenth-century theatre and vaudeville
than with those groups. I was formalistic. I used the
proscenium arch. My theatre was interior, and I treated the
audience with courtesy.*

—Robert Wilson, quoted in Arnold Aronson, *American
Avant-Garde Theatre* (2000)

I F RICHARD FOREMAN has been a SoHo theater artist who
mostly stayed home, Robert Wilson has taken his esthetics
around the world. When I first met him around 1965, he seemed a
tall gangly guy who was somewhat inarticulate and easily distracted.
Having graduated from Pratt Institute in Brooklyn, where he did
theatrical performances that are still remembered, Wilson soon
afterward moved into a loft at 147 Spring Street (that had been
previously occupied by the Open Theater, itself an artistic descendant
of the Living Theatre). He lived there until it became an office for his
foundation, moving first to the floor above and later into Tribeca. On
Spring Street, as early as 1967, he began producing theatrical pieces
that drew upon dance and spectacle without being either. One,
entitled *Byrdwoman*, had three parts. The first involved two characters
bouncing on boards in Wilson's Spring Street loft. For the second
part, Wilson rented trucks filled with hay and took the audience

around Manhattan. The third part took place outside in Jones Alley, a narrow L-shaped street that runs south of Bond Street and then east to Lafayette Street, in NoHo. "The strongest image, for me at least," Wilson remembers, "was forty figures dressed in fur coats bouncing on boards in Jones Alley." Another piece at the time, *Theater Activity*, was presented indoors at midnight in the Bleecker Street Cinema.

During 1968–1969, Wilson organized the Byrd Hoffman Foundation, named for a character in a childhood piece of his; and this not-for-profit institution became the principal sponsor of his subsequent productions. For *The King of Spain* (1969), he recruited performers from the classes in painting and body movement that he had been teaching in the New Jersey suburbs and from the frothy pool of people like himself—adventurous young artists in New York City. To mount this production, he rented the Yiddish Anderson Theater, a large playhouse on Lower Second Avenue where I'd seen Janis Joplin make her New York debut only a few years before. I remember that in this work the stage set was particularly marvelous: a Victorian sitting room with several incongruous details, such as a vertical opening in the back wall that ran from floor to ceiling. One by one, an assortment of unrelated people came on stage and either sat perfectly still or executed simple tasks largely oblivious to each other. The principal performer was a middle-aged blonde woman, who began by performing physical exercises and then droned an inimitable monologue, suggesting she might be drunk, and finally played prosaic songs on the piano. I remember losing interest until two pairs of awesomely huge, white furry legs, suspended from the theater's ceiling, moved gracefully across the front of the stage, unacknowledged by the impervious performers. The sparse audience applauded enthusiastically.

Later in 1969, Wilson presented a more ambitious piece, *The Life and Times of Sigmund Freud*, at the Brooklyn Academy of Music. With it, in my judgment, Wilson realized his mature theatrical style. He combined things that were not normally found together (not even on prior theatrical stages) and then allowed these elements to perform apart from one another. The structure echoed painterly surrealism and collage. Most actions were very slow, comparable to the speed of a baseball game without any hits; but as in the rest periods of a baseball game, elements here and there were always changing, the parts suggesting new relationships. Always something significant was happening on stage; usually Wilson offered something new to see.

In the opening tableau, for instance, an elegant young black woman sits absolutely still in a chair with a black bird perched on her hand, while a man in an old-fashioned bathing suit runs back and forth across the rear of the stage. Compositionally, the runner's continuous movement becomes a "ground bass," so to speak, for subsequent visual activity. A fake tortoise begins to move across the stage, two bare-chested women began to move slowly across the sand, a low humming background sound suggesting that this might be a silent movie. Kenneth King emerges in a baggy outfit (reminiscent of the figure in the Michelin tire ads) and performed a shadow-boxing dance, kicking up the sand. Then, a chorus of black mammies appears, in all shapes and sizes, with padded bosoms, padded buttocks, and kerchiefs, waltzing across the stage, more or less in unison, drawing deserved applause and providing a temporal climax for the tableau. Wilson's work was already much bigger than anyone else's, by the measure of the size of his staging and the number of props and people (not two black mammies, but forty!); and this taste for the extravagant remains a continuing signature.

The rest of *Freud* is similarly slow in time and rich in visual detail. Whole sections of *The King of Spain* were incorporated into this new work (the huge fur legs now waltzing in a visual-rhythmic echo of the mammies). Wilson's *Freud* production exhibited an extraordinary sensitivity to theatrical values, as well as the possibility of realizing a performance art that was neither dance nor drama but something primarily visual and architectural: an art that would articulate in the universal language of images and movements rather than in the national languages of words. Certain French critics classified Wilson's theater as "silent opera." The theater's seats were filled for *Freud*, which later had a successful European tour.

Wilson's next major piece, *Deafman Glance* (1971), was inspired by his encountering Raymond Andrews, a twelve-year-old black deaf-mute who had disrupted Wilson's class in Summit, New Jersey. One result of their friendship was Raymond's central role in this produc-

tion. It opened with a handsome young black woman killing two of
her three children, the spared one (Andrews) being lifted in a swing
and suspended high above the stage, a spectator for the entire piece.
In *Deafman Glance*, like its predecessor, the bare stage slowly fills
with people (and props) who bear little visible relation to one
another, who appear oblivious to most of the others, who perform
without words or music, and whose individual actions are mostly
done slowly. Wilson made the audience's experience more difficult by
disallowing any intermissions. One of the more stunning sequences
involves an armless dwarf with uneven legs, who draws the audience's
attention as he moves a prop around the stage. Wilson echoed Todd
Browning's film *Freaks* (1932) in incorporating such a "hidden"
human being into a public performance. I thought *Deafman* as good
as *Freud*, if not better.

The *Life and Times of Joseph Stalin* (1973) was, in my experience, Wilson's masterpiece, the culmination of his interest in silent
spectacles, as I prefer to call them. The most abundant performance I
have ever seen, *Stalin* ran for some twelve hours, with six long intermissions; it filled the stage of the Brooklyn Academy of Music with
over 140 performers and many props. Its initial three acts incorporated much of *The Life and Times of Sigmund Freud*, its fourth act
had much of *Deafman Glance*; but instead of putting Raymond
Andrews in a swing, high above the action, Wilson now had two characters, one male and the other female, playing Stalin and his wife.

Stalin, like other Wilson theater, is best summarized not in
encompassing terms but with a few memorable details. In the fifth
act, as dancers move around the stage, one performer gives an effec-
tively concise summary of dialectical materialism, itself spoken
against background music drawn from various sections of Gabriel
Fauré's *Requiem*. In the last act is a chorus of ostriches dancing in
unison. With *Stalin*, the theatrical style that Wilson had been developing—with its temporal slowness and visual abundance—reached its
apex. It had to be seen to be believed.

Residing in SoHo, Wilson had achieved a radically alternative
way of making theater: one that is predominantly visual, instead of
verbal; architectural, instead of representational; extravagant, instead

of modest; perceptual, instead of emotional; theatrical, instead of literary. Because he has realized this alternative so well, his theatrical productions rank, in my experience, among the masterpieces of my lifetime of theatergoing.

Wilson has since produced an abundance of theater both here and abroad. Indeed, going first to Europe and then to Iran in the early 1970s, he introduced European art and theater worlds to the concepts of SoHo avant-garde performance, if not SoHo art in general, making it easier for many other SoHo artists to succeed in Europe. He collaborated with the downtown composer Phillip Glass in producing the opera *Einstein on the Beach* (1975) that was probably the greatest work of its genre, new in my lifetime. He collaborated with the East German playwright Heiner Müller in a yet more elaborate musical theater piece. He produced videotapes, especially for German television, and directed classic operas for German theaters; he made sculptures and drawings that were exhibited. It could be said that he has "touch" in the sense that everything he has done has been special in some way—not necessarily excellent but surely special, much like SoHo itself. No matter where in the world he went, he always returned to his SoHo office and his nearby apartment.

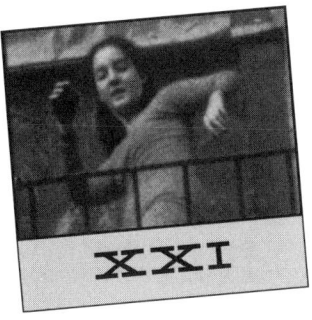

XXI

Exhibiting oneself is difficult for other people who don't feel good about their bodies. I could have been more humble—but if I'd been more humble, I wouldn't have been an artist.

—Hannah Wilke, in a statement (1985)

REMEMBERED AS Arlene Butter by her high-school classmates, she took the name Hannah Wilke from her own middle name and the surname of her first husband. Essentially a Jewish princess from Great Neck, with vocal intonations reflecting the less classy neighborhoods of Brooklyn, she transformed herself into an art-world star. I remember when I first met her early in 1970 as the girlfriend of the sculptor Claes Oldenburg, then at the peak of his artistic career. As he was driving us home with Wilke beside him in the front seat, my date at the time commented on the exquisiteness of Wilke's nose. What I didn't see at first was that the rest of her body was likewise distinguished. Little did I suspect in 1970 that she would often exhibit it, not only in pictures but in live performances. A 1975 exhibition announcement shows her with her chest bare, her lush black hair falling over her shoulders, and the top of her jeans well below her navel (long before this sexy style became fashionable among young women). Around the time I also saw her perform live at The Kitchen with just a toga around her trunk, and it kept dropping down to reveal pubic hair. In 1974, she portrayed herself as a liberated woman, telling a reporter for *New York* magazine that she divided her loft into two parts "so whoever I'm living with can't see my work and criticize it until I'm ready to show it." My first thought was that Wilke was an opportunist exploiting her good looks just as she had earlier captured a prominent artist.

It took a while for me, as well as others, to realize that she was doing something else—that she was making a female body (hers) into a changing work of art. A black-and-white photograph from a series titled *What Does This Represent/What Do You Rep*resent (1978–1984) shows a naked woman crouching in the corner of a downtown loft building, the vertical wooden panels of its walls clearly visible as such. Her spread legs expose a crotch with uneven hair lines. One calf looks thicker than the other. Her modest breasts are drooping. She looks sullen and scared with her hand on her forehead and her other arm in front of her tummy with her elbow resting on her knee. As Amelia Jones succinctly put it, "She constructs herself as literally 'cornered' by the [photographer's] gaze." No *Playboy* centerfold was she. Indicatively, later lovers were not so prominent.

Amelia Jones describes a performance I missed, perhaps still ambivalent about recognizing her work: "In a 1977 performance made for video, *Intercourse With.* . . , Hannah Wilke plays tapes of her lovers, family members, and friends speaking to her in absentia on her answering machine. Accompanying this audio track, Wilke strikes various contemplative poses, then strips off her clothing to reveal her flesh, covered with the names of those loved ones. She then slowly takes off each name, peeling away these 'others' that have spoken her as 'self.'" This was "stripping," to be sure, but psychological as well as exhibitionistic, portraying vulnerability beneath a move customarily associated with self-confidence. A few years before, she made another videotape, *Gestures* (1974), in which she moves her mouth and only her mouth through a series of erotic poses, suggesting a heterosexual acceptance of a male penis otherwise absent from her essentially narcissistic work.

Nothing established Wilke's integrity more than photographing not only her body but also her mother's after the onset of their terminal cancers. As her mother is shown with only one breast, her upper body emaciated to reveal bones, the daughter made photographs of herself devoid of head hair, her crotch hair thinned out, her torso

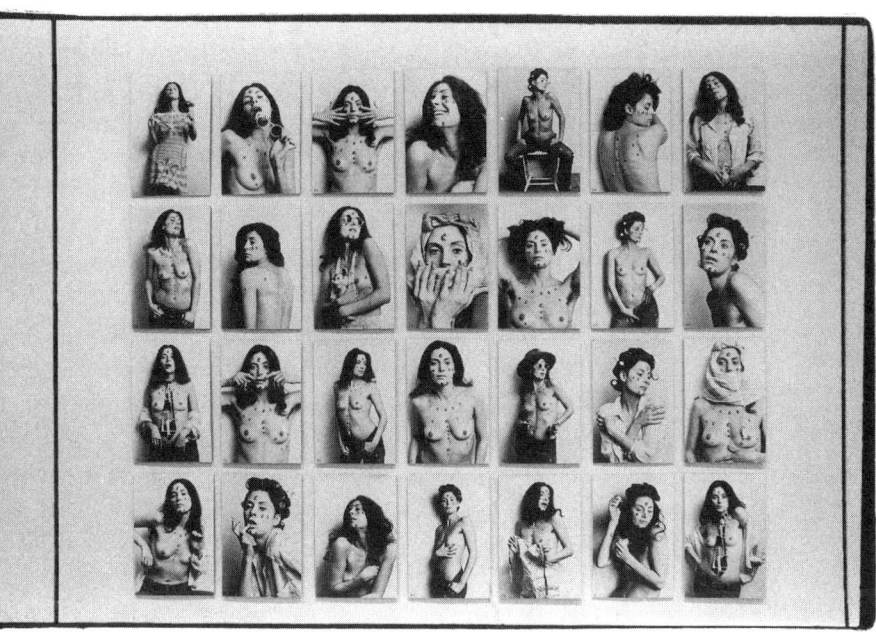

Hannah Wilke self portrait in 28 poses, September 18, 1975. Copyright Fred W. McDarrah

puffy. She made work on paper with her lost hairs affixed, titled *Brushstrokes* (1992). To quote Jones again, "Wilke is no longer to be viewed as self-absorbed beauty queen but as suffering artiste, making art out of her pain." Nearly a decade after her death in 1993, her work is remembered as finally something courageous and special. And indeed it was a feminism possible only in SoHo. It couldn't have succeeded anywhere else—certainly not in academia, probably not in Europe either. No younger person female or male has done anything resembling the arc of her career.

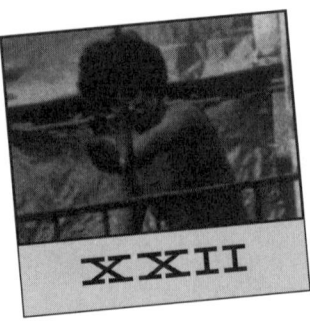

XXII

There are few spaces that offer such a range of opportunity for making a design statement as empty lofts. Structural columns, gleaming while walls, exposed radiators, windows facing unexpected views, even the web of fire sprinkler pipes, are elements that gracefully integrate into the final interior. Unrenovated lofts have become the interior design laboratories of our time.

—Suzanne Slesin, et al. *The International Book of Lofts* (1986)

T HE GREAT SoHo contribution to the practice of interior design was the residential habitation of open space in an industrial building. Isolated individuals may have done this before, but never had so many renovated so much so tastefully. SoHo artists led the way. Factory space was "gutted," as we said, prior to reconstruction from within to the owner's needs, usually to sizes much greater than those favored by commercial developers so eager to get the most profit from every inch.

Whereas ceilings in standard New York apartments were 8 feet high (and those in brownstones or luxury flats sometimes running as high as 11 feet), industrial ceilings customarily began at 11 feet and were sometimes as high as 14 feet or 16. This departure permitted the installation of levels, such as raising the floor of the kitchen area a foot or two or installing a balcony with only a bed—called, to no surprise, "a loft bed." Raising the lavatory permitted the installation of plumbing under the new level, rather than digging into the base floor.

Indeed, most newcomers put their kitchen and bathroom near the exiting plumbing lines, because nothing was more expensive and problematic than moving city water. Renovation was customarily cheaper than building afresh, especially in New York City whose complex construction laws increase costs for new buildings needlessly. Renovations were also less visible to those on the street, while industrial buildings lacked residential neighbors who might complain to some city authority about something that upset them. Indeed, tenants residing illegally wouldn't complain at all: You could bet your renovation on it.

Because space was so cheap, artists could extravagantly occupy whole floors, if not whole buildings. In 1968, Donald Judd, already successful, purchased for $68,000 a six-story corner building that was built as a store with roughly 2,500 square feet to a floor a century before. After clearing out trash at 400 bucks per floor, he claimed, he spent 13 grand on acquiring a new chimney and furnace and then thousands more on new floors, plumbing, and walls. By the early seventies, he and his family occupied the entire space with living space on three floors, his working space on two floors and the basement, and his wife's choreography studio on the last floor. Palatial was scarcely an adequate word for describing such an urban edifice. Nonetheless, in a 1974 article he is portrayed as already disliking the development of SoHo in favor of relocating to two airplane hangars in West Texas, each of which had more square footage than his entire SoHo studio-home.

As open interiors became the ideal, the typical SoHo kitchen would be exposed to the larger space, rather than hidden behind a door, and sometimes kitchen utensils would be exposed as well, rather than hidden behind cabinets. Large stoves were feasible. Some open living spaces could have remarkably little furniture; others could be cluttered. While small rugs were permissible here and there, the uptown apartment fashion of "wall-to-wall carpeting" was almost unknown. Even in lofts that could have used more floor insulation or warmth, the custom was a wooden floor, ideally well-polished. Among media artists, say, the standard mix was cheap nondescript furniture beside expensive professional equipment. Most SoHo renovations exposed the supporting interior columns (customarily every 15 to 20 feet) and the ceiling beams; a few, such as myself, did not (in my case, hiding the columns behind the walls that divided my space). Some scraped plaster from their walls to expose bricks; fewer shaved their columns to expose steel.

Anything physically (and legally) possible was feasible within an open space: a bed 4 feet high above clothing cabinets or several feet high with a ladder that incidentally became a space divider. One neighbor put a small greenhouse under the skylight in his spacious bathroom. Another suspended a trapeze from her ceiling. Track lighting, more typical of art galleries' ceilings, was common. I've seen a sauna in one loft and a Jacuzzi in another. Humongous bathrooms were not uncommon. One of my favorite renovations has interior walls of cinderblocks, which are superior to the customary sheet rock not only in dampening sounds but also in preventing fire.

The renovation I designed for myself was likewise unique and beyond the imagination of an interior designer. Distracted by daylight, needing an extra wall to separate my workspace from the bedroom when I stayed up late, I wanted an essentially windowless room for reading and writing and so I made one 17 feet by 20 feet. (This book was written from a desk from where I cannot see outside.)

Bedrooms were sometimes incorporated into the residential space, which was barely separate from areas devoted to artistic work. I've seen loft spaces with beds in the middle of the living space, sometimes across from a large couch or a dining table, always making me speculate about when and if its occupants ever made love. (For practical reasons, children often got their own rooms.)

Another option for SoHo renovations was an abundance of tall and/or wide windows that had previously made daytime industrial work possible without the expense of electric light. As curtains were unpopular, natural light could fill a residential loft from sunrise to sunset. Plants, often large plants, became popular, the artist Don Corrigan once quipping that "plants are to SoHo what lawns are to suburbia." Exposing one's interior to the world, which might have been more problematic in a slum, became more feasible in a low-crime, one-industry neighborhood, especially since the only people who could peer into your windows from their own high floors belong to the same cultural class(es). (Nonetheless, a month after we moved in, a supremely athletic cat burglar came into our loft through a third-floor window, having climbed up the shutters that were installed outside our back-building windows for both security and protection from occasional dangerous weather. Seeing him at the entrance to our sleeping area, we screamed, and he scampered back out the window and down the shutters. The following day, a cop specializing in loft security came to our place and looked around puzzled. Amid the piles of books and papers, abstract art and junky furniture, he found, as he said, "nothing to steal.")

Whereas most mid-block floor-through lofts had windows only in the front and the back (and mid-block part-floor lofts, like my own, had windows only on either the front or the back), those in corner buildings were perceived to be more attractive for having windows on the longer side of the loft as well as the shorter, if not three sides. If a loft had windows on all four sides, usually because it was on an upper floor of a building with lower structures beside it, that advantage was usually featured in, say, the opening line of a real estate ad. Top floor lofts could have skylights. So could those whose back ends, say, became a sort of roof below floors that were set back. If skylights hadn't been installed for industrial purposes, the SoHo resident often added his own. Since backyards were customarily only 10 feet deep, rather than the 30+ feet required for residential brownstones, those desiring gardens used not the backyard but the roof.

Needless to say, just as SoHo art has been featured in art magazines since 1970, so have SoHo residential lofts been pictured since then in periodicals and books devoted to interior design. An article about one's loft could be as important as a favorable review of one's art. Indeed, my own supremely cluttered space made the front page of the Home section of the *New York Times* on September 5, 1985, under the banner of "The Problem of Living with Too Many Books" and then again in the *Times* Sunday magazine section some sixteen years later; but that's another story remembered elsewhere in this book.

Once the SoHo example was publicized, industrial spaces around the world were independently renovated, *The International*

Book of Lofts (1986) documenting the new fashion. In Paris in 1985, I attended a party held in my honor not in the kind of attic atelier favored by French artists a century before but in a grand airy space in an abandoned factory on the outskirts of town. I saw similarly large studios in West Berlin and later in the former East Berlin. To judge from construction canopies extending into the street, buildings in SoHo proper are still being renovated. What those recently renovated lofts look like I do not know. Photographs in the design press nowadays no longer feature SoHo. Not knowing the new people of twenty years ago, I'm no more familiar with RNNPs, who are Really New New People.

I thought about doing a paragraph about the development of interior design of the most distinguished boutiques—how they evolved from funky Paracelso, even before I arrived here (in 1974), which sold previously owned antique clothing mostly to women, whose proprietors have always been uniquely dressed; through the Gallery of Wearable Art that was so prominent in the mid-1980s, with live models in its West Broadway windows on weekends; to Comme des Garçons, whose austere space on Wooster Street and clothes mostly in black, brown, and gray reflected neighborhood minimal esthetic and accompanying severe tastes; to Prada in 2000, whose extravagance is almost obscene; but so detestable are most of these stores to my older co-op partners, along with other veteran neighbors, that I feared they would stone me to death before I could move out. I do vividly remember a co-op tenant about to relocate uptown, where she belonged, telling me that she would "need to buy new clothes with colors." About the cosmetics stores, which invaded SoHo during the 1990s, there is nothing for me to say.

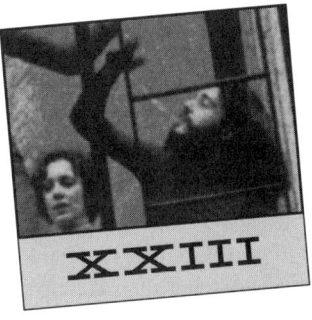

XXIII

[Cindy] Sherman's brilliance at translating the critical preoccupations of her time into purely pictorial currency has made her a success among collectors, critics, curators, and the general public. Her talent is for making the ubiquitous "issues" and "theory" of the early 1980s art world into compelling and subjective works of art.

—Ellen Handy, in *Contemporary Photographers* (third ed., 1995)

THERE ARE THREE stories of photography in SoHo. One line involves artists trained in photography, who published their work mostly in magazines and then books and incidentally exhibited. A second includes photographers who from their professional beginnings concentrated mostly on the creation of books, incidentally publishing in magazines and exhibiting in galleries. A third involves artists trained mostly in visual art who exhibited their work in galleries before all else.

Representatives of the first line extended more artfully the traditional endeavors of journalistic photography, some of them using the large loft spaces available around SoHo to house their darkrooms beside their living spaces, noxious chemicals notwithstanding. Residing, respectively, on west Van Dam Street and on Bond Street in NoHo, both Annie Leibovitz (b. 1945) and Robert Mapplethorpe (1946–1989) first became known for their pictures of celebrities in mass magazines, especially *Rolling Stone* in her case, *Andy Warhol's Interview* for him, and eventually *Vanity Fair* for both. Each took

photographs that essentially flattered their subjects. One striking departure for Mapplethorpe was African-American male nudes depicted to
look sculptural. One Leibovitz specialty was enticing celebrities to
pose in unfamiliar ways. A famous picture portrays John Lennon
naked, his left hip turned toward the camera, his knees drawn up to
his chest, kissing his wife Yoko Ono on the cheek, who is fully
clothed in black, her long black hair extending upward from her
head. One technical difference between the two photographers is that
nearly all Mapplethorpe is black and white; Leibovitz prefers color.
Another difference is that only Mapplethorpe gets an entry in the
1988 edition of the compendious Colin Naylor encyclopedia,
Contemporary Photographers (1988), even though Leibovitz's pictures
had been visible for over a decade by then. Both would eventually
have museum exhibitions, and each managed to become independently famous. My enthusiasm for their work is limited. Other notable
SoHo photographers for magazines included Neal Slavin, who specialized in sports; and D. James Dee, whose specialty was photographing artists' (his neighbors') works. (Don't forget that the great New
York City photographer known only as Weegee [né Usher/Arthur H.
Felig, 1899–1968] lived just east of SoHo-to-be, on Centre Market
Street, one block long just behind the old Police Headquarters on
Lafayette Street, surrounded during his time there by stores selling
police uniforms and firearms.)

　　The epitome of the second line, Ralph Gibson (1939), started
publishing books in 1966, but not until he got to New York and settled in SoHo did he found Lustrum Press and, in the great SoHo tradition of artists' self-respect, publish through his own imprint the tril-
ogy on which his reputation is based: *The Somnambulist* (1970), *Déjà
Vu* (1972), and *Days at Sea* (1974). His model appeared to be *Les
Américains*, published here as *Americans*, by Robert Frank, who incidentally lived some of the time on Bleecker Street in NoHo. Over
thirty more books of Gibson's pictures have subsequently appeared,
sometimes under his own imprint, mostly published by others here
and abroad, in sum establishing him among the most important photographic book-artists. Eclectic in his choice of subjects, Gibson
defines his style by sharp contrasts between black and white. The

largest retrospective of his photography is not a museum exhibition but yet another book, *Deus ex Machina*, published initially in Germany.

Another book photographer working in SoHo, Mary Ellen Mark, published her first book, *Passport* (1974), with Lustrum Press before producing a succession of books for various publishers both large and small. The book *Mary Ellen Mark: 25 Years* (1991) is a handsome retrospective; *Mary Ellen Mark 55* (2001), a paperback selection. One of her earliest solo exhibitions was at Castelli Graphics, where Gibson had exhibited as well as early as 1976, which was located not at the major dealer's West Broadway megagallery, but at a satellite a few blocks away in a large Broadway building that predominantly housed businesses other than galleries.

Photography entered SoHo galleries previously known for only painting and sculpture initially in a venue that John (not Ralph) Gibson named after himself. Indeed, he tried to create from disparate individuals a movement that he called variously Narrative or Story, promoting it as the hottest, newest thing during the 1970s. What made the photographs into unique gallery objects were the artists' words about them, customarily handwritten onto the face of the picture. The epitome was a series meditating on the alphabet by Peter Hutchinson (b. 1930), a British artist, who produced booklets in addition to art for walls. Among the younger downtown visual artists working with photographs in this way were Bill Beckley (1946) and Roger Welch (1946). Little did anyone imagine at the time that some art galleries in SoHo would soon be exhibiting only photographs.

Yet younger, Cindy Sherman (1954) has frequently denied the appellation of "photographer" for herself, indicatively preferring to be known as an "artist who uses photography." From the start of her precocious New York career in 1977, she exhibited photographs and only pictures, devoid of writing, exclusively in art galleries, initially within a four-artist exhibition in 1978 at the publicly funded Artists Space, where she also worked at the front desk. When the executive director of AS cofounded a new, nonprofit SoHo gallery called Metro Pictures, Sherman was one of the first artists given her own show, in her case annually from 1980 to 1985. The 1981 show in particular

prompted a rave review in the *New York Times* by Andy Grundberg
that gave her overnight credibility, as only the *Times* can, with institu-
tionalized curators. The following year, a one-person exhibition
toured several European museums. In 1983, before she turned thirty,
Sherman had a one-person retrospective at the St. Louis Art Museum.
In 1984, Akron Art Museum initiated an exhibition that toured, while
two Japanese museums had their own Sherman shows. In 1987, New
York's Whitney Museum gave her a show. Within a decade, the tra-
jectory of Sherman's career was truly meteoric.

Her stunning, immediately persuasive innovation consisted of
photographs of herself impersonating a wealth of roles through costumes and makeup. Often mistaken as self-portraits, these were rather
self-dramatizations. Her first principal subject in black-and-white photographs from the late 1970s was solemn women in B-level
Hollywood movies. As her 8" by 10" prints superficially resembled in
format the publicity "stills" released by Hollywood studios, they raised
questions about self-publicity at the same time that they could be
seen as ironically mocking conventional "starlet" poses. The project
had the collective title of Untitled Film Stills; the prints were individually numbered. It was not for nothing that a later retrospective at the
Museum of Modern Art was personally subsidized by the pop star
Madonna, who has likewise exploited costume and makeup for
changing female identities. Back in 1969, Michael Kirby, wishing to
demonstrate the inherent contentiousness of the art world, noted that
only twice in his experience did everyone he knew think a certain
artist was doing an extraordinary work, if only briefly: The first example was the sculptor Lee Bontecou around 1959; the second, Claes
Oldenburg in 1966; Sherman around 1981 would rank as a third
example. For all three, needless to say perhaps, unanimous sympathy
evaporated within the following decade. Indeed, as late as 2002, my
co-op neighbor Daile Kaplan, a photographic historian who runs the
photography department at the Swann Galleries in New York,
declared to me flatly, "I really disagree. Sherman is not a photographer."

My longtime friend A. D. Coleman, by some measures the dean
of American photography critics, takes a more critical look at

Sherman's (and by extension other SoHo photographer's) achievements. He wrote to me in response to an earlier draft of this section:

> "SoHo Photography" was produced in large part by people whose astute analysis of the art scene had indicated that marketing photographs as objets d'art was easiest when the maker thereof was defined as an artist and not a photographer and the object itself was described as something other than a photograph (e.g, documentation of a performance), or was presented by its maker and his/her epigones and shills as connected to any lineage other than that of the medium of photography. And that those labeled "artists" could command greater attention, respect, authority, and money than those labeled "photographers," because the art world's entrenched disdain for photography somehow survived the acceptance of photographs as collectible and museum-worthy objects.

Coleman's conclusion is neat, if true, but what is unclear, at least to me, is how premeditated, rather than inadvertent, this successful SoHo exhibition strategy was.

Later in the 1980s, Sherman was using color to portray other familiar contemporary female figures: stereotypes, essentially. The delicious irony was that a woman with such an indefinite appearance, as revealed in the few "straight" photographs of her, could with a wealth of prostheses assume so many distinct images. "In 1983–84," according to Ellen Handy, "she began to explore and erase the boundaries between fashion photography, contemporary femininity, and fine art photography, by photographing herself in high fashion clothing, in a series of images commissioned by a fashion designer for advertising purposes, but also exhibited by Sherman as her work." Later photographs appear to portray psychological states, again familiar as human visages, but unfamiliar as images exhibited in an art gallery. Perhaps her most extraordinary series is *History Portraits* (1988) in which, thanks to more sophisticated makeup and costuming, as well as such appurtenances as false female breasts, she photographed herself as images from art history, such as women in portraits by Ingres and other classical painters. (How she realized these is almost inconceivable, if, as is claimed, she works by herself as her own cameraperson. The ratio of "mistakes" must be astronomical.)

Though Sherman's intentions might have been modest, her pictures generated a wealth of heavy thoughts about representation and roles. Indeed, the texts in several exhibition catalogs devoted to her work seemed to rival each other for high-falutin' weight. Gathered together in the twenty-first century, they would make a monumental but finally hilarious anthology of late-twenty-century art jargon. Whether Sherman was victimized by her overinflating admirers is a question best left to future historians.

The steady advance in her art within her first public decade created the image of Sherman as an artist on the verge of scaling previously unknown heights. Instead, she stalled by the 1990s, much like SoHo itself, removing herself from her images, instead focusing upon various types of prostheses (which I thought might become her principal theme), sex toys, gargoyles, plastic medical models of body parts, and so forth. Though these similarly untitled photographs were likewise given only numerals (much like Opus numbers in music composition), one felt that they needed a more suggestive linguistic platform. No human image would be allowed to succeed, or compete with, her own. Presented together with her earlier images, whether in exhibitions or books, her later work (done past the age of thirty-five) seems contrived. Sherman also made a feature film, *Office Killer* (1997), that bombed, though admiring reviews can be found.

Gather together the catalogs of several Sherman museum exhibitions, as I have done, and you'll notice that the same few images are reprinted again and again, revealing the limitations so far of her oeuvre. (One question not answered is whether the museums have unique prints or does Sherman produce multiples of her masterpieces?) Nonetheless, only in SoHo, with the general commitment to expanding the acceptable options in both making and exhibiting art, could her earlier photographs be exhibited in galleries normally devoted to arts other than photography. Once Sherman's earlier work was accepted, downtown galleries could exhibit such artist-photographers as Andreas Serrano and Louise Lawler, among others.

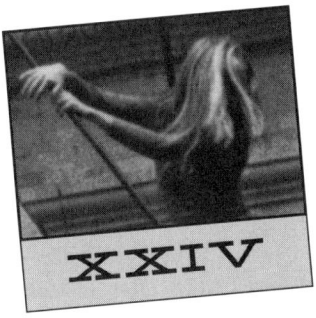

XXIV

AS AN AVANT-GARDE arts community, SoHo was particularly hospitable to the art forms that were new in the 1960s and 1970s: video, holography, and book-art (aka Artists' Books), among others. I can recall that, once the portable video recorder became available around 1967, several adventurous artists, most of them trained in visual arts, purchased them. Robert Whitman, then residing on Mulberry Street east of SoHo proper, used one for an outdoors performance piece that he produced in Long Island at that time.

As Davidson Gigliotti remembers, most of the pioneering New York videomen lived not in SoHo but on the Lower East Side, which was at the time the epitome of a cultural bohemia, incidentally accounting for why much early video activity reflected the radical political aspirations of either (or both) the New Left and the futurism of, say, Buckminster Fuller. Gigliotti says, "In those days we saw video as a different practice; related to art, certainly, but also embedded in broad cultural concerns. We wanted to change the world, of course. Still do, actually." The contrasting figure was Nam June Paik, always residing in SoHo, who seemed more interested in exploring the radical possibilities of the medium (and later making radical social gestures, such as dropping his pants on the greeting line at a White House reception for the prime minister of South Korea). Paik's singular achievement is acknowledged elsewhere in this book.

Art based upon videotape, rather than the manipulation of monitors, made its first appearance in an exhibition at Howard Wise Gallery in 1969 featuring *Wipe Cycle* by Frank Gillette and Ira

Schneider. An image directly in front of the installation was recorded on tape and then played back 8 seconds later on four black-and-white monitors (so long ago was this done) and then 16 seconds later on a second set of four monitors. Thanks to a simple switching mechanism, the identity of each set of monitors continually changed. I felt I was in the presence of an autonomous intelligence, which is to say a kind of robot. *Wipe* Cycle was a stunning piece when first displayed and no less impressive a generation later, in 1989, when I saw it again in an exhibition in West Berlin.

As Gigliotti recalls, filmmakers were more inclined to live in SoHo than video artists, and many of the former were hostile to video: "Hollis Frampton, for example, was polite about video, but he didn't think it would go anywhere. He didn't like it because you couldn't hold the videotape up to the light and see the image. Some filmmakers were not so polite about it. We were treated as arriviste by most— Mr. Nobody from Nowhere, as one person put it. Certainly they were right. We had no background, and no one had ever heard of us. We just popped up on the fringes of the artworld with these video cameras and wouldn't go away."

The initial presentation venue for video was the Kitchen. Once it relocated to Broome Street, it opened within its space a video library that was available for anyone to use, in part extending its mission of supporting lateral movement by SoHo artists out of the "fields" in which they were originally trained. (When video was new, nearly all its artists were trained in other arts.) Down Broome Street at #454, likewise upstairs, was Global Village, which presented only video, beginning with alternative news coverage in 1970, especially at Friday night screenings open to everyone, eventually including my own early video work in 1978. During the 1970s, the Anthology Film Archives, the command center of avant-garde film, also had a program of video screenings run successively by Shigeko Kubota and Bob Harris. It was here that my videotapes were first screened in a solo show late in 1975.

Starting in 1978, some SoHo video was distributed to the rest of Manhattan by a regular program available only on cable television, SoHo TV, essentially produced by Jaime Davidovich, implicitly demonstrating that cable with its narrow-casting could distribute a different kind of television program from the mass merchandizing of network broadcasting.

The art of holography, roughly three-dimensional photography, likewise publicly available for the first time in the mid-1960s, came to SoHo with Lloyd Cross, a Canadian, who established his studio in a sub-basement at the northwest corner of Prince and Mercer Streets (for long afterward an abandoned factory building, now the site of the opulent Mercer Hotel). As holography at that time depended upon finding a floor devoid of vibrations (that would upset exposures that could take as long as a minute), Cross had to dig deep. "Visiting Lloyd was a little like visiting the mad scientist's laboratory," Gigliotti recalls. "A descent by elevator deep into subterranean depths, a walk through a narrow labyrinth, led to a large, well-lit sandbox with mirrors on sticks embedded in it."

Returning to San Francisco around 1972, Cross soon afterward developed the holographic innovation still connected to his name, the multiplex integral hologram that combines white-light transmission holography with conventional filmmaking to produce a moving three-dimensional image. A classic example shows an attractive brunette blowing a kiss to the spectator who moves his or her body laterally in front of the image. Hart Perry, initially a film animator, remembers shooting the film of Salvidor Dali for Cross's first multiplex. In 1977, Cross produced with the dancer Simone Forti a 360–degree multiplex *Striding Crawling* with her appearing as a tiny figure performing characteristic moves. (It was revived in 2001 for a Whitney Museum exhibition on *The Projected Image*.) Later Cross helped Perry construct a multiplex machine from his optical printer housed above a bar on the southeast corner of Broome Street and West Broadway. At this last production facility I made in 1978 a multiplex of myself in collaboration with Perry, *On Holography*, the imagery consisting only of large letters whose words compose syntactically circular sentences about holography.

In 1976, Rosemary ("Posey") Jackson established the Museum of Holography on Mercer Street, just north of Canal. A year later the museum acquired *Holosphere* (1972), a technical journal formerly published by a laser manufacturer. Later came *The Whole Message*, a newsletter whose title was an English translation of the Greek word "hologram," and an on-site kiosk selling literature and trinkets. Early on the museum's staff was Fred Unterseher, who soon afterward wrote *The Holography Handbook* (1982), with whom I myself worked during a production residency at the museum in 1985. Not only were holograms regularly exhibited there for decades, but the museum had an educational program that introduced the new medium to children. In its basement was a production studio much like Cross's, located where vibrations were minimal and heat was scarce, but that at MOH had more advanced tools, such as a professional optical bench and an NRC metal table, rather than the sandtable. Down there, on its concrete floors, I spent much of December 1989, a legendarily freezing month in the history of New York City, producing my own holograms as a guest artist. In the mid-1990s, the museum closed, its collection sold off to MIT, another sign of the end of Artists' SoHo.

Two complements to the Museum of Holography were Rudi Stern's Let There Be Neon, which was a West Broadway store resembling a museum devoted entirely to art made with neon light, and the Museum of Colored Glass and Light, long in a second floor loft at 72 Wooster Street, that displayed extensions of stained glass, mostly by the space's owner, Raphael Nemeth, who illuminated his work not by sunlight but electric lamps. "None of the pieces in this collection are for sale," read a sign in his gallery, "because Nemeth feels the continuity in the development of his process would be broken." How quaint such sentiments seem today. Nonetheless, by the late 1990s, both of these galleries were gone as well.

Among the other important light artists in SoHo was Stephen Antonakos. Discovering neon around 1960, he has since made it his principal medium. Whereas Dan Flavin used this other medium of fluorescent light for its peculiar kind of glow, what Antonakos loved in neon was its colors. First he added neon tubes to his assemblages; then he let the lamps stand by themselves. Later he had them fill an entire room, defining a space wholly with light. In 1973, he made the radical move of placing ten large neon works outdoors around the architecture of the Ft. Worth Museum, making the entire building into a prop for a giant light sculpture. Though neon has always been popular in commercial signage, Antonakos appropriated it for modern art by using it abstractly, typically for curved lines apparently suspended in space. Most of his work in recent years has been for public spaces, where they customarily appear without his name attached: on the south side of West 42nd Street between Ninth and Tenth Avenues in Manhattan; in the Exchange Place PATH station in Jersey City; in the Pershing Square station in Los Angeles; and in the Providence Convention Center in Rhode Island. Typically, they are visible from greater distances than most public art. Unfortunately, none appear in Antonakos's own neighborhood of SoHo.

Another important new art developed in SoHo was artistic machines, which has been my term for kinetic sculptures propelled by motors. James Seawright, who had a studio next to Paula Cooper when she opened her initial SoHo gallery in 1968, joined her a few years later in purchasing a Wooster Street building, where she made the ground floor into her gallery while he took a whole floor mostly to store all the electrical parts necessary to assemble his "sculptures," as he preferred to call them then. The best of them were autonomous machines whose movements responded to extrinsic stimuli. The twelve tall columns in *Electronic Peristyle* (1968) responded with varying sound to the presence of spectators within a raised sloping platform 15 feet in diameter. In the middle was an elegantly crafted transparent globe perhaps two feet in diameter containing an electronic jungle that included twelve photocells pointing outward, like cannons from a turret. As spectators moved about the platform, they interrupted light beams and touched off photocell signals. These signals, prompted by a continually varying process, rapidly articulated sounds from speakers in the twelve columns. Later Seawright works included walls of rectangular mirrors, each a few feet wide and high, tilted at various angles to make the scene before it into a kind of cubist picture. Thirty years ago, I thought him among the most promising artists in America. Soon afterward, he became in his mid-thirties a professor at Princeton University, where he eventually chaired the visual arts program, his art languishing, the culture of Princeton apparently defeating SoHo, in a pattern more typical of poets who

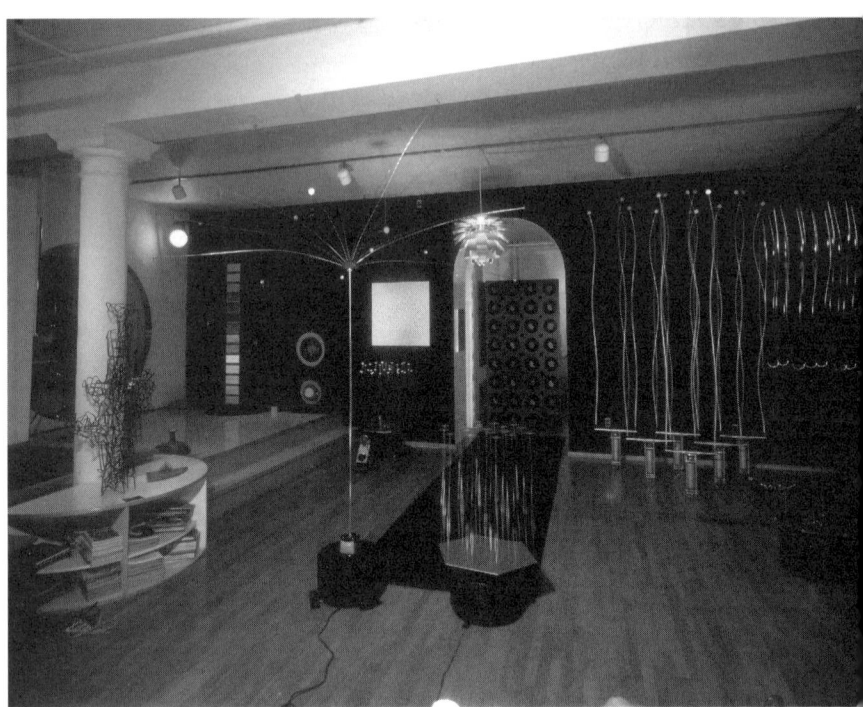

Wen-Ying Tsai's family loft. Photo by Si-Chi Ko, courtesy of the Tsai family

publish a strong first book and then, rewarded with a cushy job, become unproductive campus celebrities.

Wen-Ying Tsai, the most accomplished technological artist of them all, began with slender vertical rods with tops the size of bottle caps. A motor at their base made them vibrate within a narrow field. Once he subjected them to a rapidly flickering strobe light in a darkened space, the vibrating rods appeared to dance. When the rate of flicker changed in response to either sounds in the surrounding space or the spectator's proximity to a sensing device, the dancing changed as well. A strong kinetic illusion, these established Tsai's reputation in the late 1960s. After sojourns in Cambridge, Massachusetts, and Paris, Tsai and his family settled in 5,000 square feet of SoHo space on the corner of Broadway and Prince Street. Visiting their loft there was always a thrill. Between his front door and his kitchen was a sunken tub that received water from vibrating shower heads attached to the ceiling. When the falling water was illuminated by a strobe light, the droplets danced up and down. At certain strobe speeds, the droplets appeared to be moving upward apparently violating all rules of gravity. *Upwards-Falling Fountain* (1979), as he called it, creates an illusion that had to be seen firsthand to be believed.

In his workshop was a yet larger water sculpture, *Living Fountain* (1980–1988), with a shower head 3 feet in diameter plus three concentric circles of water jets all installed above a basin 12 by 16 feet. Here the strobe is designed to respond to combinations of changes in audible music, random sensors, audio feedback controls, and a computer program. For the traveling Computers and Art Exhibition, Tsai chose G. F. Handel's *Water Music*. Needing yet more space for his stupendous creations, the Tsais purchased a barn near Woodstock, New York, and later came to forsake SoHo for a whole building in the flat-iron distinct further north in Manhattan. One of the minor tragedies in the history of SoHo was that technological art wasn't exhibited here. Indeed, it was hardly seen elsewhere in New York, except for an occasional exhibition at the Bronx Museum in the 1980s or at a short-lived gallery in IBM's midtown building.

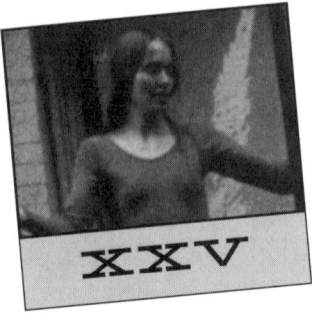

XXV

The basic thing about modernism in literature is that it recognized, and insisted upon recognizing, the materiality of language as a source of whatever happens in literature, rather than emphasizing its power to communicate ideas, or anything like that.

—Harry Mathews, in an interview (1999)

ALTHOUGH WRITING alone was not among the categories qualifying an artist for legal residence in SoHo proper, a good deal of literature was produced there, much of it obscurely published and barely known, even decades later. The distinctive characteristic of SoHo literature was its close relation, both stylistically and socially, to new ideas in the other arts. More precisely, SoHo writing was concerned, like other SoHo arts, with issues of minimalism and abstraction, of extreme fragmentation; with alternative scale and coherence, of patterning and difficulty; questions of nonart and anti-art, perceptual stretching, and the exploration of media other than one's initial mastery (which, for writers, would be words for printed pages). Another SoHo ideal has been unique signature—that a work should look or sound like yours and no one else's—at a time when most aspiring graduates of university writing programs were encouraged to resemble one or another accepted masters. It follows that SoHo writing was not about expressionism or about classicism, not about "poetic feeling" or realistic portrayals.

Both the art and literature of SoHo were concerned with discovering the radical possibilities of one's art, rather than the exploration of familiar conventions. To put it differently, SoHo writing approached Art and still remained Literature. Much of it was necessarily self-published, often in editions of a few hundred copies, in contrast to the number of several thousand, which commercial publishers tell you is the minimum they must sell to "break even." Indeed, some of it was never published at all, Carl Andre, better known for his sculpture, only exhibited typed sheets of paper 8 ½" by 11", usually at the Paula Cooper Gallery, while refusing (perhaps shrewdly, not to diminish their value as "art") requests by others to print them.

The verbal texts that we associate with the polyartistic movement Fluxus are early examples of SoHo writing. Many of them were published by George Maciunas, often to include in boxes along with strictly visual materials. Just as John Cage was a major influence on Fluxus, so it could be said that he was the father of SoHo literature (as well as the titular deity of some strains of downtown music). On the north side of Houston Street has long lived one of the great American experimental writers, Madeline Gins, producing extraordinary books both in her own name and in collaboration with her husband the artist Arakawa—among them, her own *Word Rain* (1969) and *Helen Keller or Arakawa* (1994); and their *The Mechanism of Meaning* (1988) and *Architecture: Sites of Reversible Destiny* (1994).

Many SoHo authors worked in arts other than writing: Claes Oldenburg doing sculpture and performance; Carl Andre, Alison Knowles, Agnes Denes, and Rosemarie Castoro publishing writing in addition to exhibiting sculpture; the visual artist Jennifer Bartlett publishing *Cleopatra I-IV* (1971) and a full-length novel *History of the Universe* (1985) that reflects the influence of Gertrude Stein who likewise learned to advance writing through her experience of visual art. Frances Alenikoff and Kenneth King doing dance and choreography; Jackson Mac Low, poetry and music; and myself doing video, book design, electroacoustic music composition, and holography. Had e. e. cummings lived into the 1970s, when he would have been in his eighties, he would have epitomized a SoHo writer. As he exhibited his paintings and drawings and his wife was a recognized photographer, Cummings could have easily qualified for the official city certificate required to reside within SoHo.

As an example of SoHo-style writing, consider these sequences from Frances Alenikoff's long poem "Chronicles" (1981):

application

communication

consummation

santification

or, simply:

fail

wail

Agnes Denes's "Hamlet Fragmented" (1971) is a pioneering attempt to use a computer to reorganize the language of Shakespeare's classic, thus opening:

O, throw away the worser part of it,

And live the purer with the other half,

Good night, but go out to my uncle's bed

Assume a virtue if you have it not,

Later including proposals for replacing certain words, resulting with lines such as these:

Players ready?

,   mother, here's   metal   attractive.

Only to conclude with blocks of numerical codes supposedly used to generate the remarkable text.

Much other SoHo writing appeared within visual works, sometimes in works wholly of words, more often as accompanying texts. As noted before, photographs often had short texts handwritten on the face of the image to make them appear personal, as distinct from typeset captions appearing underneath. Robert Morris, best known for his sculpture, also a distinguished essayist on sculptural issues, incor-

porated longer prose texts into a series of metal tableaux, 29" by
38 ¹/₂" by 7" deep.

To the image of compartments he put into the lower left-hand
corner a text that reads in its entirety, including the title:

Tomb for a Dismembered Body

The Torso is said to repose beneath this lacy white trellis. And that rock-
ery or grotto over there? I was told it marks the resting place of the
pelvis. But I am not sure; nothing is marked. Beyond those trees are two
small pools, just visible there to the left. Yes, for the feet. Who laid out
these gravel paths? I was not told that. Yes! This is the maze you heard
about. Don't ask me why it was covered with mirrors. Or why that mist
from the top keeps them wet, I would prefer if you did not enter. I can't
be responsible. No, the head is not visible at the center. It is deep in the
ground beneath one of the walls. So I have been told. That grouping on
the hill of bronze flag poles and flags? Yes, for the hands. I don't know
what the colors of the flags mean. A swamp? You were told of one? I
would agree, it is somewhat dispersed layout. But, apt, you say. I'm sure
he would be pleased to hear it.

All of these examples appeared in a 1982 anthology of mine, *The
Literature of SoHo.*

Like cummings before them, SoHo's writers evolved plural professional situations, where they could do one art at one time and
another at a different time, much as cummings tended to paint during the day while writing in the evening. Coming to know how easily
a creative person can move from one art to another, I was scarcely
alone in objecting to the use of artistic categories to characterize people, rather than work. Even if they make writing or sculpture, people
aren't necessarily "writers" or "sculptors," especially if they made
both. As far back as 1975, I objected to the epithet "artist's books,"
new at the time, which was initially meant to distinguish them for
writer's books, because the authors of "artist's books" had gone to art
school or exhibited something somewhere once upon a time. The
genre should have been called "book art." Having personally created
videotapes as well as film and writing, I think I know at firsthand the
technical as well as creative differences between video and film, say,

as well as between both and writing. However, I came to resent such person-centered definitions as "writer" and "filmmaker," not only because they shortchanged the extent of my creative activity but also because they restricted it. That is to say, I am not a "filmmaker" when I make films and a "writer" when I write. I am, like cummings before me, a creative person involved in a variety of artistic situations. I do not change heads in going from one art to another; I scarcely change clothes. Trust the tale, not the teller—consider the work, not the biographical label. Also, professional categories function to make disciplinary transgressions into a kind of pseudoevent—a so-called poet's film is no different in essence from anyone else's film, whereas a so-called artist's book is, all current rationalizations to the contrary notwithstanding, still a book.

Another kind of SoHo writing was the visual artist's thoughtful essays about art issues. These appeared occasionally in the slick art magazines but more often in small-circulation journals published within SoHo, largely for SoHo (as distinct from the slick magazines). Examples included *Art-Rite*, *Artworkers News*, and *The Fox*, among others. Some of the best of these SoHo essays were reprinted in the genuinely pioneering anthologies compiled by Gregory Battcock until his premature death—among others, *Idea Art* (1973), *New Artists Video* (1978), and *The Art of Performance* (1984, posthumously coedited); others appeared in more specialized books like Ira Schneider and Beryl Korot's *Video Art: An Anthology* (1973). Perhaps the best single anthology of such writing appeared not in this country but in Europe in *Germany—On Art/Uber Kunst* (1974, bilingual)—never to be reprinted here, inexplicably. Another anthology connecting some SoHo literature to the larger world of American avant-garde writing is Alan Sondheim's *Individuals* (1977). For a brief spell, the press at the Nova Scotia College of Art and Design, of all places, was issuing books by SoHo artists, including Claes Oldenberg's *Raw Notes* (1974), Yvonne Rainer's *Work 1963–1973* (1974), Simone Forti's *Handbook in Motion* (1974), Steve Reich's *Writing about Music* (1974), and Carl Andre and Hollis Frampton's *12 Dialogues 1961–1963* (1983). For an even briefer period, some of these volumes were distributed closer to home by the New York University Press.

Among the masterpieces of book-art books, consider several Sol LeWitt made when he was residing on Hester Street, on a Chinatown edge of SoHo. *Arcs, Circles, & Grids* (1972) is a rigorous sequence of 196 drawings on square pages that suggest a narrative solely through the changing shapes of lines. For *Autobiography* (1981), he took guilelessly simple small photographs of all the objects in his studio, correctly suggesting that for purposes of an autobiographical book the sum of them reflected his life just as much as any prose narrative. In the 1970s and 1980s, he frequently persuaded institutions exhibiting his work to print a book of his in lieu of a catalog. Some were saddle-stitched chapbooks; others were thicker and perfect bound. The sum of them represents to my mind a unique artistic/literary achievement. Published in minimal editions, these books are scarce, even from Antiquariats, to recall the German epithet for high-class used book dealers. For a while, LeWitt sent new ones to me, still deserving my gratitude. (I've resisted offers from dealers to buy them, so important do they remain to me.)

From the time I relocated to SoHo, with thrice as much interior space as I had before, I produced many examples in this book-art genre: a newsprint chapbook composed entirely of numerals, *Numbers: Poems & Stories* (1974); the same text in two radically different formats, *One Night Stood* (1977); palm-sized ladderbooks composed of geometric drawings that metamorphosed over a sequence, *Modulations* (1975) and *Extrapolate* (1975); an abstract narrative composed only of a systematically recomposed single photograph of myself, *Reincarnations* (1981); and sequences of geometric drawings, acknowledging the influence of the LeWitt books: *Constructs* (1975), *Constructs Two* (1978), *Fifty Constructivist Stories* (1991), *Intermix* (1991), and *Constructs 3–6* (four volumes, 1991), among other titles. I began to have one-person shows of my book-art books in 1979, the oeuvre reflecting the quick effects of my move to SoHo. In 1985, I received a senior grant for this work from the visual arts program of the National Endowment for the Arts. Had I stayed in the East Village (or, worse, stayed uptown), believe me, this work wouldn't have been done at all.

Looking back, I estimate that SoHo writing has so far had less impact on native literature than, say, SoHo painting had on American art, not only because it was more radical than the norm but also because books appearing from noncommercial publishers are rarely recognized in the critical media and the writing classes, to our misfortune. The great bookstore for indigenous SoHo writing was Printed Matter, mentioned before. One could find there much of the work described here. However, by the time Printed Matter moved to West Chelsea during the 2000–2001 season, few residing in SoHo were producing SoHo writing any more.

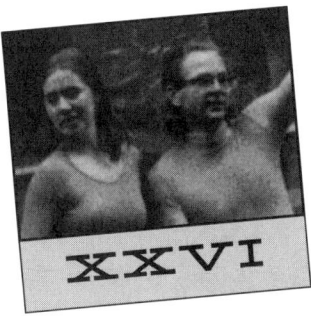

XXVI

Paik opposed the idea of television as a defined and limited medium. For him, television was a process to be explored and a performance to be executed through the constant energy of his imagination and his art against the powers of conformity. Paik saw television as interactive and it became for him a kind of performance object.

—John Hanhardt, *The Worlds of Nam June Paik* (2000)

ORN IN KOREA IN 1932, Nam June Paik (pronounced Pike, like the fish) went to high school in Hong Kong before studying music at universities in Japan and then in Germany, where his work earned early support from both John Cage and Karlheinz Stockhausen at a time when the two titans were more predisposed to agree than disagree. The latter, no pushover for enthusiasm, published this recollection of a Paik performance in the early 1960s:

> Paik came onto the stage in silence and shocked most of the audience by his actions as quick as lightning. For example, he threw beans against the ceiling which was above the audience and into the audience. He then hid his face behind a roll of paper, which he unrolled infinitely slowly in breathless silence, against his eyes so they became wet with tears. He screamed at the same moment he switched on two tape recorders with a sound montage typical of him, consisting of women's screams, radio news, children's noise, fragments of classical music, and electronic sounds. Sometimes he also switched on an old gramaphone

with a record of Haydn's string quartet version of the *Deutschlandlied*.
Immediately back at the stage ramp he emptied a tube of shaving cream
into his hair and smeared its content over his face over his dark suit and
down to his feet. . . .

At another performance, in a Cologne "atelier" belonging to
Stockhausen's wife-to-be-then, Mary Baumeister, Paik leaped from the
stage into the audience to cut John Cage's tie with scissors and smear
both the composer and his associate, the pianist David Tudor, with
his favorite stuff: shaving cream. In New York, at George Maciunas's
modest Canal Street loft (ironically called Fluxhall after Kunsthalle),
Paik presented *Zen for Film* (1962–1964), a memorable masterpiece
of minimalist/conceptual moviemaking—approximately 1,000 feet of
clear 16mm film projected onto a screen for thirty minutes. "Without
images or sound, Paik's film became a tabula rasa for the viewer's free
assocations," writes Michael Rush. "With each additional screening of
the film, scratches, dust, and other chance events of film projection
inevitably occurred, thus rendering the film new, in a certain way,
each time."

From the start of his theatrical career, Paik had established a pre-
disposition for extravagance and audacity that would continue. One
example, his 1975 performance titled *Lesson* in a Fluxus anthology
staged at 80 Wooster Street, I have already mentioned. In another
concert on that premises, he broke several 78 rpm records, no doubt
obtained nearby in the Canal Street junk shops, parts of which he distributed to spectators, signing them in an ic(r)onic gesture. (I still
have one.) Generous with his handwriting, Paik usually signed exhibition catalogues he sent to me.

After several comparably aggressive performance pieces in
Europe, many of them in Fluxus festivals, Paik installed in 1963 the
first gallery exhibition ever of television sets in Wuppertal, Germany.
Their live-time imagery he altered by manipulating the broadcast signal through the use of magnets, among other techniques, creating
continuously distorted, abstract images from representational pictures.
It was an innovative move, not to be forgotten as photographs made at
the time display decades later a quality that seems not only uniquely
televisual, so to speak, but classic. "Paik saw the cathode-ray tube as a

compositional device," John Harhardt wrote in his catalog for a Paik retrospective in 2000, "a surface that through distortions, transformed the received broadcast image."

One detail of his biography that should not be lost was that initially he worked for roughly three years at an electronic music studio in Cologne, producing audiotapes before he made video. The latest museum catalog identifies four "1/4–inch" and thus reel-to-reel tapes made between 1958 and 1962, their titles reflecting Paik's ambitions at the time: *Hommage à JohnCage: Musik für Tonbänder und Klavier*, *Etude for Pianoforte, and Prepared Piano for Merce Cunningham*. Simply, Paik was among the first to realize a lesson since lost—that training in high-tech music might provide a better preparation for video than education in, say, film and visual art (and thus that video production courses more appropriately belong in music schools than art schools). Among other first-rank video artists likewise trained initially in composition and electronic music is Reynold Weidenaar.

Though Paik continued producing audacious live performances, some of them involving genuine danger, his video activities had greater impact. In Peter Moore's 1965 photograph, Paik's Canal Street studio resembles a TV repair shop with an open television chassis in the foreground and several monitors scattered in the background. Evidently, he had discovered that just outside his front door on Canal Street was New York City's principal source of electronic (and other) junk. Late in 1965, Paik showed at Café au Go Go a videotape made with an early portable video camera he had purportedly purchased earlier that day from a Manhattan music store. In the mimeographed sheet printed for this event, he promised with prophetic insight: "In my videotaped electrovision, not only you see your picture instantaneously and find out what kind of bad habits you have, but see yourself deformed in 12 ways, which only electronic ways can do." Exploiting those new technologies of camera and tape for their esthetic possibilities different from those offered by cathode-ray tubes alone, Paik incorporated them into his first one-person exhibition at the New School in the same year. (I repeat the story of Paik's early use of portable video equipment because it is canonical, repeated in several history books and exhibition catalogs, though my own recollection is that portable video recorders were unavailable before the summer of 1967.)

For the announcement of his 1968 exhibition titled Electronic Art at the Galeria Bonino on 57th Street, smack in the middle of uptown dealing, Paik reproduced an electronic schematic, introducing a striking image, soon to become more familiar, to an art-gallery audience that, unlike electrical engineers, largely hadn't seen one before. Reviewing the exhibition in the *New York Times*, the shamelessly retrograde critic John Canaday reported accurately, "Mr. Paik is exhibiting a dozen or so TV sets, each one violated by its own electronic attachment to deform the image beyond anything you can imagine, no matter how bad your reception is." He continued, "But in most cases the screen becomes a field of operation for totally abstract images, in motion, composed sometimes of wonderfully organized lines of light, and sometimes of curious hazy, flow shapes." Paik had four more solo shows at Bonino, one as late as 1974, and although nothing sold, the gallery's owner testified that these shows gave her space a visibility otherwise unavailable. One piece, Grace Glueck reported, "was wanted by a collector who intended to donate it to the Museum of Modern Art. But, as Ms. Bonino recalls with a shrug, the Modern refused it." (The piece is now owned by the Stedelijk in Amsterdam.) Indicatively, other large NYC museums have been more respectful of Paik than MoMA.

In 1968, Paik was among the first artists-in-residence at the Boston public television station WGBH, where he incidentally developed a Video Synthesizer that, extending his original video-art principle, could radically transform an image fed into it as well as generate kinetic images strictly indigenous to it. In these respects, the video synthesizer resembled the audio synthesizer developed a few years before, most prominently by Robert Moog. In the 1970s, Paik was the principal beneficiary of the Television Laboratory established in New York City's public television station, WNET. (Out of this video hothouse came early executives of the strictly commercial channel MTV, their taste in otherworldly electronic imagery directly reflecting their contact with Paik.)

While keeping his SoHo address, Paik began to work and sometimes live elsewhere, first as artist-in-residence at SUNY at Stony

Brook in 1967, later at the California Institute of the Arts, where he established a video department that continues. Eventually a professor at the Kunstakademie in Düsseldorf, Paik became the epitome of not the artist-without-a-country but the artist-from-many-countries as he once represented Germany at the august Venice Bienale and at other places in both the United States and his native Korea, the cultural officials of each nation eager to capitalize on his international reputation as the pioneer video artist. He also received a load of grants, initially from the John D. Rockefeller III Fund with its Asian cultural programs; later from the Rockefeller Foundation, whose arts director had in the early 1970s designated Paik to be the avatar for video art in the West. Aware of his titular role, he would often attend newcomers' video screenings, including mine, sometimes dozing off, generously dispensing compliments without jeopardizing his royal status.

Limitations in his spoken English notwithstanding, Paik also published English-language statements and manifestos that could be frequently reprinted:

> Someday artists will work with capacitors, resistors, and semi-conductors as they work today with brushes, violins, and junk. (1965)

> Imagine a future where *TV Guide* will be as thick as the Manhattan telephone directory. (1973)

> [The Versatile Color TV Synthesizer] will enable us to shape the TV screen canvas

> as precisely as Leonardo

> as freely as Picasso

> as colorfully as Renoir

> as profoundly as Mondrian

> as violently as Pollock and

> as lyrically as Jasper Johns (1969)

For his numerous exhibitions and performances, Paik developed several strategies that were often repeated. One involved putting tele-

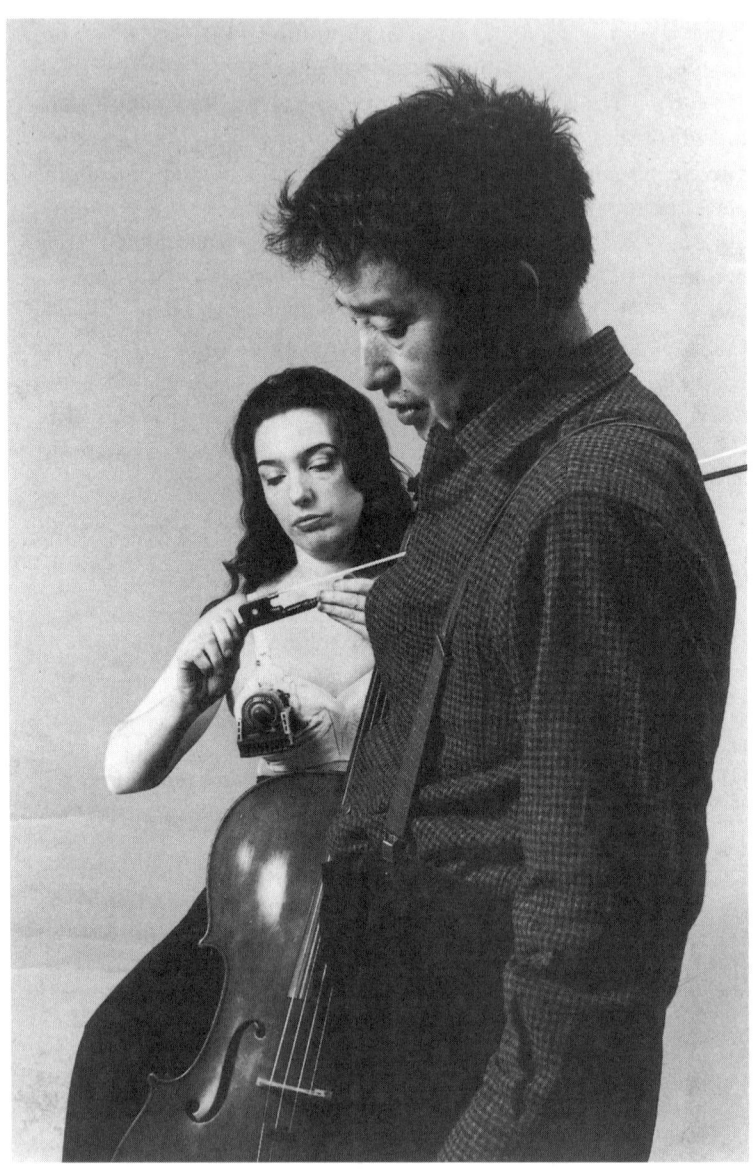

Nam June Paik and Charlotte Moorman wearing TV bra. Promotional photo, photographer unknown. Courtesy of Nam June Paik and Anthology Film Archives

vision monitors into unexpected places: amid live plants, into furniture, in a robot, or on a bra worn by the cellist Charlotte Moorman (1938–1992), his principal collaborator in live performances during her lifetime. Another, later strategy required an abundance of monitors, often dozens of them with mixtures of simultaneous or contrasting imagery, climaxing with the use of over 1,000 of them, extending approximately 60 feet high, for an installation at the 1988 Seoul Olympics. Displays such as these defined the genre of Video Sculpture that Paik pioneered. A third involved a wealth of images that were indigenously televisual, so to speak. Reproduced in bulk, in color, many to a page, as on the cover or in a color signature of the catalog produced for his 1982 retrospective at the Guggenheim, or page after page, as in a German book prepared for his 60th birthday, *Eine DATA base* (1993), these remarkable images alone would grant Paik a secure place in contemporary visual art. He also silkscreened images from his videotapes about John Cage and Merce Cunningham for limited editions of playing cards produced in Japan (1978, 1981).

Other recurring strategies include performances that are audacious and yet fundamentally silly, such as the Fluxus events described before, and *Candle TV* (1975), where a live candle burns inside the shell of a television set; or placing fish tanks in front of a row of monitors, the live animals purportedly "humanizing" the technology. (I wish I were joking about these lightweight visual equivalents of verbal one-liners.) Ever since *Global Groove* (1974), Paik's videotapes have depended upon juxtapositions of initially unrelated images, which is to say collage, to identify a modernist structural formula, certainly innovative in the 1920s, that had by the 1960s become distinctly old-fashioned, certainly in other arts. [Since I'm no great fan of Paik's videotapes, I should mention that John Hanhardt, his most loyal curator, identifies four major works "for television," as he puts it (implicitly distinguishing them from video for exhibition): *Global Groove* (1974), *Guadalcanal Requiem* (1977), *Allan 'n' Allen's Complaint* (1982), and *Living with the Living Theater* (1979). To my taste, the most sympathetic tape is Paik's dense appreciation of New York City, *Suite 212* (1975, reedited 1977).]

Limitations notwithstanding, Paik was the first video artist to have a full-scale retrospective at the Whitney Museum of American Art in 1982. (Its curator, John Hanhardt, later ensconced at the Guggenheim Musem, mounted a yet larger Paik retrospective in 2000, this featuring lasers.) Into the 1980s, no major video exhibition was credible without including Paik, and if a general exhibition of recent art had a token video, it was usually something by Paik. Precisely because the most sophisticated American television stations and private foundations concentrated so much of their resources on Paik's career, there has been reason for both jealousy and disappointment among his colleagues.

For all of his artistic prominence as an international art celebrity, few in SoHo (or anywhere else) have emulated his essentially goofy sensibility. Of no one else in SoHo can it be said, as I've read of Paik, "He speaks five languages badly." (These are, for the record, English, Korean, Japanese, French, and German.) Many in SoHo (and elsewhere probably) can testify to the experience of hearing him become increasingly excited until his English sentences become incomprehensible. Even his chronic narcolepsy is remembered with humor. My favorite anecdote recalls his request for an afternoon nap in a couch in the office of a museum mounting an exhibition of his work. "Must make some esthetic decisions," he declared as he dozed off. With such writing as "Danger Music for Dick Higgins" ("Creep into the VAGINA of a living WHALE"), Paik contributed to the obscure tradition of Conceptual Dance. Suffering a debilitating stroke in 1996, he would winter in yet another new home, this in Miami Beach, Florida, returning to his SoHo loft in the summers, often simply sitting on the street in a folding chair, his wife Shigeko Kubota and his male nurse beside him, to spread good cheer among old friends and new admirers.

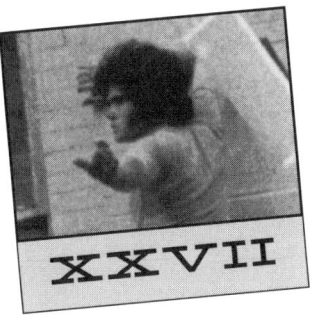

XXVII

The subject of my art is light itself—the discovery and
materialization of forms and structures contained in light.
Using sunlight and starlight as its source, the artwork
manifests experiences of primal solar color, and star
geometry in sculptural form.

—Charles Ross, in a statement (2002)

C HARLES ROSS WAS already established as a technologically
sophisticated sculptor before he came to SoHo. With an
undergraduate degree in mathematics before he took an M.A. in
sculpture, both from Berkeley in the early 1960s, he was the only
visual artist I knew in the mid-1960s to read *Scientific American* over
a solo dinner in a restaurant. His initial specialty was optics, or optical
effects, initially with clear liquid-filled prisms, often large, that
refracted light in surprising ways. Especially in arrays, these sculptures
were quite spectacular; and when exposed to natural sunlight, the
rich spectrum of refracted light would change continuously in
response to the moving of the sun (actually the turning of the earth).

Early into SoHo, he purchased half a floor in George Maciunas's
initial 1967 co-op at 80 Wooster Street. In the same year, Ross joined
the stable of artists at the Dwan Gallery in New York where both the
Minimal and Land Art movements originated. In 1971, Ross initiated
on the roof of Fluxhouse Cooperative II a prototype called Solar
Burns that took time for nature to complete.

A few years later he sold his share in Fluxhouse Cooperative II to
finance the purchase of a much larger entire top floor across Wooster

Street, at a time when, since property was cheap, humongous space was regarded as an easy measure not of wealth, as later, but artistic ambition. (Remember that only a decade before, Robert Rauschenberg's 3,000 square feet seemed huge.) Part of his new studio was set up to create additional prisms and test them. "In order to design spectrum events that occur at different times of the year, each prism must be specifically tuned to the sun. This process of tuning a prism is done by placing small prisms into an architectural model that has been attached to a sun-angle machine. The sun angle machine, which I developed early in my career, duplicates the movement of sunlight on any day of the year in any location on the planet. Thus by experimenting with the placement and angle of each prism I am able to accurately choreograph specific spectrum events which will occur in the final piece." In other words, in SoHo he has a contraption that can replicate the movement of the sun anywhere in the world.

Another portion of Ross's top floor loft is devoted to a garden of exotic tropical plants and cactuses, some of which have thrived under a skylight for twenty-five years. Prisms installed in several of the windows are tuned to direct the sun's spectrum through the plants. "The result is an oasis," his companion Jill O'Bryan told me. "The amount and time for watering each plant has been carefully calculated and is marked on the calendar. Ross's mathematical precision keep the plants healthy and happy," creating a sense of primary Nature among the second nature of industrial construction. Out of mathematical precision comes not only art but an attentiveness to plants.

Ross exhibited in galleries outside SoHo and within well into the late 1980s; but as his work was getting larger, he needed to think about where else to go. As architects appreciated his work, he began to work in public spaces, completing in 1985 for the Plaza of the Americas in Dallas a large solar spectrum sculpture where washes of color at much as 40 feet in length shift from red to violet.

Back in 1972, the architect Moshe Safdie had approached Ross about creating a spectrum work, as he calls it, for a synagogue that Safdie was building in the Old City of Jerusalem, but disputes within the client community killed that project. Instead, the collaboration was revived twenty years later when Safdie installed Ross's Solar

Spectrum in the chapel at the Harvard Business School.

In 1993 *The Year of Solar Burns* was commissioned by the French Ministry of Culture for permanent installation in the fifteenth-century Chateau d'Oiron in the Loire Valley. The "solar burns" are portraits of sunlight literally drawn by the sun itself. To create these images Ross places a wooden plank under a large magnifying lens. As the sun passes across the sky (or the earth turns), it burns a mark across the plank. Changing weather patterns act to modulate the burn: sunny skies produce a broad smoke flare, passing clouds leave unburned interruptions. Out of cloudy days come blank boards. The prototype for *Solar Burns* was made on the roof at 80 Wooster Street two decades before.

From 1994 to 1996, Virginia Dwan, his sometime gallerist, collaborated with Ross and the architect Laban Wingert to create the Dwan Light Sanctuary for the United World College in Montezuma, New Mexico. Ross proposed a unique solar spectrum space—a round chamber whose dimensions and sloping walls are based on astronomical relationships and seasonal angles of the sun. Twenty-four large prisms produce orchestrated spectrum events that circulate through the space, changing by the hour and with the seasons. A square window frames the pole star.

His major project over the past three decades has been not a commission but an ambitious earthwork done wholly on his own initiative. Atop a small mesa Ross purchased eighty miles from Santa Fe, New Mexico, he is constructing *Star Axis*, "an earth/sky sculpture and a naked eye observatory," as he calls it. Its outside dimensions will be 11 stories high and $1/10$ of a mile across. "Star Axis creates an intimate experience of how the earth's environment extends into the space of the stars. Each element of *Star Axis*—every shape, every measure, every angle—was first discovered by astronomical observation and then brought down into the land–star geometry anchored in earth and rock."

Not unlike other prominent SoHo artists whose work is mostly public commissions done elsewhere—most notably, Stephen Antonakos and Kenneth Snelson—Charles Ross still spends most of the year back home in SoHo where he keeps his archives, creates new work, develops his unfinished proposals, tends his loft garden, and makes documentary videos about work installed, alas, mostly elsewhere.

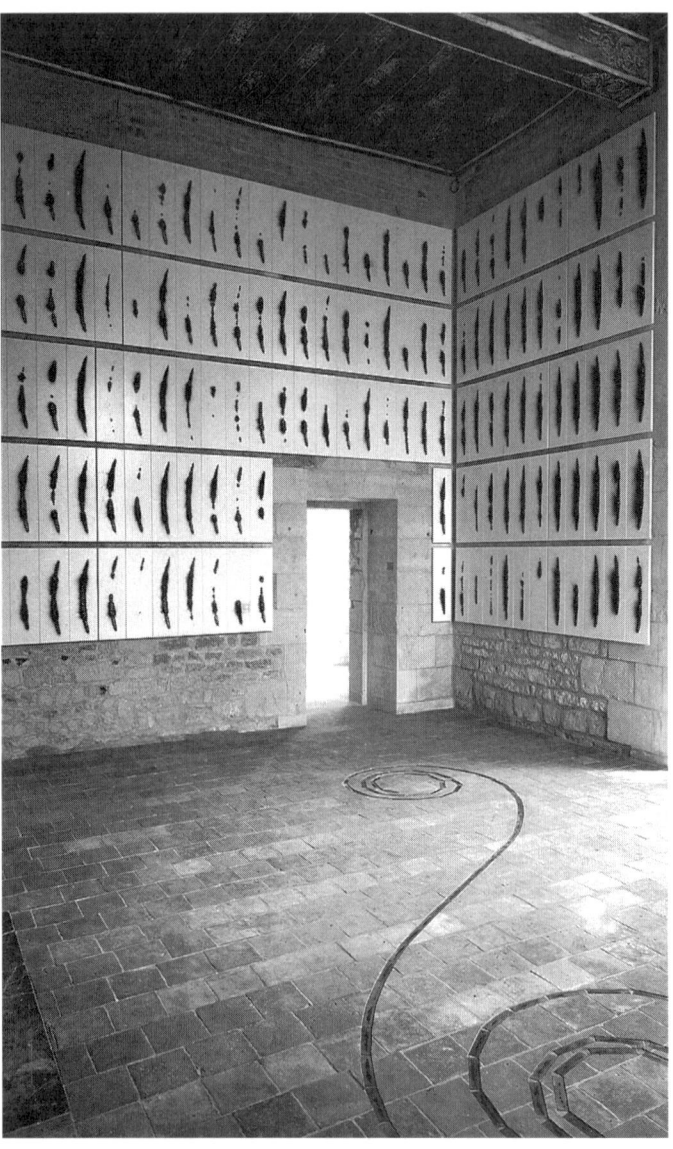

Charles Ross, *Year of Solar Burns*, Chateau d'Oiron, Oiron, France, 1993. 365 burns, 10" x 30" each. Wood, oil paint, focused sunlight, bronze. Photo courtesy of Charles Ross

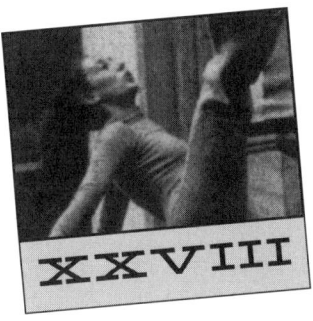

XXVIII

There is no other word for it—SoHo is a phenomenon. For European time standards, the speed at which this industrial slum, even though slated for demolition, has become the final point of the Western avant-garde is nothing short of mind-boggling.

—René Block, introduction to *SoHo: Downtown Manhattan* (1975)

O NE MEASURE OF the vitality of a cultural community has always been the number and quality of publications originating within it, as distinct from those started by outsiders trying to capitalize on the prominence of a moniker. For instance, the *Village Voice* was a newsprint weekly founded in the mid-1950s by people residing within Greenwich Village, initially to provide them with cultural information about their community. (Eventually, it also became a national newspaper.) The *SoHo News*, by contrast, was founded in 1973 by an outsider, a sometime rock concert promoter, in part to exploit the success of the *Voice*, with a similar size and similarly weekly publication schedule. Though the offices of the *SoHo News* were on Broadway below Houston Street, nearly all of its editors lived outside SoHo; most of its writers probably did as well. Having contributed a few pieces to its pages, I can recall my editor's skepticism toward the fact that I actually resided in SoHo. It died in 1982. Later, several glossy art magazines settled in and around SoHo, even though some of them had originated uptown (or in California). Perhaps their editorial outlook changed in the wake of relocation; perhaps not.

The true SoHo publications were written by people residing there, largely for fellow artists who, if not living there as well, spent much of their spare times hanging around its streets. Previous small-circulation artist periodicals published in the New York area included *Possibilities* (1947), a one-shot edited by John Cage, Harold Rosenberg, Robert Motherwell, and Pierre Chareau; Ruth and John Stephan's *Tiger's Eye* (1947–1949), which also printed writers along with reproducing art (and was remembered in an exhibition at Yale University in 2002); Harry Holtzman's *Transformation* (1950–1952); *It Is* (1958–60), edited by Phillip Pavia; and *Scrap* (1959), whose four issues, each condensed on a single sheet of paper, were published by Sidney Geist.

Most of the SoHo artist-for-artist periodicals were cheaply produced, often at local print shops. The printer I remember best was Expedi at 110 Greene Street with its Chinese foreman and Chinese staff, with its constantly blaring Chinese pop music providing an exotic background soundtrack for any of us working there. Among the first SoHo artist magazines was *Avalanche* (1968–1976), square in format printed on glossy paper, like *Artforum* at the time, but slightly smaller in size, devoted to new developments in video and performance. Its owner/publisher was Willoughby Sharp, whose presence in SoHo has been sporadic. Les Levine's *Culture Hero* (1968) began strongly with editorial formulas later adopted by *Andy Warhol's Interview*, only to disappear while the latter prospered. *The Fox* (1974–1975) was created by Joseph Kosuth and Sarah Charlesworth, young lovers at the time, with verbose pretheory "theoretical" articles printed on newsprint but nonetheless perfect-bound between card-stock supposedly to give its words additional weight.

By contrast, *Art-Rite* (1972–1979), was tabloid-sized newsprint from front to back, edited by Edit DeAk and Walter Robinson (commonly called Mike), as they passed into their mid-thirties. The former recalled in 1998 that their unpretentious looking publication "came from the people, establishing our own voice, our own style and category." Its single most consequential issue was devoted to a symposium about Artists' Books (aka book-art).

Art Workers News Letter (1971) initiated a sequence of magazines sponsored by the National Artworkers Coalition, later called Coalition for the Community of Artists. "Its original purposes were to create a union-like organization," Elliott Barowitz remembers, "that would offer health care, insurance programs, jobs counseling and jobs, information on health hazards in the studio—handbooks on health and legal issues, business acumen, etc." With these purposes in mind, the magazine and its successors mixed practical information about artists' materials, especially those with previously unacknowledged dangers, with independent book reviews. Its mandate seemed to be intelligence, as distinct from opinion. With a move to new offices on lower Broadway, it was renamed *Artworkers News* only to change its name again to *Art & Artists* in 1983. Among the contributors beginning their careers as art writers in its pages were Donald Kuspit, Gerald Mazorati, and Adam Gopnik. It ceased publishing in 1989.

There were also SoHo magazines devoted to the other arts, such as Jonas Mekas's *Film Culture* (1955), which followed its founding editor and the Anthology Film Archives through successive addresses including one in SoHo; Tom Borek's dance magazine *Eddy* (1973–1978); Beryl Korot and Phyllis Segura's *Radical Software* (1970–1974), whose focus for eleven issues was video as the new medium was emerging; *Holosphere* (1972–1990) and *The Whole Message* (1977) for holography, mentioned before. *Ear* (1973–1991), for avant-garde music, began strongly in California only to die west of SoHo.

This survey scarcely exhausts the catalog of artists' publications emerging from SoHo. I remember a literary magazine named *Benzene* (1980–1985), edited by Alan Bealy, which published my typographically unconventional "Seductions" in its initial issue; Art Spiegelman and Françoise Mouly's *RAW* (1980–86) for sophisticated comics; Judith Aminoff's *Cover* (1980–1983); the collectively edited feminist art magazine *Heresies* (1977–1993); *New Observations* (1981–2000), which was founded by Lucio Pozzi who passed it on in 1987 to Diane Karp, and had many guest editors through over 100 separate issues; Anne Turyn and Brian Wallis's *Top Stories* (1979–1985); Phil Mariani and Brian Wallis's *Wedge* (1982–1985); Tom Lawson's *Reallife* (1979–1992); Bob Witz's Appearances (1978–1987); Mike Golden's *SAW* (*SoHo Arts Weekly*) (1984–1986);

Just Another A..hole (1978–1987) produced in various print and audio formats by the writer Barbara Ess sometimes with assistance from the composer Glenn Branca; Stephen Soreff's *AGAR* (*Avant-Garde Art Review*) (1981–1991), which "is intended to add the areas of prediction, speculation, and suggesting to existing art commentary"; Betsy Sisler's *Bomb* (1981–   ); Josephina Ayerza's *Lacanian Ink* (1990–   ), and Abe Lubelski's NY *Arts Review* (1995–   ); all of them reflecting the cultural hothouse that was Artists' SoHo. Indicatively, only the last three survived into the twenty-first century. While newspapers are necessarily forgotten, artists' magazines should not be. What the sum of them accomplished in contributing to the intelligence of Artists' SoHo would make a valuable doctoral thesis.

One anomaly was *October*, a quarterly incidentally founded in SoHo in the late 1970s and still going into the twenty-first century. Essentially an academic journal, edited by professors for professors, it was eventually sponsored by a university press, as one of its founding editors moved out of SoHo. Though it occasionally published extended essays about and even by SoHo artists, it seemed to belong to another world when it began and certainly has resided there for most of its life.

Among the national magazines edited around geographic SoHo, though scarcely reflecting Artists' SoHo, are *Interview* (formerly *Andy Warhol's Interview*), *Art in America*, *Harper's*, *Nerve*, *Paper*, *Tight*, *Leg Show*, and *Juggs*. To those who know the last three, no description is necessary; for those unfamiliar with them, a description is likewise unnecessary. To culturally open territory come odd bedfellows.

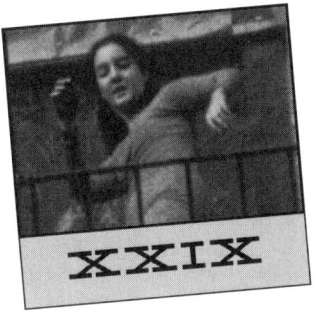

XXIX

*What Soho did for me, truthfully, was open my mind to
seeing art and talking about it endlessly. It also sharpened
my eyes, and it offered a community of like-minded people,
who were willing to judge and criticize each other. It
allowed us to think of our ideas as art, or at any rate, to
work them out according to the then existing laws of art.
After all, Soho was Art, and we were Soho.*

—Hanne Tierney, in a letter (2002)

BORN IN GERMANY in 1940, emigrating to the United States
when she was nineteen, Hanne Tierney came to SoHo in
the early 1970s as a mother of two kids and wife of a mathematics
professor, incidentally working part-time at a charcuterie and
bartending in SoHo and Tribeca. The permission to reside in SoHo—
the family's artist's certification—came from her work, not his. Her art
began with children's books published both in America and German-
speaking Switzerland. Thinking about "three-dimensional storytelling,
when the viewer could see in one full swoop what it might have taken
pages and pages to write about," as she put it, "brought me to the use
of symbols as stand-ins for human actors. The next step, working with
puppetry, soon developed into a systematic exploration of a theater
without actors—the beloved hobby horse of the early Symbolists."

As her children grew, Tierney developed a puppet theater that
she did entirely on her own, not only making the equipment but also
speaking the voices while she visibly manipulated from a control
panel on one side of the stage as many as 100 strings. She worked

initially with literary texts by Oscar Wilde, Anton Chekhov, Maurice Maeterlinck, Frederico Garcia Lorca, and Gertrude Stein, as well as her own stories. At first the figures on her stage resembled humans; later, in a brilliant departure, she used cloths of various colors, suspended by thin strings from eye loops in the ceiling, to stand for people and qualities. As they typically move through the air as words are spoken on their behalf, shrewd lighting makes the apparitions elegant, if not beautiful. Simplicity of production notwithstanding, the result of Tierney's departures was a chamber theater at once abstract, tactile, kinetic, and so highly original that it must be seen to be appreciated.

Her concept was so attractive that by 1982, while her kids were still at home, she had performed at the Guggenheim Museum, the Whitney Museum, the Sidney Biennial, and the Berlin theater festival. In the 1980s, she received grants from the National Endowment for the Arts and participated in several Jim Henson world-class puppet festivals.

In 1999, after two decades of squatting temporarily in other people's venues, Tierney, in the great tradition of SoHo theater artists, opened her own exhibition and performance space. However, Five Myles was not in SoHo, alas, which had become too expensive for a new theater, but in a abandoned garage on the edge of the Crown Heights section of Brooklyn, implicitly importing SoHo ways into other parts of New York City. Had she not resided in the SoHo hothouse, this theater, let alone her art, would probably not have developed at all.

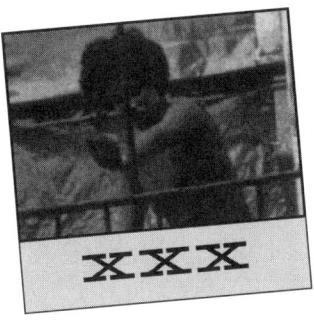

XXX

*It wasn't until I left home to go to college that it really hit
me that most adults don't do art or anything related to it.*

—Lun-Yi Tsai

C HILDLIKE THOUGH artists, especially unmarried artists, tend
to be, actual children were scarce in Artists' SoHo, at least at
the beginning, as most couples weren't married and those that were
legally hitched were too devoted to their careers or too poor to think
about having kids. There were no children residing in my building
until the 1990s, though one of my partners had children who lived
with their father. Lacking children to befriend other children, I got to
know artists' kids through their parents. Among the first remembered
by me were the tall twin sons of the technological artist Wen-Ying
Tsai mentioned before—Lun-Yi and Ming-Yi. At a Christmastime
party in the late 1980s one or the other asked my advice about writing
his application to college, I guess on the grounds that a professional
writer had superior intelligence about this particular subliterary form.
(I assured them that I didn't.) In their respect for the imaginary
competences of arts professionals the Tsai twins were very much
products of the Artists' SoHo hothouse.

Born in 1970, Lun-Yi and Ming-Yi went to junior high at the
United Nations School and as teenagers took the subway daily to the
Bronx High School of Science, a hothouse of a different academic
sort. Lun-Yi then went to Tufts, where he majored in math, in which
he also took an M.A., before becoming a visual artist who had a one-
person show of paintings both representational and geometric in 2002

at the National Arts Club in New York City. "There weren't many kids in SoHo," he recalled. "My friends from school lived either uptown or in Queens. Growing up in the home of a full-time artist also separated us from our classmates. The visitors to our home were writers, museum curators, collectors, musicians, and other artists. In our building except for one restaurant owner and one fashion model, everyone did art. It wasn't until I left home to go to college that it really hit me that most people don't do art or anything related to it.

"From my parents and their friends, we developed an instinctive feeling for art—its role in society and its value and importance as a human activity. In school, while the other children talked about pop stars and movie stars, my brother and I argued about whether Kandinsky was better than Miro. I always felt that I had the inside story on art, that I knew something that not even my art teachers knew, much less my peers. To me, the extreme dichotomy between school and after-school was just the way the world was made. I had the idea early that art was life and that great art could teach me all I needed to know about life. I always thought that I could learn more from walking around the galleries of SoHo than sitting at home doing my homework.

"There were a lot of interesting exhibits. There were immense paintings and then tiny paintings. There were sculptures that jutted out of walls and sculptures that just leaned against them. There were video installations; neon lights; plastic, glass, wood and steel concoctions. All kinds of materials were being used. When we entered them, the bright wooden floors would creak beneath our feet. The smell of the varnish and the oil paints became a pleasant smell for me and to this day when I go into my studio to work, that smell brings back those memories. I also saw piles of all kinds—rocks, clothes, garbage, etc. People were really pushing and trying to find something.

"In junior high, I started exploring the galleries every day on the way home from school. I walked all around and went into anything that looked like it had art. Galleries were opening and closing every season. I never bothered to keep track of their names and didn't really pay attention to the artists' names either; for me, it was all about the work. The impressive works I remember and sometimes even took

photographs of. Today, I occasionally see young artists doing something that I saw years ago in SoHo when I was a teenager."

What Lun-Yi learned early was the quality of esthetic experience.
"The first thing that comes to mind when I think of my childhood in
SoHo is the view from my window. My room faced the Prince Street
side of our building and through the wired glass I could see the bars of
the fire escape and then the red facade of the building across the street,
which was recently the Guggenheim downtown. Looking up into the
distance, I would see the off-white side of the New Museum building
against the sky. Its empty windows, covered now and then with polyeth-
ylene, were always in disrepair. When I was in high school, this view
inspired me to write poems in French on my mother's European IBM
selectrix. I would sit at my table while the late afternoon light on that
building in the distance would give me a vague sense of yearning filled
with nostalgia and loneliness. Since then, I have always been fascinated
with light on buildings especially late afternoon light on old buildings.

"I got my first camera, a Nikon FM, on Election Tuesday,
November 2, 1982. The first thing I did was take pictures of our
neighborhood. I hid the camera in my jacket since it was pretty
expensive and took it out to take pictures only when I was sure no
one would come up behind me and snatch it. We did this on Sundays
when the streets were empty. The brilliant winter sun would flood the
streets; the wind would be in our hair and we would look for interesting buildings to take pictures of. I shot exclusively in black and white.
I always tried to take photographs without people in them and sometimes we would wait for a long time so that everyone would get out of
the way. These days, it's impossible to take such pictures in SoHo.

"It wasn't only the space outside, but also the loft space in which
we lived that gave me an appreciation for the two most important sine
qua non of the visual arts—light and space. The large windows of my
father's office and the living area let the bright morning sun pour into
the whole space. None of my fellow classmates had anything like that.
They lived mostly in tiny claustrophobic apartments or houses with
views of gray buildings or alleys. It wasn't until much later when I
started to paint seriously that I realized how much I needed my own
well-lit space to think and create.

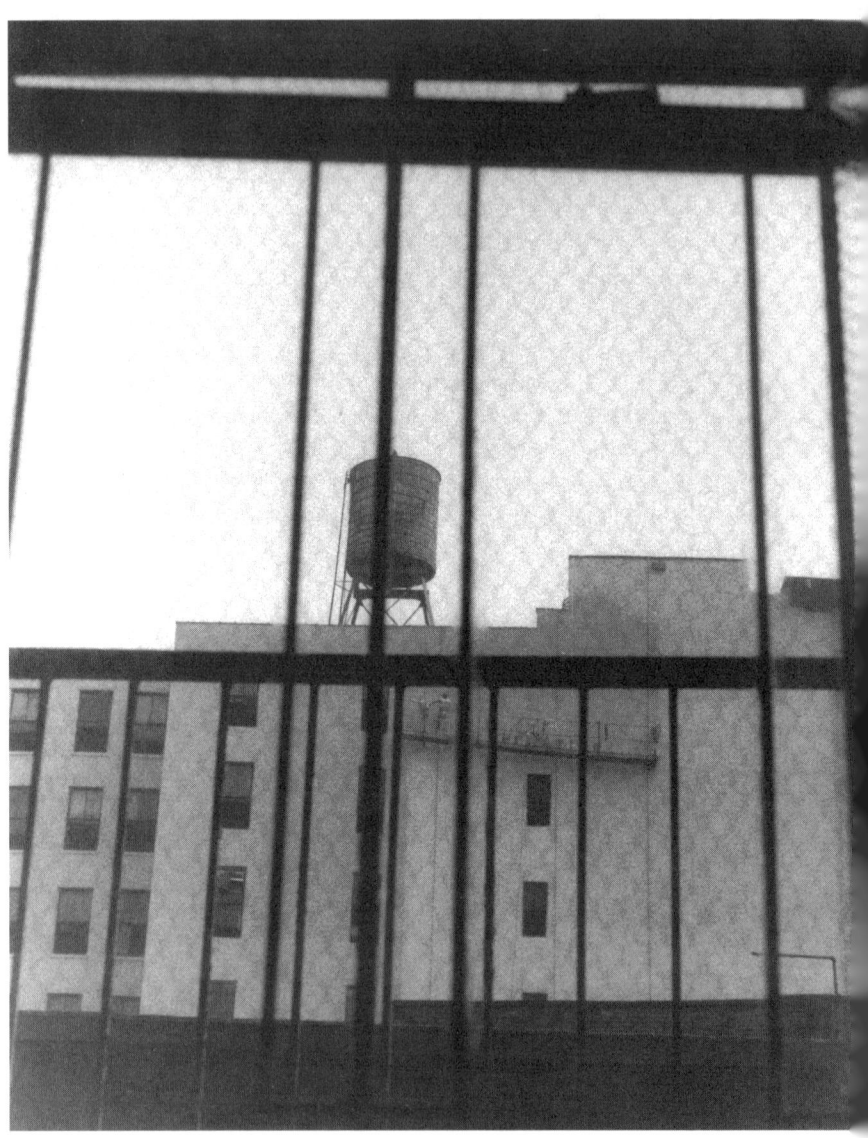

Old SoHo Window, the view from Lun-Yi Tsai's bedroom window with water tower on top of New Museum building, removed in 1990s. Photo by Lun-Yi Tsai, 1983

"I've always known that I would be an artist. It was the most natural choice for me; as a child, almost every adult I knew was an artist of one kind or another. Growing up in SoHo when it was a 'cultural hothouse' made me understand that art isn't something you see in museums or read about in books—it's something that is alive and thriving. When I left SoHo, I began to understand its lesson and its uniqueness and how fortunate I was to have lived in it in those years. If I had grown up in any other part of America or even in any other part of New York, I would not be even close to the person that I am today. As an artist, I would not have nearly the depth, knowledge, and instinct for art that I acquired somewhat serendipitously as a child by being at the right place at the right time." Hell, I wish I'd grown up in the Artists' SoHo hothouse. Blooming might have come a lot sooner.

The children of artists are probably scarcer in SoHo nowadays than kids whose parents do other things. Coming back from school in the afternoons, neither can have the pleasure, or education, that comes from hanging out in galleries. High-end retailers just don't make aspiring artists.

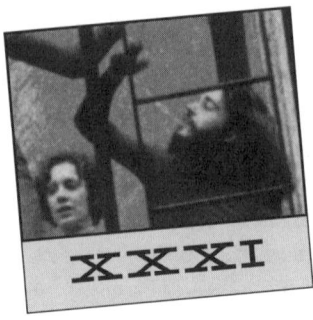

XXXI

T HE IDEA OF SoHo as an artists' hothouse first entered
general consciousness in newspaper reports about art
exhibitions and then in slick magazine articles usually featuring loft
interiors before it appeared in films. The bibliography to Seeman and
Siegfried's *SoHo* (1978) mentions *New York Times* articles by its art
critic Grace Glueck in 1969 and 1970 and then two in 1971. *Life*
magazine, then more prominent than later, had a five-page spread
titled "Living Big in a Loft" in its issue of March 27, 1970. "Behind
these grubby façades lurks an artists' colony," gushed the anonymous
writer. "Sixteen-foot ceilings, 45-foot rooms, and community spirit."
Charles R. Simpson records the alarm of SoHo's pioneers: "It was a
house-beautiful spread [that] blew our cover, so there was no point in
laying low. A Village person did the research, and we couldn't talk
them [sic] out of it." Not until 1970 did articles about SoHo appear in
the *Village Voice*, typically looking more north than south and thus
deprecating the alternative neighborhood much as it had deplored
the East Village a few years before.

   In the early 1970s, articles became more plentiful as apprecia-
tions of SoHo architecture appeared in the professional periodicals
Historic Preservation, *The Society of Architectural Historians Journal*,
and *Architectural Forum*. A writer named S. T. Edens recognized
SoHo's alternative spaces in a short article in *Art in America* in 1973.
The first major feature in my memory appeared as a cover story in
New York magazine, May 20, 1974, with a pull-out map, a brief
appreciation of SoHo as "the most exciting place to live" by Dorothy
Seiberling, long the art-scene chief for *Life* magazine, some advice on
SoHo shopping by Elin Schoen, and an extended report on "lofty liv-

ing" by Joan Kron, then beginning her career as what we've come to characterize as a lifestyle writer. *Town & Country* published in September 1977 an appreciation by Ellen Bilgore with a sequence of thirty-six small photos of a handsome investment banker's wife named Daily Pattee in various SoHo venues. In my own mind these last photos told a larger public a truth known to us—that SoHo was a neighborhood safe for well-dressed women traveling alone. That wouldn't have been said in such a slick magazine only a few years before.

SoHo appears in Wim Wenders's feature film, *The American Friend* (1977), some of which takes place in a loft on West Broadway between Spring and Prince Streets. SoHo functions in Paul Mazursky's *An Unmarried Woman* (1978) as the alternative world attracting the protagonist, an abandoned Upper East Side housewife. Meeting a painter played by Alan Bates, the no-longer-married woman, played by Jill Clayburgh, begins an affair with a sort of man unknown to her before. Though I've heard various local lofts identified as appearing in the film, I recognized for sure the corner where the Clayburgh character vomits into the trashcan as perhaps 50 feet away from my front door. At the time, as well as two decades later, *An Unmarried Woman* was lauded for realistic characters and feelings. I remember thinking at the time that its tragic honesty would discourage cross-river contacts, thank god. On the other hand, more than once I noticed that a suburban woman visiting a single male artist's loft in the early 1980s, especially if alone, often expected some sexual adventure in the course of hospitality. Can I be alone in noting that Mazursky made this film immediately after *Next Stop Greenwich Village* (1976), which had a male outsider perhaps reflecting himself, who wrote both films, the director having his protagonist change gender, so to speak, as his camera moved downtown.

SoHo also figures in Martin Scorsese's *After Hours* (1985), where a computer worker, played by Griffen Dunne, invites a pretty young woman, just met, played by Rosanna Arquette, to tour SoHo with him—a move not unreasonable at the time. However, when his money inexplicably flies out a window, the protagonist is stuck in a modern semblance of the Emerald City in the Land of Oz (or of Dante's hell). He encounters a female sculptor who makes paperweights from cream-cheese bagels, an array of thieves (Cheech and Chong), crazies, female sadomasochists (Linda Fiorentino), punks, and even an angry mob trying to kill him as a thief. A loaded dialogue between the protagonist and a nightclub bouncer echoes passages in Franz Kafka's "Before the Law." Why pick on SoHo, you ask? It seems that Scorsese, who grew up in Little Italy a mile to the east and later moved to Tribeca a mile to the southwest, was among the first to portray how oppressive, aside from flamboyant retailers, the neighborhood could become. *After Hours* was, in fact, filmed at the Emerald Bar on Spring Street well west of SoHo, in the Spring Street subway stop just east, and at the Moondance diner at 80 Sixth Avenue just beyond its southwest corner. Some consider *After Hours* among the best surreal urban nightmare movies, the neighborhood inspiring a dystopia of itself. It went on to win Scorsese a best director award at the 1986 Cannes Film Festival. I'm told that SoHo appears in such short-lived Hollywood films as Adrian Lyne's *9 1/2 Weeks* (1986), ostensibly about a sadomasochistic relationship between a Wall Street heavy and an art gallery lightweight; Andrew Davis's *A Perfect Murder* (1998), which portrays a rich commodities trader whose young wife turns unfaithful; and Jerry Zuker's *Ghost* (1990). *Ghost*, set in a building on Prince Street between Wooster and Greene, stars not only Demi Moore, Patrick Swayze, and Whoopi Goldberg but special effects by an entity called Industrial Light and Magic (apparently reflecting SoHo, but not of it).

But I haven't seen these films, I'm no more interested in Hollywod produce than I am in nonartist's SoHo.

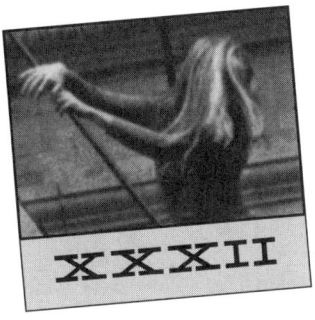

XXXII

A DIFFERENT SORT of SoHo, and SoHo art, appears in Michael Snow's *Wavelength* (1967), which is in many ways the classic representation of early SoHo. For forty-five minutes, a stationary camera zooms down a long narrow space 80 feet long to several large windows overlooking a street, incidentally revealing unfinished walls and a rickety floor. Fairly early in the film, a young woman supervises the moving of a bookcase into the space. Leaving temporarily, she returns with another young woman; together they listen to a radio. In P. Adams Sitney's summary, "Midway through, a man breaks glass (heard off-screen) through an unseen door and climbs the stairs (so we hear); he enters the studio and collapses on the floor, but the lens has already crossed half the room, and he is only glimpsed; the image passes over him. Late in the film, a girl returns, goes to the telephone, which, being at the far wall, is in full view, and in a dramatic moment which brings the previous events of the film into a narrative nexus, calls a man, 'Richard,' to tell him there is a dead body in the room. She insists that the man does not look drunk, but dead, and she says she will wait downstairs. She leaves." Plot continues to be minimal, though the representation is rich.

Notwithstanding its esthetic contributions to the history of avant-garde film, identified in Sitney's pioneering critical history, *Visionary Film* (1974), *Wavelength* portrays a different sort of interior preresidential space, essentially a threadbare loft, all captured with a minimal curiosity that looks paradoxically intelligent in representing the neighborhood in its earliest times. Simply, this is how SoHo looked before artists' renovations set in. (Otherwise, the Michael Snow classic, for those who don't know, is *La Region Centrale/The Central*

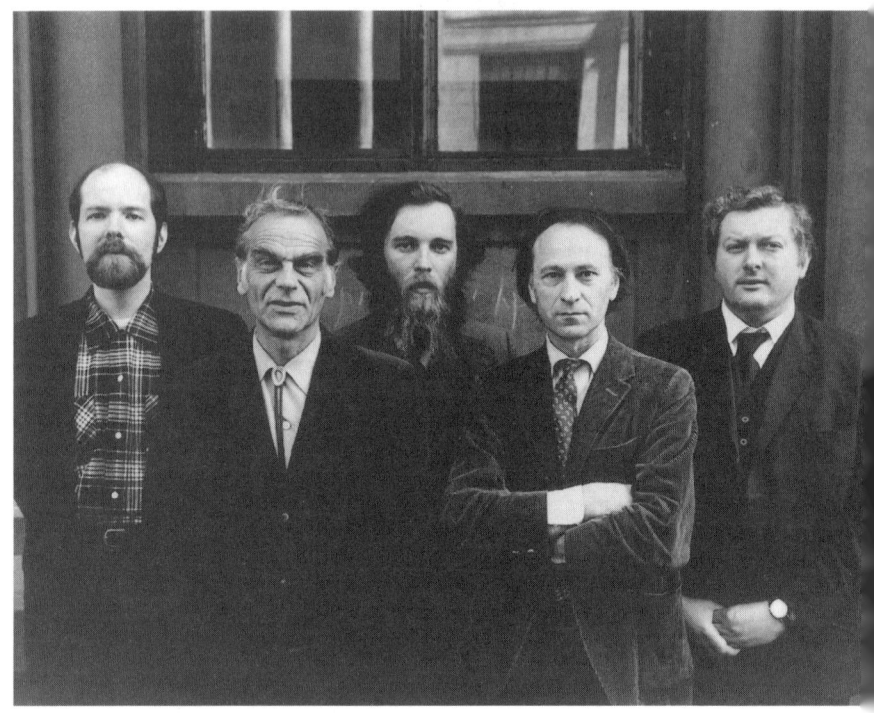

Anthology Film Archives Film Selection Committee: Ken Kelman, James
Broughton, P. Adams Sitney, Jonas Mekas, Peter Kubelka. Photo by Stephen
Shore, courtesy of Anthology Film Archives

Region [1971], which does something similar for the superficially bar-
ren terrain of northern Quebec.)

The only regular film theater within SoHo proper in the 1970s
was the Film-Makers' Cinematheque, which became Anthology Film
Archives in 1974. Anthology showed new avant-garde films along with
classics; in both respects it educated many of us in a highly selective
canon, "the essential cinema," put together by a committee of its
founding members. Once it closed too soon (to be relocated to the
East Village in 1980), some of its kind of programming was continued
at the Film Forum, more properly in Tribeca, which offered more
conventional "art-house" programming aimed at a larger audience.

Around the time Film Forum moved a few blocks uptown into the West Village, a complex of several screens opened in the basement of the Cable Building on the northwest corner of Broadway and Houston. With an entrance and exits on Mercer Street, the Angelika, as it was called, presented some avant-garde films at the beginning, usually after midnight, before focusing upon the sorts of uptown movies that get favorable reviews in the uptown newspapers. Not unlike earlier SoHo restaurants aimed at outsiders, the Angelika exploited the fact that in the evenings, SoHo became a parking lot for B&Ters. (Taxi drivers also exploited this fact, as those driving a night-time shift would park their cabs in SoHo sometime after midnight, expecting to find empty street space in the course of leaving them for the morning drivers who would unlock the parked cabs well before the witching hour of 8 A.M.)

Sometime in the early 1990s, I recall that television advertisements were shot on my street perhaps once a week, often for Japanese clients. Most of them featured handsome well-dressed young people against an industrial background, somewhat misrepresenting a neighborhood that was becoming increasingly middle-aged and looking less and less industrial. However, by the 2000s I began to see fewer film-production trucks on the street, assuming that the production companies had followed the galleries and perhaps the handsome well-dressed young people into West Chelsea instead, I guess because it now looks more like SoHo used to look than SoHo currently looks.

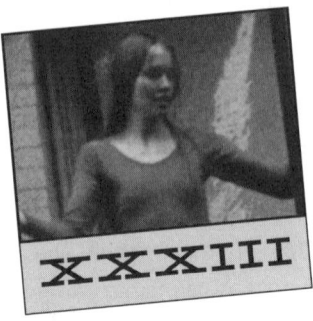

XXXIII

*Their music was different because they were different.
Schooled in the aesthetics of pop music and art, Sonic
Youth combined their punk education with an intense
experimentation that changed everything from the
instruments they played to the people who heard them.*

—John Rocco, "Sonic Youth," *A Dictionary of the Avant-
Gardes* (1999)

*Suicide are now so firmly installed in the rock canon, it's
hard to remember the scorn they once provoked. Prior to
the release of their debut album in 1977, Suicide played
barely half a dozen shows over as many years, and most of
these performances resulted in riots owing to [Alan] Vega's
confrontational stage persona. . . . Some say Suicide were
the ultimate punks, because even the punks hated them.*

—Simon Reynolds, *Village Voice* (February 5, 2002)

SONIC YOUTH is the classic name of a pop-music group that
began in 1981 in SoHo's outer precincts defined by the clubs
Max's Kansas City on lower Park Avenue and CBGB on the upper
Bowery (which is by geographical definition north of the flea-bag
dormitories). Its founders were the guitarist Thurston Moore, who
also sang, and his wife-to-be Kim Gordon, who played bass and guitar
and sang. Moore had previously participated in other groups; Gordon,
an art school graduate, had befriended such downtown artists as Dan

Graham and Jenny Holzer. After early collaborators departed, Moore and Gordon added Lee Ranaldo, a guitarist/singer, who later published books of his poetry, as would Moore, much as Kim Gordon would establish a clothing business. These three made an eponymously titled mini-LP released in 1982 by Neutral Records, a label founded by downtown NYC guitar/composer Glen Branca, himself an avatar of abrasive and loud music based on rock, noise, jazz, and high modern composition in the tradition of Frank Zappa. The latter acknowledged as his principal musical guru Edgar Varèse (who lived on Sullivan Street in Greenwich Village, just north of Houston).

Not unlike classical avant-garde musicians in the 1980s, Sonic Youth went abroad, in their case to London, to overwhelming success. Their uninhibited performance reportedly impressed even the punk-loving British. They attacked their junk-shop guitars, oddly tuned, with egg beaters and screw drivers, echoing the sounds of John Cage's prepared piano. When they returned moderately triumphant to New York City in 1984, Steve Shelley joined the band as the permanent drummer.

Sonic Youth issued a series of challenging discs on smaller labels until the legendarily successful record entrepreneur David Geffen contracted them in 1990. "This was considered insane by many on watch as there was really no history of independent underground bands succeeding within the realms of the corporate music industry," Thurston Moore wrote in the booklet for their record *A Thousand Leaves* (1998). "They released the LP *Goo* in 1990 and then *Dirty* in 1992. Both LPs were chock block full of heady, heavy swirl and strum." Meanwhile, individual SY members were issuing discs under their own names. Moore and Gordon also published a literary magazine *Ecstatic Peace!* (2001–2002), whose first four issues were to their friend Charles Potts, a veteran smallpressman, "a throwback to the '60s."

By 1997, Sonic Youth built its own studio downtown, just as SoHo theater artists had earlier built their own venues. Similarly, they released discs in the atavistic EP format (45 rpm) on their own label SYR. "This music was extrapolated," Moore continues, "mostly instrumental forays into wild improvisatory meditations and sub/conscious structural creations." In 1997, they played in Lincoln Center's Avery Fisher Hall, a temple of classic music, under the title "Guitar Futurism," the second word acknowledging their avant-garde predecessors.

Their *Goodbye to the 20th Century* (two discs, self-released, 1999) features pieces by such avant-garde heavies as John Cage, Christian Woolf, James Tenney, Takahisa Kosugi, and George Maciunas between tracks attributed to Kim Gordon and the rock musician Jim O'Rourke, who later became an official member of the band. The SY daughter Coco Hayley Gordon Moore performs Yoko Ono's *Voice Piece for Soprano* by screaming three times within twelve seconds. Reviewing the discs for *High Times*, John Rocco found "weird noise, out-of-body narration, wild improvisation, everyday sounds like a paper bag being crumbled, and enough space clatter to rebuild the Death Star."

Like Zappa before them, SY didn't forget the avant-garde tradition as they banked their fortune. The albums released around the turn of the century had titles such as *Murray Street* (2001) that acknowledged their downtown Manhattan roots. I once met Moore unintentionally on the checkout line at a classy NoHo book and record store when, standing in front of him, I spontaneously complimented his selection of records. Later, after I learned who he was, I also found out that his collection of records (certainly) and books (perhaps) exceeds my own. No grunge is he.

Scarcely as successful as Sonic Youth, Alan Vega was born in 1948 and is thus older than all the principals in Sonic Youth. Named at birth Alan Bermowitz, he grew up Jewish-Catholic in the Bensonhurst section of Brooklyn before moving to Manhattan and abandoning his birth-surname as a young man. He differs from most of the other individuals featured here in that I didn't know about him before writing this book. Friends had to identify his importance for me, most prominently with art exhibitions at O.K. Harris in the early 1970s and musical work, mostly during a post-punk tradition, beginning at the Mercer Arts Center that became the Kitchen.

A free spirit from his professional beginnings, he founded around 1969 A Project of Living Artists Museum on Broadway and Waverly

Place, in a building since superceded by NYU, and then in the basement at 133 Greene Street, which, thanks to historic district constaints, still stands. The former address, Lucy R. Lippard remembers, "was invaded by the FBI after an invitation was sent out to come to discuss how to 'kidnap Kissinger.' In 1970, they posted a series of [Ad] Reinhardtian questions about the morality of the art world." Vega told me recently that, "The space was kept open 24 hours a day for artists to exhibit, dance, play music, or do anything else that they felt was art." This ambitious promise was strong enough to warrant grants from the New York State Council on the Arts in 1970–1971 for $12,600 for "operating expenses of this center of cultural activities which sponsors meetings of artist groups, workshops, and exhibitions," in addition to $4,600 for "a workshop in live sketching; film showings, dance recitals, and poetry readings; and free exhibit facilities for artist groups concerned with relating the arts to society." Those sums were good money for a very young man in those days. Had Vega continued at his initial profession, he could have been the director of a multimedia alternative space like the Kitchen.

The Greene Street basement was likewise open around the clock, in part because people sacked out there, including Alan. "For the longest while, when I had to pass through SoHo, it used to make me cry. I had a whole life down here, 1970 to '76. We used to hang out on the stoop, jam all night; and nobody cared around the noise. Suddenly, people start giving you looks like you don't belong there. You know it's time to move on." Meanwhile, as "Alan Suicide," he exhibited floor-based light sculptures at O.K. Harris from 1972 to 1976. A decade later, Barbara Gladstone would open her SoHo gallery with an "Alan Vega" exhibition that featured cross-shaped wall sculptures. A book about this work has appeared in France as *100,000 Watts of Fat City* (1998) with an introduction by no less an art celebrity than Julian Schnabel. With characterisic self-defeating bravado, Vega told a British newspaper in 1998, "The stuff I make is very Suicide: it's all in the shape of crosses. I use lights, wire, and wood, superimposed with images of athletes or Mike Tyson. I sell it to rich people in Texas who don't realize there's usually a good old New York cockroach stuck on the bottom. That is always a great joy to me as I take their ten grand." Rarely does Suicide miss an opportunity to play Suicide.

"One group performing at the Project was a fifteen-piece jazz band called Reverend B, featuring Martin Rev on electric piano. Working at the time with electronic soundscapes, Vega, with his early drum machines, joined Rev with his cheap Japanese keyboard, forming a two-man group named Suicide, remembered as "the first synthpop duo," which differed from the other emerging punk groups at the time first in excluding guitars and then in being more extreme. Only in his vocals and his favoring of a regular, if excessive, drumbeat did Vega acknowledge the pop-music tradition in the eponymous first album that was released in 1977. Among other deviances, even in the hypertolerant pop-music world, they called their live performance a "punk mass," an epithet at once pretentious, blasphemous, original, and ironic. Thanks to their raucous performance style and riots following their appearances with The Clash, Elvis Costello, and even The Cars, Suicide became to some "the most unbookable group of all time." The downtown media artist G. H. Hovagimyan remembers, "The keyboard player generated constantly permutating blues runs and progressions while Suicide sang, moaned, and shouted out lyrics to no one in particular. He would riff on the 'Ballad of Frankie & Johnny' in the descriptive equivalent of jazz man on a jam. Suicide's music was the underside of Phillip Glass' *Music in 12 Parts*."

Their second studio album, *Martin Rev and Alan Vega*, appeared in 1981. Meanwhile, Vega released *Juke Box Baby* solely under his own name. The anonymous author of an unauthorized Internet fan site explains, "Vega's endlessly echoed voice sounded eerily rockabillyish over Phil Hawk's minimal guitar work. The menacing drumbeats in 'Bye Bye Bayou' dragged Creedence [Clearwater Revival] up to date, and threw them into the East Village jungle. 'Ice Drummer' was the supposed euphoria that preceded hypothermia." Though the album disappeared back home, it was very popular in France, reportedly topping some charts, much as other major SoHo figures scarcely known became more prominent in Europe at that time.

For the 1980s, Vega formed a more orthodox band that was signed by Elektra, which apparently thought he would give them a big disco hit with *Saturn Strip* (1983) that was produced by Ric Ocasek of The Cars. Since money from that disk didn't fall from the sky, Vega needed to battle with Elektra for two years to produce *Just a Million Dreams* (1985), the company at one point trying to throw him out of his own recording sessions and take over control of the final production. Dropped by the label, Vega toured Europe, again to more success than he had ever seen back home.

In 1988, Vega and Rev re-formed Suicide to record their third studio album, *A Way of Life*, and then did a European tour together. Meanwhile, Vega had joined his wife-to-be Liz Lamere, a corporate lawyer (and later a lawyer-recruiter) who moonlighted as a rock-band drummer, to take three years producing *Deuce Avenue* (1990), which deviated yet further in lacking conventional instruments completely. In 1993, Vega produced another solo album, *New Raceion*, and a book, *Cripple Nation*, containing art, lyrics, and other texts, both of them published by Henry Rollins under his 2.13.61 imprint. I hear in Vega's best discs a marvelously flexible and various singing voice that depends excessively upon (or is defeated by) a loud drum machine, though I sense that others might find strength in what sounds to me like weakness.

The Vega/Suicide fan site summarizes his subsequent career: "All went quiet until 1995 when Vega let *Dujang Prang* out of the bag to creep around the darker corners of rock'n'roll, scaring the children with weird mechanical noises, driving beats and the howling of a tortured soul on vocals. The Suicide revival and an odd-job hook up with Alex Chilton took up most of his time until mid-1998 when, in collaboration with Messrs. Vaisanen and Vainio of Finland's Pan Sonic, he formed VVV and released *Endless* (1998; Mute/BlastFirst). A great swinging album of doom'n' drone in the old style, it would make a fine accompaniment to one's descent into hell. A brilliant return to form from the patron saint of self-immolation." Only scarcely more knowledgeable now about Alan Vega than before, I couldn't have written a more succinct summary if I tried. Having heard several of his current CDs, I recommended the self-anthology, *Suicide: Alan Vega*, published as "Artist Anthology Number One" by 213CD and introduced by the label's proprietor, Henry Rollins, himself a punk celebrity. I'd still like to see Suicide-Vega-Bermowitz perform live.

Although personally short, round-faced, and affable-looking, Vega has been among the most intimidating punk artists, as well as among the less visible, perhaps because he eschewed "the smart career move" of dying young. (And, since he has already passed fifty, it's way too late now.) These professional aberrations probably account for why neither he nor his group is mentioned in, say, Greil Marcus's big book on punk, *Lipstick Traces* (1989), among other purportedly canonical texts about radical rock. Nonetheless, by the twenty-first century, the continuing musical influence of Bermowitz/Vega/Suicide can be heard in the most extreme groups gathered under the epithets of "noise" and "punk." In 2002, Jeffrey Deitch Projects, the last word in its name echoing that of Vega's alternative space of three decades before, mounted another exhibition of "Suicide" art in SoHo. As Simon Reynolds describes this work: "Densely tangled garlands of lightbulbs in all different colors and shapes, the pieces are festooned with pop jetsam: toy guns and monsters, porno cards, kitschy religious trinkets, and photos of movie stars snipped from glossy mags."

Success *d'estime* and success *d'argent* are the two sides of SoHo culture, not only in pop music but also in the other arts. Some earned one without the other; a few won both.

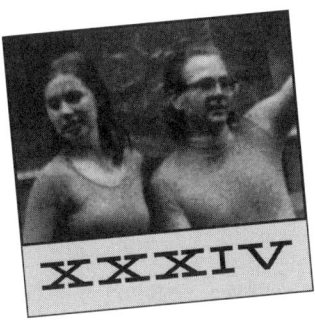

XXXIV

*The dog piss has changed into young overdressed/down folk
with designer dogs—it's a designer neighborhood—most
mom and pop stores belong now to small or big
conglomerates—rents are $20–50,000 per month—canvas
shoes replaced canvases—one street beggar murdered and
one still sings Sam Cooke songs—the dog shit is piling
up—now most vendors sell jewelry.*

—Steve Dalachinsky, on a postcard (2002)

A s Jaap Reitman epitomized traditional bookstore-selling in SoHo, the poet Steve Dalachinsky has represented since 1976 the activity of alternative peddling on the rent-free sidewalks, usually on Spring Street between Wooster and Greene, most recently across from Reitman's terminal location. With only a table and merchandise kept in his apartment a few blocks away, he has for more than a quarter-century displayed a selective stock of records, beat literature, and his own books. Beside him often, especially on weekends, is Harry Nudel, a truer antiquariat, as the Germans would say, who keeps his stock of quality literature in his nearby residential loft. As far back as the 1970s, SoHo's street merchants offered classier stuff than, say, those around Sixth Avenue south of 8th Street, who had disparate collections of books mostly gleaned, I'm told, from those recently deceased; or those around St. Marks Place in the East Village, who were recycling stolen merchandise. (The neighborhood joke in the East Village was that if your apartment was robbed, you could usually find your former personal possessions on a nearby street the next week.) By contrast, the street booksellers outside the NYU Bobst Library opposite the southeast corner of Washington Square have a more selective stock designed to appeal to students.

Visual artists of all kinds and qualities have exhibited on SoHo streets—paintings, sculptures, photographs, jewelry—usually featuring their own creations. Other regulars include peddlers of expensive art books, all shrink-wrapped, offering such large discounts from official "list" prices that one rightly wonders how they get their stock at sub-wholesale prices. More recently, I've seen outlandish hats and expensive handbags. By the 1990s, I found that, especially on Saturday afternoons, the sidewalks of SoHo have become so clogged with peddlers and their browsing customers that residents such as myelf are forced into the street to get at normal walking speed from one place to another.

All these street sellers capitalized on the abundance of shoppers, especially after 1980, who liked to cruise through SoHo with money burning a hole in their pockets. While most of their moolah went to the overpriced boutiques, some was spent on books and art sold on the street. Whereas other SoHo street merchants needed to get a license from New York City, booksellers did not, because of a liberal interpretation of the First Amendment. Thanks to a street agitator/painter named Robert Lederman, visual art was likewise exempted, even if it satirized, as Lederman's often did, the current city mayor.

Dalachinsky remembers, "A neighborhood pioneer gypsy street vendor, I moved to the corner parking lot [Spring and Wooster] that is now a flea market and then had a friend sell next to me as she did in my first location. Then the two-pair-for-five-dollar sock sellers started coming, and with them came the police. Because I did not exclusively sell books, I sometimes got screwed by the cops, once even taken away. More and more people began to sell on the street, bringing more and more problems and police due in part to the SoHo Partnership," which is a neighborhood beautification cooperative that employs sometime welfare recipients to empty garbage cans and clean the streets.

Working the street as he does, Dalachinsky remembers physical changes in the neighborhood. The ledge at Kochendorfer's store for knife and tool sharpeners was removed to discourage tourists from sitting on it and street merchants from laying out their stuff. Art supply stores, such as Jaime Canvas, likewise disappeared. So did well-stocked hardware stores and bodegas. Wally's Ice Cream Parlor became Le Petite Café. Dalachinsky recalls as well Jean-Michel Basquiat as a young black man of Puerto Rican and Haitian descent who called himself Samo: "I used to chase Samo away from my corner on West Broadway and Spring, where he sold hand-made postcards. He was a real brat. If only I had those postcards now." One street memory of mine is that around 1975 on Friday afternoons a fishmonger would pull up in his truck on the southeast corner of Broadway and Houston Street selling fresh fish to Catholic workers still forbidden to eat meat that day.

The neighborhood likewise attracted a wittier class of street beggars than was customary in the city. One of them once solicited my money for "The Southampton Mortgage Company." I recalled a cellist playing (rehearsing?) J. S. Bach suites on warm days and once came upon a brass quartet who found a marvelous resonance on SoHo streets devoid of car traffic. Chinese masseurs hit the neighborhood with their knee-chairs around the year 2000. I could tell that SoHo must be more attractive than other city neighborhoods when I found a street beggar on every block and even witnessed screaming territorial wars among them, knowing full well that independent entrepreneurs, such as street beggars, avoid neighborhoods they find inhospitable. (For one thing, SoHo residential buildings lacked doormen to scare them away.) For Dalachinsky, one prototerminal epiphany came when "a woman walking her dog allowed the dog to piss on my cart full of LPs. When I pointed this out to her, she rudely replied, 'He [meaning the dog] belongs here and you don't.'"

By the 2000s, the principal product offered on SoHo streets was jewelry, which Germans call Schmuck, its vendors nouveau to SoHo no doubt capitalizing upon a liberal interpretation of Art. And so it went in Schmucky SoHo.

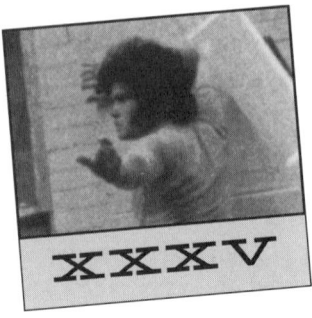

XXXV

THOUGH SoHo in its prime as an artists' colony did not attract political radicals, the industrial slum that preceded SoHo was a no-man's-land briefly providing refuge to the Students for a Democratic Society. As Steve Tappis remembers it, "In the late spring of 1968, right after the student strike at Columbia University, New York Regional SDS was evicted from its offices on Union Square West. After a few weeks in a new office we were again evicted. We found out that the FBI and the New York City Red Squad pressured the landlords to get rid of us. It seemed impossible to find a new office.

"Virginia Admiral, a long-time peace activist and friend of mine, was in the process of renovating a loft in SoHo. She suggested that SDS purchase a loft to use as a permanent office. She recommended 131 Prince Street which was being converted from industrial space into a residential artist co-op." As this was one of George Maciunas's earliest projects, the price for the back half of the fourth floor, 30 feet by 60 feet, or 1,800 square feet, was attractive: only $3,100. An additional $1,500 or so was spent by SDS on renovating the space. Then as later, the neighborhood was no less amenable to political "deviance" than marginal sexualities.

"I led a fund-raising effort," Tappis continued, "and, because of the high profile of the Columbia strike, we raised the money and purchased the loft. We set up a print shop and used the space for offices and meetings." Paul Kielar, a theatrical producer/director who had purchased the front half of the same floor and renovated his portion through the summer of 1968 when only cloth sheets separated his space from the back, remembers the sound of young people copulating in the back space, as well as visits by overage hippies who asked questions and collected SDS literature and thus were clearly FBI men. "One of the more sensible of the SDS was a young man called Charlie Simpson," a carpenter, who subsequently published a sociological study of SoHo. Local policing, on the other hand, was slight in SoHo at the time after working hours, because the cops were slow to realize that some people were renovating the spaces behind closed crummy front doors.

"I started a print shop with the help of a crazy but brilliant guy named Art Rosenberg," Tappis remembers. "His mission in life was to help start print shops for peace groups. He showed up with two old presses and a few cartons of parts. We took the parts from both presses and pieced together a functioning 10 x 14 offset press. We made a vacuum table with an old refrigerator motor that we found in the street and we burned plates with a $10 bulb for a sun lamp. We got an old camera from some group in Boston and we made a small darkroom. So the entire print shop cost less than $1,000 to build from scratch." Since the American principle of freedom of the press is best available to those who own one and SoHo housed many printers at the time (while none now), the First Amendment was especially sacred on its streets.

In the wake of a notorious deadly explosion of a townhouse on West 10th Street on March 6, 1970, the other owners at 131 Prince Street, justifiably anxious about harboring their SDS partner, attempted to persuade it to sell its half-floor and move into a smaller space in the building's basement. "At first they balked and objected," another partner still residing at 131 Prince recalls, "but once we explained our concerns to them and, better, a potential purchaser appeared, they yielded."

"Soon after that," Tappis continues, "because of factional splits in SDS, other organizations took over the basement space." More specifically, one co-op partner remembers, "The first takeover took place when the Weathermen forcibly took the space away from the SDS people. Some months later, the original SDS people in the middle of the night, broke through the cinderblock wall they had originally built, and smoked out a few Weathermen who might have been sleeping there. I recall the smell of smoke. The operation must have been well planned, as the SDS people had brought along a quantity of new cinderblocks and rebuilt the wall so that by morning all was peaceful again." Paul Kielar remembers going down to the basement and encountering five guys with wrecking equipment. "When I asked them what was going on, they assured me, 'Don't worry. We're taking over. We're the good guys.'"

Sometime around 1970, another group assumed control of the basement space, printing their literature on the sometime SDS press. "There was another middle-of-the-night break-in," recalls Emmanuel Ghent, a psychoanalyst who is also a composer. "When people arrived in the morning, they discovered that their printing press had been stolen. It couldn't have been moved in one piece; someone must have known how to dismantle it. The entire operation, including using the freight elevator to get the pieces upstairs to a waiting truck, took place without anyone already living in the building hearing anything amiss." The basement was later rented to an artist who for many years lived there, truly sub rosa (as subterranean spaces in SoHo are no more legal for residence than ground floors). On this last libertarian cause, as on many other residential issues, SoHo residents were customarily very tolerant.

The final irony is that the ground floor storefront of the same building that had once belonged to the jazzman Ornette Coleman for use as a performance space and later to the Meisel Gallery (for representational art) was in 2001 rented to the high-end international jeweler Cartier—that's right, Cartier!—so different had Prince Street become in thirty years. Oh yes, the 1,800–square-foot space was at the recent rate of $600 per square foot, worth more than a million dollars in the twenty-first century, which would have given the sometime student radicals a handsome profit (and capital gains tax to subsidize later FBI operatives) had they had the foresight to keep it.

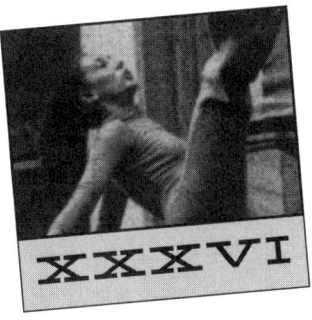

XXXVI

*The New York SoHo may be the first neighborhood in the
history of the Western world to which prospective residents
are required, as an article of municipal law, to convince the
authorities that they have some plausible claim to the title
"artist."*

—Stephen Koch, "Reflections on SoHo" (1975)

T HE LAWYER JERALD ORDOVER began to represent visual
artists in the early 1960s. Some were recommended to him
by Ivan Karp, a childhood friend, then working for Leo Castelli. As
happened to good lawyers in the days before they could advertise,
some clients recommended others, including Edward Avedisian, John
Chamberlain, Frank Stella, Barbara Rose, and, in 1965, Castelli
himself. Meanwhile, when the proprietors of CAMI Hall uptown
wanted to cancel the cellist Charlotte Moorman's contract for her
1966 avant-garde festival, she called on Jerry, as he was commonly
called, for help. He interceded and the concerts continued.

Already representing avant-garde music along with new art, Jerry
then took on dance companies and performance artists primarily to
set up nonprofit corporations necessary for both tax-exempt status and
most grants from public funders. Popular beyond belief, he often
served on the nonprofits' board of directors. The Performance Group,
then in its heyday, connected him to Judith Malina and Julian Beck,
the founders of the Living Theater, when they returned to the United
States in the late 1960s. He came to represent them as well through a
variety of legal problems that forever dogged the group, all at no fee.

As everyone who has ever worked with Jerry knows, his principal strategy for dealing with conflicts and legal problems was less contention than negotiation, patient negotiation, often deflecting the more combative temperaments typical of his artist clients.

When artists began to move into SoHo, Jerry handled rental leases. He advised George Maciunas on purchasing entire buildings. When Maciunas purchased on his own, he recommended Ordover to represent individual artists wishing to join Maciunas co-ops. Though representing a new client in negotiations with a former client could be considered improper for a lawyer, nobody minded then or later. After all, Jerry was a neighborhood icon who had no significant sustained competition. He could have been elected SoHo's Solomon (aka Community Judge), had such a position existed. Starting with Paula Cooper and Ivan Karp, Jerry also represented art dealers both established and aspiring in negotiating the purchase or leasing of large exhibition spaces in SoHo. He negotiated artist/dealer contracts, public and private art commissions, and agreements for editions of artists' prints. In addition to helping develop the contract form for the U.S. government's Art in Architecture program of mandating art in all new federal buildings and negotiating public art agreements on behalf of artists, he figured out how to buttress legally Lawrence Weiner's conceptual art that consisted entirely of statements: words only words, apart from distinctive typography, calligraphy, or any other esthetic enhancements. "Since the works consist of words and phrases which can easily be reproduced in any way, in any medium, I serve as Larry's official certifier of ownership of his works," Ordover told me. "No one can pass off a lawyer's letter concerning an artwork as an artwork."

When I questioned this last sentence, I got from Ordover this inspired response: "Such a letter, the subject of which happens to be an artist's artwork, can't be treated, presented, offered, labeled—or passed off—as an artwork in itself by a third party. (The only exception, and its really a different matter, rather than an exception, is if the lawyer, the writer of the letter, declared that his letter was a work of art or submitted it to the art world as a work of art; but no one has tried to sell one of my letters.)"

"In the case of my letters acknowledging the sale or a transfer of works by Lawrence Weiner, in which the title of the work was set forth, my identification of the work was in effect a reproduction of the work, but not by the artist-creator of the piece. When such a letter came from Lawrence Weiner, signed by him, some collector-recipients tried to treat the letter as a separate work or art by him and displayed it or even offered it for sale as such. It would be quite a stretch for anyone to try that with a letter from this or any other lawyer." Got it?

"When so many artworks these years are based upon the use of commonplace objects or commonplace words, Weiner's asking me to issue certifying letters for him was partially based on my being a lawyer—it lent some gravitas to the letters; but they could as easily have come from his wife, his studio assistant, his bookkeeper, or his daughter, or one of his dealers because no value judgment is being made. However, once it became established that the Larry Weiner certificates were coming from a single authority, the importance and status of the certificate would be established." A unique legal-esthetic imagination these last moves surely took.

Loving the artists' colony that was developing, Ordover moved just west of SoHo in 1973 and brought his office into his home four years later. A regular presence at SoHo art openings, no more pompous than his clients, Jerry often accepted art in payment, amassing a substantial collection (while complaining into his retirement that some of his clients failed to honor his invoices). He represented so many SoHo artists at one time or another that more than once his negotiating skills functioned to get two combating sometime clients to settle their differences amicably. While not entirely kosher in this last respect, he was successful, thanks to his temperament, at keeping life among the SoHo artists mellow. Admiring artists but preserving personal distance (say, eschewing artists as lovers—freeing himself from compromising alliances), he kept SoHo legally clean. Every artists' colony should have a Jerry Ordover—or two. If earlier ones did in America or elsewhere, I don't know, because artists' lawyers aren't remembered in the history books; but repairing neglects, along with making the invisible visible, suits my temperament here and elsewhere in this memoir.

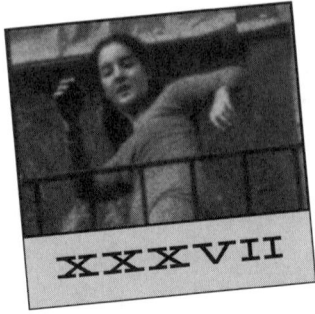

XXXVII

SOHO, SIMPLY *SOHO*, is the name of a commercial novel published in 1981 by Doubleday, a publisher with an acquired confidence about establishing best-sellers based upon a century of experience. The book's author is C. L. Byrd, who is identified not within the book itself but only on the dust-jacket flap as "the pseudonym of two writers closely involved with the New York art world." Two years later a paperback edition appeared from Bantam. I didn't notice either of those books when they first appeared. Nor does anyone I know remember the title, as *SoHo* was published not for us SoHoites but for the American masses. A postal card that was sent recently to "C. L. Byrd" at Doubleday, asking him/her for real identities, did not get a reply.

Two decades after its publication I discovered *SoHo* inadvertently via an Internet search engine and purchased a used copy that had previously belonged to a library in Stony Creek, Connecticut, between Branford and Guilford, east of New Haven. The library slip attached to my copy's back page reveals it was borrowed nearly twenty times between 1981 and 1983, one satisfied Connecticut reader perhaps recommending it to another, and then only several times since, before it was marked "withdrawn." My own sense is that the novel was meant to be a movie, as it portrays good-looking people often engaged in sex. On the other hand, the book's commercial failure probably dissuaded large publishers, always subservient to precedent, from doing later similarly conventional novels set in SoHo. That accounts for why few known to me have appeared since (though here I might be as ignorant of successors as I was of this).

In my copy is pasted the promise, apparently from promotional literature, of "a multigenerational saga of a family of Jewish immigrants and their success in the worlds of business and art. When Eli Dansky, a six-year-old Russian Jew arrived in New York with his mother in 1913, the area of Manhattan just above the financial district was known as 'The Valley,' for its lack of tall buildings created a dent in the soaring skyline. But in the next generation things were to change for both the family and the area—fortune and family feuds for Eli, the bohemian atmosphere for a rapidly growing cultural and artistic center for SoHo. When finally the family future seemed assured, the past reappears, as haunting and dangerous as the empty shells of buildings surrounding the Danskys. Rich in period detail, with colorful characters and an intriguing plot, the novel, recounting the family's rise above its immigrant origins, will appeal to a broad spectrum of readers: New Yorkers, Jews, immigrants, and art lovers alike." Thus, SoHo is seen from the perspective of entrepreneurs who came before World War II and their children who become involved with artists in the 1970s. If the Danskys were based upon a real SoHo family, I don't know who the models might be.

SoHo apparently did not appeal to many readers; a best-seller it surely wasn't, unfortunately, because it has knowledgeable descriptions of the neighborhood in the mid-twentieth century, including characterizations of the kinds of individual entrepreneurs who dominated a turf beneath the radar of large corporations—not only manufacturers of buttons and small landlords, like the Danskys, but also gallerists and restauranteurs, not to mention artists both successful and not. Mike Fanelli's venue is accurately described as "a small, friendly bar—like a saloon in a fin de siècle photograph—with signed pictures of boxers hanging on one wall. The customers were predominantly blue-collar workers from the neighborhood, though it was hard to distinguish them from the artists among them, who wore proletarian denim shirts and dungarees or overalls."

Consider this detailed, accurate evocation of Canal Street on a weekday in 1966: "A number of stores had, in effect, burst and spilled out onto the street, so that their wares were displayed in irregularly ascending rows of trays and boxes—some resting on trestles, some on other boxes—in the way that fruit and vegetables were arranged out-side old-fashioned greengrocers. In front of one store were containers of vacuum tubes, condensers, transformers, loudspeaker cones—everything the radio or hi-fi enthusiast could require—the price of each item boldly stated on a hand-lettered card. Another shop offered plumbing supplies—mundane objects that became exotic isolated out here on the street—and a third displayed sneakers, sandals, and sev-eral kinds of work boots, all crowded onto a kind of miniature bleach-ers. A cascade of legal pads, ledgers, typewriter ribbons, old calendars, pencil sharpeners, ink pads, and desk lamps overflowed from an office supply company. Nearby were rolls of garden hose, brass rods, hack-saw blades, nuts and bolts, latches, flying pans, bathroom cabinets, casters, door handles, toilet paper holders—the contents of a hard-ware store that had been turned inside out—and next to that a clut-tered assemblage of electric motors in all sizes and shapes." This is so wonderful I wish I had written every word.

Having read the book from beginning to end, all 511 pages, dur-ing a long airplane flight, with sufficient open time to be bored with the soap operatic machinations of a family, I still wonder who wrote this *SoHo?*

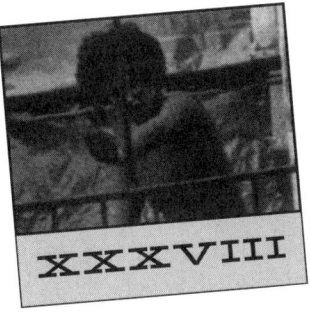

XXXVIII

*Less in known and more is written about SoHo than
perhaps any neighborhood in the world.*

—Douglas Davis, "SoHo du Mal" (1975)

S OON AFTER THE sometime industrial area just south of
Houston Street became known as SoHo, the neighborhood
southwest of it became known at Tribeca, its name a compression of
Triangle Below Canal Street, with Broadway to the East, the Hudson
River to the West, and Chambers Street on its south. Though Tribeca
superficially resembles SoHo as a residentially renovated industrial
neighborhood, it is actually a different community open not just to
artists but nonartists as well. If the buildings of SoHo housed printing
and garment manufacturing, the principal historic business of the
Tribeca buildings, particularly in its western precincts, was food, such
as my relatives' olive oil importing business at the corner of Franklin
and Hudson Streets.

Few art galleries were established in Tribeca, and they didn't last
long. In the early '80s, the city permitted exhibition spaces only on
the north-south avenues, excluding them from the quieter east-west
side streets, the intentions of some planning genius once again being
counterproductive, as all were discouraged. However, that move alone
did not prevent Tribeca from resembing SoHo. The architect Richard
Gluckman once told me that Tribeca galleries failed because collectors' limousines couldn't get through the bumper-to-bumper New
Jersey-bound crosstown traffic on Canal Street on Friday afternoons.
Since his offices were located in Tribeca and gallery design was per-

haps his most renowned specialty, Gluckman spoke with a certain authority and considerable regret. Conversely, the B&T crowds that invaded SoHo particularly on weekends skipped over Tribeca. Precisely because its streets were less commercialized, Tribeca attracted expensive restaurants, likewise exploiting the fact that industrial parking hours left the streets open at night. It also was more hospitable than SoHo to national celebrities desiring privacy, such as John F. Kennedy, Jr.; actress Cher; comedian David Letterman; sculptor Richard Serra; and actor Robert DeNiro (whose father, a painter with the same name, and mother, Virginia Admiral, were early residents of SoHo).

More than once I've wondered why local professional athletes haven't purchased residential lofts, more likely in Tribeca than SoHo proper, given not only their wealth but also their need for space for their own exercise equipment and perhaps a sauna; but then again, perhaps athletes have settled there, with minimal publicity, as SoHo and Tribeca commonly lack doormen susceptible to newspaper gossip reporters. The tennis star John McEnroe once had a gallery in SoHo, accounting for why I would see him on the street; but he reportedly lived uptown near Central Park. Somewhere I read that Phil Jackson, now pro basketball's most successful coach, had a loft in the West Village above an auto facility when he played for the New York Knicks around 1970. So different was his bachelor residence from that of his teammates that more than one recalled that they visited him once and only once.

In the 1980s, the initial putative successor to SoHo for art galleries was the East Village, which defined precisely a neighborhood with 14th Street on the north, Houston Street on the south, the Bowery on the west, and some indefinite boundary on the east, because the areas east of First Avenue, successively Avenues A to D, were thought to be progressively less hospitable to strangers, no matter how art-loving they were. At first it was claimed that the new galleries there showed an art less formal and formalist than that predominant in SoHo. Actually, the work was also smaller, much smaller, because the storefront exhibition spaces were smaller, much smaller, than SoHo's industrial arenas. (Around this time, MoMA mounted a large Kurt Schwitters show that struck me as "very East Village" pre-cisely because so many of the pieces on the walls were less than 2 feet by 1 foot.) As exhibition venues, they resembled the old 10th Street, only a few blocks to the west—in John Canady's phrase, "small, close, low-ceilinged compartments in bad to moderately good repair." However, the East Village didn't survive as a gallery showcase, I always assumed because its scruffy bohemians looked too inhospitable not just to the limo drivers but to the sorts of moneyed people who purchase art. Some of the more successful East Village gallerists, such as Jay Gorney and Pat Hearn, subsequently relocated in SoHo before moving onto West Chelsea.

West Chelsea was a more propitious venue because it resembled SoHo in the 1960s as an industrial slum with few residents and many underutilized commercial spaces yet larger than those in SoHo and customarily devoid of interior columns that marked SoHo (because the West Chelsea buildings were constructed later). The pioneer was the Dia Foundation, which had begun in SoHo and still kept spaces there. At 548 West 22nd Street—not between Eighth and Ninth Avenues, where several top-floor ateliers are still visible on the south side of the street, but in the formerly deserted precincts west of Tenth Avenue—Dia renovated in the mid-1980s an entire large warehouse, 40,000 square feet in sum, to exhibit a few favored artists. Brilliantly designed by Richard Gluckman, an architect whose austere style influenced other gallery renovations in West Chelsea, the Dia Center for the Arts also sponsored pseudoacademic lectures and poetry read-ings of comparable academic sorts.

Before the 1990s were over, other galleries once based in SoHo had moved their showcases to this neighborhood: Sonnabend, Gagosian, Metro Pictures, Barbara Gladstore, Charles Cowles, Jay Gorney, and even Mary Boone (after a brief foray uptown), among others, collectively illustrating that art dealers can be as portable as Bedouin with their tents. Following immediate precedent, most of them took ground-floor spaces that were open to passersby. Some SoHo gallerists received moving money from well-heeled retailers who, especially in the late '90s, desperately wanted to purchase or assume long leases on SoHo space. The number of galleries in West

Chelsea exceeded the count ever in SoHo at any one time, just as the SoHo number exceeded that of 10th Street or uptown, the increase in all cases reflecting the greater size of the New York art world and the ever larger number of people wanting to exhibit. Likewise relocating to Chelsea, amid the taxi garages, delivery services, and warehouses that remained, were the Kitchen, Printed Matter, several co-op galleries, and even those merchants whose claim to advanced taste had once depended upon a SoHo address, such as the expensive clothing retailer Comme des Garçons.

Whether West Chelsea's preeminence in retailing new art will survive as long as SoHo's cannot yet be determined. One difference between them is that Chelsea quickly became too expensive for emerging artists to relocate there as well (although some doing small-scale work purchased modest studios-without-toilets in buildings with many rooms, such as at 624 West 26th Street), so it would never become the productive artistic hothouse that SoHo once was. By the beginning of the new century, emerging artists tended to reside instead on the other sides of Manhattan's rivers in Williamsburg to the east (accessible to Chelsea on the L subway line that ran across 14th Street) and Jersey City to the west (delivering to Chelsea on the PATH train that stopped along sixth Avenue). As the critic Robert C. Morgan discerned about Chelsea, "Instead of the artists living and working in lofts above the galleries (on street level), there was virtually no shared geographical space. Instead they were divided by several miles, ghettoized, in fact. When together in SoHo—at least at the outset—no one thought of money as significant. But now that art is playing second fiddle to money, Rome is burning—albeit slowly—on the other side."

Scarcely a replica of SoHo, West Chelsea had become something else. With proximity to the Hudson River came winter winds that can be quite fearsome, especially down long side streets. Whenever SoHo veterans greeted one another in West Chelsea, someone would inevitably remark that getting to new art's new neighborhood was a pain in the ass. Indeed, it was. For a while some Chelsea galleries sponsored gratis a passenger bus that ran from SoHo to West Chelsea on Saturday afternoon, so onerous did the trek initially seem; but once the new art scene was established, the bussing scheme was abandoned. The critic Robert C. Morgan once warned that two successive brutal winters could scare off not only art lovers but also art buyers, but that hasn't happened yet. If so, where would the art galleries go next? My hunch is that the more portable dealers might first try the 50s west of Tenth Avenue, were it not yet renovated, though it too is susceptible to those damned Hudson River winds; or WeVar, or Varest, which is west of Varick Street but north of Canal, a sort of uptown but downscale Tribeca, that has some monstrous shipping facilties and a new office building contructed by the London advertising firm Saatchi and Saatchi. Worse, the galleries would instead disperse throughout Manhattan, which would never again have a center for retailing new art.

One truth not to be forgotten is that none of these art neighborhoods were designated for artists or galleries. In no case did some city, state, or federal mucketymuck(s) decide that SoHo, Tribeca, the East Village, Williamsburg, or West Chelsea should be the appropriate location for an art world. In each case, artists and gallerists simply moved in, redefining the urban terrain long before city officials adjusted to the fact of their being there. Likewise, in no case were major real estate developers involved, mostly because the neighborhoods were all at their beginnings unacceptable to the bourgeoisie. Developers could not expect government agencies to cooperate with subsidies, rezoning favors, and other benefits in neighborhoods commonly thought to be, as they were at their beginnings, worthless to everyone except urban pioneers. (I have read here and there that artists were shock troops, the special forces, the commandos, for major New York City real estate developers, their names all familiar, but don't see how that can be true, since these neighborhoods are all too small compared to downtown or midtown Manhattan. That accounts for why the names on construction and reconstruction in SoHo and Chelsea were invariably unfamiliar.)

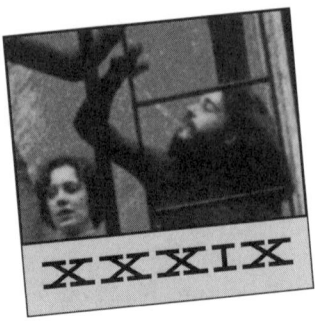

XXXIX

I sit here in this old house alone.

—Edmund Wilson, *Upstate* (1971)

MY SOHO LOFT became famous for a day in 1985, when it appeared at the top of the front page of the widely read *New York Times*'s Thursday Home section. Accompanying a feature article on "Living with Too Many Books" was a photograph of me sitting beneath towering shelves tightly filled with paperbacks. Whereas most features in the *Times* are forgotten a few days afterward, this has often been remembered, mostly by those likewise possessing an abundance of books, especially if they had, like myself, discovered that an urban loft could accommodate thousands of books as easily as an apartment or townhouse with many rooms. Not unlike SoHo itself, I received from the august *Times* more recognition for my interior decoration than for my art or writing. The article said I had 10,000 volumes, which was roughly accurate at the time, assuming that books are on average one inch thick, because the only figure authorized by me was "956 running feet" of shelving containing books. Those more experienced insist that the count must since have approached 15,000; that's what the Italian collector Egidio Marzona told me around 1998, with the authority of someone owning, he testified, 60,000 volumes.

What the size of this library mostly reflected is not that I "collect" books, because I don't, but that I've worked my way through several intellectual fields. After taking degrees in American civilization and American history, I became interested in literature and literary criticism; later, I wrote about other arts. By contrast, no one pursuing a single discipline would need so many books at home. A second fact shaping the size of the library is professional independence. Whereas professors can rely upon a university library, I could use only the New York Public. However, not only is its stocking erratic, but even the famed research central at 42nd Street is missing many items listed in its catalog. A third is that more than 2,000 contain something of mine. The last, and probably most important, fact is that moving to SoHo gave me enough interior space.

The only rational reason for having such a populous library is that I prefer to do research at home, with my own annotations, much like other SoHo artists preferred to work a few feet away from their beds; but by the late 1990s the problem became that I no longer always knew where to find a title I wanted. If the book had been mine for a while, and it hadn't been moved, I could probably locate it; but if the book were new to me, or had been moved to make way for the expansion of something else (typically books authored by me, which was the most rapidly expanding category), it could escape my search. Whenever this happened, as it did increasingly for a while, I felt the need to sell off some books or, more reasonably, relocate into a larger space.

Most people entering my loft for the first time would exclaim, "So many books." A few said, "So many records," usually indicating implicitly that they were already accustomed to seeing a lot of books. Since long-playing records are slimmer than books, they take up less space per capita, and the last time I measured there were 35 running feet, which I suppose amounts to 3,000 records, or a fairly reasonable figure of one hundred per year for thirty years. Over the past two decades I have accumulated many audiocassettes that have their own shelves. I have perhaps several hundred compact discs and even some DVDs and a single videodisc (though no machines for playing either of the latter). More recently, I've been recording, on the slowest VHS speed, movies that I consider part of my personal culture; and my collection of these videotapes could fill another wall. The abundance of culture, let me confess, makes me feel comfortable. As I live alone, no one is bothered if I play music and speech nearly all the time.

More than once I've rationalized that I'm squirreling away for the time when I am not so eager to work. However, as a full-time culture-worker, I can't afford to be ill and so never am.

The space itself became a kind of factory, all of it eventually organized for the production of what I do. Since nothing currently manufactured here has been particularly remunerative, there was no one else to be the janitor (or the boss). Way in the back was a windowless space, between 10 feet by 20, in which were located five desks. The one with the typewriter was initially for my most serious writing but, once I got into word processors, it was used only for correspondence. The second with a drawing board tilted up at an angle was for editing and proofreading. A third and a fourth accumulated papers from projects in progress. Whatever function I once had in mind for the fifth now escapes me. It seems mostly used to support my feet when I want to lean back while proofreading. In the corner of this room was an extra bed that was meant for naps but was hardly used. (When I first lived here, there was someone else; after 1985 or so, I was warned, there was insufficient room for anyone else.) Along one short wall were deep shelves that housed my biannual accordion files of professional correspondence (implicitly waiting for an archive's offer that could not be refused); beneath it was a deep shelf of mailing supplies. Next to the typewriter desk were four tall filing cabinets containing projects still in progress. As a steam pipe ran upward through this room, it was also the warmest space, especially during winter nights, when the rest of the apartment cooled down.

The next room, likewise windowless, was meant to be the "reading room." On one side of my favorite butterfly chair was the dialing machine and an answering machine; on the other side was a radio-amplifier attached to both a cassette player and a new CD machine. Across the room was a television that I came to watch more often once I acquired a VCR that enabled me to see programs I would have missed and incidentally fast-forward through commercials and promotions. I also placed the two-piece projection television here that was given to me by someone with insufficient space for its 6-foot screen. Behind the chair was a wall full of unread books, my assumption being that a new book could not be shelved with others of its kind until it has been "processed," as I say, with annotations and a sheet of notes. Along sidewalls of this reading room were yet more shelves that extended under a tilted table that I use for drawing. Underneath yet another table, now filled with towers storing dozens of compact discs, was my great uncle's 1929 edition of the *Encyclopedia Britannica*, which remains one of the few books I inherited, as opposed to acquiring on my own initiative. On the door to this room were tacked two pieces of paper, one forbidding smoking, because there was no natural ventilation, the other a publisher's royalty check for one dollar, reminding me that my activity has scarcely been profitable.

On the other side of this door was the dining room, or what was once a dining room, with a long table, surrounded by several chairs (and bookshelves on all the walls behind it); but since I haven't entertained for many years, the table tended to contain a miscellany of things that I was moving in and out of the house. Across from it on a large desk were two computers: the antique Kaypro that until the mid-1990s I preferred for writing, and a new one, a Mac, which was initially for rewriting because its keyboard always felt alien. By the year 2000 I acquired Internet access and discovered that, if I turned on my computer immediately after arising, I no longer needed coffee or tea to become fully alert. In this dining room that had become a writing room were two computer-driven printers that gave the boss (lacking a secretary) far neater typescripts and business letters than he could ever produce at the typewriter. Beside the printers was one of the dozen radio receivers distributed throughout the house, so that sound was always within reach. Here too was an extension telephone that was usually unplugged, because even if I were not sleeping I'd still rather not have my concentration interrupted and, better yet, would rather not seem impolite if it were.

Behind it was the bedroom, with a queen-sized bed along one wall and a television along the other. This room I kept largely free of books, for fear they would distract me as I was trying to get to sleep (just as the writing room in the back is also free of books). On the bedroom floor was a large metal cabinet whose horizontal shelves, 3 feet by 4 feet, contained prints of my own visual poetry and numerical art. Atop the cabinet, likewise lying prostrate, was a box containing a traveling exhibition of my work (even though it hasn't left this house in years). One of the two bedroom windows was completely covered, its sill used instead for storage; the other was customarily curtained, as it looked out on the back of another building.

Adjacent to the bedroom, with four unadorned windows that looked out over the roof of a single-story restaurant, was the living room, the largest single space in my loft and, in a comparative sense, the least occupied. It had shelves not only along its walls, but an island of shelving in the middle. Here too were several works of art that I've collected over the years: a large black-and-white painting by Suzan Frecon, a kinetic sculpture by Einno Rutsaalo, a wooden car by Paul Zelevansky, and the magnificent six panels, 6 feet high and 14 feet across, of inked black words on white doors that are John Furnival's *Tour de Babel Changées en Pont*. In this room were also visual works of mine: black and white canvases and prints, with either numbers or words, mostly mounted high above the bookshelves, just below the ceiling; and, on a revolving stand, the first of my two major holograms.

The Furnival panels divided the living room couch and coffee table from a back area that contained audio editing equipment and a small film viewer placed between pickup reels for 16 mm footage. It is here that I and at times student interns worked on my principal creative project for the 1980s: separate *Epiphanies* for audiotape and film. In the corner of this space I put a reading area, with a strong lamp, a chair, and a radio/record player.

To enter my hallowed domicile, I needed four keys: the first to open the door to the building, the second to unlock the elevator to go to my floor, the third to unlock the deadbolt to my apartment door, and the fourth to open that door. Just inside that door was a hallway with bookshelves running along both sides. Directly over the front door itself was another shelf that ran to the ceiling. Beyond the hallway was a kitchen with the refrigerator on one side, a stove and sink on the other, and bookshelves between them. In the middle were two chains suspended from a mirrored rig near the ceiling, their ends normally hooked together, from which, if I unlocked them, I could display my more recent holograms. Exhibiting them, you see, required

20 feet of open space that by the late 1980s was available here only between the refrigerator and the stove. At the end of the sink was a pair of bookshelves, stacked back to back and placed perpendicularly to the wall. At the end of this shelf was a small table where I fed myself and kept my vitamins.

A few years ago the Internal Revenue Service questioned the rather large percentage of the monthly maintenance fees that I deducted as a business expense. To justify my claim that so much of my apartment was used exclusively for professional work, my account-ant asked me to shoot a roll of 35 mm black-and-white film that was developed on a single contact sheet. Looking at the thirty-six little photographs of my loft, the accountant asked skeptically, "Does it always look like this?" I assured him that it did. "Oh, this won't be a problem," he said—and indeed it wasn't.

In general, I was reluctant to invite strangers here. The books were intimidating, I knew, and as such were likely to have negative effects on the spontaneity of guests. Others came to regard the apart-ment as a kind of candy store, pulling things out without putting them back where they belong, thereby causing needless difficulty the next time I needed a certain title. I could go on; but after all, this apartment is not a showplace: it was really a factory in a residence principally for me.

This was where I preferred to spend most of my middle-aged days, rising late, refusing to answer the doorbell or telephone until I finished working, staying up well into the night reading and writing. Being in the back of the building, away from the SoHo street that sometimes had industrial traffic, my place was unusually quiet. Even though I worked nearly all the time when at home, it is here that I slept best. At a party in the early 1980s I was asked about my principal recollection of myself between the ages of seven and ten. As I replied—playing in my room with my toys—I realized that was how I spent most of my time then (and now) as well. My favorite "summer place" was the ninth-floor roof, where I could read and nap undis-tracted, which we called Silver Beach after the color of its protective coating. Every day that I could spend entirely at home, without ever leaving, I regarded as a logistical success.

With such a profound devotion to my SoHo loft I came to identify with other writers who were similarly rooted in the places in
which they lived and worked—Lewis Mumford in Amenia (N.Y.),
Edmund Wilson in Talcottville (N.Y.), Donald Hall in Danbury
(Conn.), Stanley Edgar Hyman in North Bennington (Vt.)—except
that my artist's retreat within the city epitomized SoHo, an artists'
colony smack in the middle of New York City. I could never understand why anybody would ever want to own a second home. For the
same reason that I never went away during the summer, not even for
a weekend in "the country," I sublet only once; because as this apartment contained my life, damage it and you could damage me. A few
years ago, I gave it a name much like those given to British manor
houses, because to me it was indeed a castle—Wordship—and chris-
tened myself its Earl. The place where I now live, a thousand feet
away from New York City's best beach, has a library 100 feet long and
10 feet wide—enough continuously open space with shelves on both
sides and islands in the middle for all my books, records, tapes, discs,
and files, not to mention works of art on the walls above the shelves.
Having acquired a SoHo taste for abundant interior space, I wanted
yet more but had to go elsewhere to find it. Conversely, had I not
experienced the SoHo alternative in interior design, I probably would
have thought of a series of rooms. My new abode is called Wordship
II until it becomes Wordship, much as XYZ, Jr., eventually becomes
XYZ when XYZ, Sr., is unfortunately forgotten.

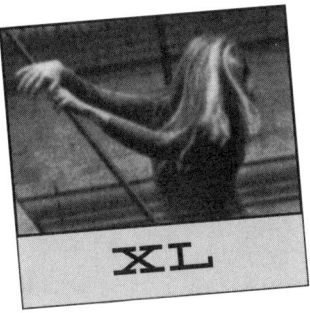

XL

As the Village became better known and more generally
sought as a place of residence, it lost the cheap rents which
made it particularly attractive to artists and writers.

—Caroline Ware, *Greenwich Village, 1920–1930* (1935)

IT SEEMS IN RETROSPECT that from the moment I moved into SoHo, back in 1974, the art world residing there has been threatened. One early sign was the arrival soon afterward of restaurants and gourmet food stores whose wares were not aimed primarily at the neighborhood but rather at the B&T folk. I can remember early in the 1980s counting most of the people on the street one Saturday afternoon, and realizing that they were walking too slowly as though they didn't live here. Never again would locals predominate on weekend afternoons. Sometime later, slow walkers began to dominate the sidewalks even on weekdays, creating inadvertent obstacles for us natives wanting to walk quickly from one place to another. "Get a horse," I wanted to scream at them.

In 1979, real estate prices went up, SoHo thereafter attracting, I conjecture, people who weren't primarily artists, implicitly discouraging the immigration here of young people resembling who we were only a few years before. They went, instead, to the East Village and then the Lower East Side. Next came a section of Brooklyn named Dumbo (Down under the Manhattan and Brooklyn Bridge off-ramps) before Williamsburg and later Bushwick. By the late 1990s, young artists favored Jersey City, among other outlying spaces, many of them wishing they lived not in SoHo but in Brooklyn.

Thanks to a legal document called "The SoHo Letter," nonartists from the mid-1980s could buy and rent in SoHo as long as they agreed in advance to be financially responsible for any legal problems that resulted. (None ever suffered.) SoHo became a high-priced neighborhood still dominated by people who were classy, but scarcely rich except perhaps in "paper profits" in real estate or art owned for decades. SoHo became a unique community, even within New York City, in housing millionaires beside those who are economically marginal, the former at their best trying not to be boorish. The newcomers usually dressed like us, as we couldn't possibly dress like them.

As late as 1996, in a Columbia University graduate school study commissioned by Sean Sweeney as director of the SoHo Alliance, drawing upon its mailing list, 56 percent of the respondents were working artists. (In NoHo, the figure was 40 percent.) A futher fact was that by bourgeois American standards their average income was subnormal. Indeed, perhaps no other place in the world has so many people with illiquid assets amounting to more than a million dollars (property, art), while their net incomes are less than thirty grand (including me).

What remained in SoHo—what would always remain in SoHo because it was legally protected—was the magnificent historic architecture. Surviving examples include the cast-iron facades at 480–92 Broadway, 28–30 Greene Street, 47–49 Mercer Street, 427–29 Broadway, the Singer Building at 561 Broadway; the later, more Romanesque style of 484–90 Broome Street; the oldest building in the neighborhood at 107 Spring Street; and ornate details everywhere for those who care to look. Such architectural masterpieces are not to be found in Chelsea, or anywhere else.

Those with more particular tastes can date the death of SoHo to the appearance of a hairdresser on Prince Street in the late 1970s, or the revamping of Fanelli's into a yuppie bar in the mid-1980s, or the closing of the restaurant Food that catered to neighborhood tastes and employed SoHo people. (It was the last SoHo store I patronized regularly.) An eatery patronized by both artists and laborers, the nonalcoholic semblance of the classic Fanelli's, was a sort of coffee shop on the southeast corner of Canal Street and Broadway. Called variously

Dave's Corner, Dave's Restaurant, and Dave's Lunch, depending upon which sign you read, it was open all night, every night, promising not only clumsily cooked diner food but "the world's best egg cream," or at least the best indigenous chocolate cream drink in lower Manhattan, served by soda jerks who knew they dispensed a superior product. When Dave's Whatever disappeared I don't remember. In its place was for a while a Chinese noodle restaurant, also open all night. Around 1995, I'm told, the space was subdivided to become "a knock-off perfumeria, a handbag stall, and the only Mexican pizzeria on Canal." I've known artists who, upon returning to SoHo after a decade or more away, remember Dave's strongly enough to ask me to meet them there. "It's gone, it's gone," I must tell them, like so much else we once loved.

I recall now that, for a long time, nearly everything regularly patronized in my daily life from stores to friends to cultural venues was within walking distance. Once this was no longer true, I knew that the community once loved by me had begun to disintegrate. Perry Meisel, an NYU professor residing just north of Houston Street, thinks the shift came with a change in orthography—when "Soho" replaced "SoHo" in even the more sophisticated press. Others will no doubt cite Jaap Reitman closing his bookstore after more than twenty years, the Museum of Holography disappearing after an equally long run, the end of the Whitney Counterweights, the arrival of the plush Mercer Hotel or the superplush SoHo Grand Hotel, or the disappearance after decades in the year 2000 of the healthy eatery called Whole Foods (to be replaced by yet another boutique).

My own sense of SoHo's cataclysmic change came around 1985 when a slick magazine asked for a report on my neighorhood. I wrote not about galleries but high-ticket retailers, mostly of clothing and then furniture, who were cunningly exploiting the neighborhood's reputation for advanced taste. What had been SoHo for South of Houston had become ShoMa for Shopping Mall. Around 1990, I noticed that corporations selling art prints across the country, such as Martin Lawrence or Dansen, had in SoHo small street-level stores that had few visible customers. Curious about this apparent failure in merchandizing, I learned that such chains benefited from adding

SoHo to their address collection that includes Palm Beach, Palm Springs, Greenwich, and similarly moneyed locations. A decade later, nearly all the retail chains selling clothing or design to wealthy people had outlets in SoHo, some of them likewise visibly devoid of customers, supposedly for superior credibility in their other locations. I thought of offering my own SoHo address to any retailer offering the highest price and not requiring that I vacate, but couldn't figure out how and where to sell my virtual proposal. SoHo had become such a classy imprimatur that SoHo soda, SoHo shoes, and the SoHo Press had nothing to do with geographic SoHo, let alone Artists' SoHo.

Sometime in the 1990s, the neighborhood was flooded with cosmetics stores, selling a more expensive kind of artistic paint; but unlike ground-level stores selling art or high-end furniture that had few visible customers, these Lipstick District retailers attracted crowds of shoppers, or at least browsers. Another index around 2000 was the proliferation of skinny women, taller than I am, customarily strolling alone in eye-enticing outfits on SoHo streets, walking as only fashion models can, their long legs resembling scissors (or castrating implements), in turn reflecting the arrival of modeling agencies in SoHo. In 2001, especially in the wake of the destruction of the World Trade Center only two kilometers south, SoHo had enough empty ground-floor spaces to prompt fear for its retailing future. Then, in mid-2002, Apple Computer opened a spectacularly designed outlet exclusively for its products that was so successful, at least at drawing walkers off the street, that it seemed likley that other computer retailers would follow. Those slower to acknowledge SoHo's decline can point to the emigration en masse throughout the 1990s of not only the commercial galleries but the alternative spaces to West Chelsea, which has, at last report, become the center of art merchandising (but not artists' living). Around 1999, the media mogul Rupert Murdoch (yes—him) purchased a penthouse across the parking lot from my building; two years later, a branch of Cartier, the uptown jeweler, opened around the corner from me. By the twenty-first century, the great experiment in creating a large artists' colony within the city had come to an end. And it was time for me to move on.

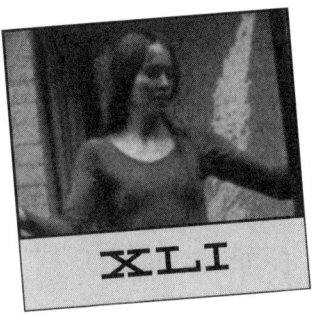

XLI

Bibliography

Nowhere else in the world is there such a concentration of artistic endeavor.

—Helene Zucker Seeman and Alanna Siegfried,
SoHo (1978)

BOOKS ABOUT ARTISTS' hothouses are remarkably few. Caroline Ware's *Greenwich Village* (1935, twice reprinted, as recently as 1994) is a sociological study of a lower Manhattan community that writers and artists made world famous. Given a disciplinary academic bias, it devotes much less attention to the artists, dubbed "The Villagers," than to ethnic groups incidentally there. In SoHo, as noted before, there were no ethnic groups, let alone any other residents, before the artists came. A stronger book is June Skinner Sawyers' anthology *Fiction, Poetry, and Reminiscences, 1872–2002, A Greenwich Village Reader* (2001). On early American bohemias, see Albert Parry's *Garrets & Pretenders* (1933) and Ross Wetzsteon's *Republic of Dreams Greenwich Village: The American Bohemia, 1910–1960* (2002). The epigraph from Harold Rosenberg comes from *The Tradition of the New* (1959); that by Fran Liebovitz from "Soho: or Not at Home with Mr. Art" (1983), reprinted in Michael Marqusee's *New York: An Illustrated Anthology* (1988); that from Philip Glass from Lee Morrissey's *The Kitchen Turns Twenty: A Retrospective Anthology* (1992).

For an intimate cultural memoir, I've always treasured Malcolm Cowley's *Exile's Return* (1937), which I read in college. Others admire Anatole Broyard's *When Kafka Was the Rage* (1993) and Dan Wakefield's *New York in the Fifties* (1992). John Gruen's *The New Bohemia* (1967), an Upper West Sider's gossipy report on the East Village as it was developing (before it reached its cultural apex), is most useful now for implicitly distinguishing a bohemia from an artists' colony.

Mary Emma Harris's *The Arts at Black Mountain College* (1985) portrays interactions between artists and teachers, as well as artists and artists, at the most extraordinary arts college ever in America. At BMC, however, the setting was rural, rather than urban; and the number of people involved was less than a thousand, with less than a hundred there at any one time, rather than, as in SoHo, in the thousands. In the university that was Artists' SoHo, as noted before, there was no administration.

For a general history of lower Manhattan, see Mike Wallace and Edwin G. Burrows' *Gotham* (1998), Lloyd Morris's *Incredible New York; High Life and Low Life of the Last Hundred Years* (1951), Lucy Sprague Mitchell and Clara Lambert's *Manhattan Now and Long Ago* (1934), and Timothy G. Gilfoyle's *City of Eros* (1992) for its documentation of downtown prostitution. Betty Kray's *Four Literary-Historical Walks* (1982) includes "A Walk through the SoHo Historical District with Walt Whitman."

For images, consider John A. Kouwenhoven's *The Columbia Historical Portrait of New York* (1953), Huson Jackson's *New York Architecture* (1952), Nathan Silver's *Lost New York* (1955), Alan Burnham's *New York Landmarks: A Study and Index of Architecurally Notable Structures in Greater New York* (1963), Ada Louise Huxtable's *Classic New York: Georgian Gentility to Greek Elegance* (1964), *Cast Iron Architecture in New York* (1974) by Margot Gayle and Edmund V. Gillon, Jr., and all three editions of Norval White and Elliot Willensky's *AIA Guide to New York City* (1968, 1978, 2000), whose contents, images, and even basic design have changed over the decades.

Helene Zucker Seeman and Alanna Siegfried's *SoHo: A Guide* (1978) remains very informative, if dated. Among its most valuable elements are the street-by-street inventories of buildings identifying their prominent postindustrial/commercial occupants at that time and a chronological bibliography of books and articles about SoHo. The Rapkin Study was published as *The South Houston Industrial Area* by the New York City Planning Commission in 1963. SoHo's early history is remembered in Charles R. Simpson's *SoHo: The Artist in the City* (1981), James R. Hudson's *The Unanticipated City: Loft Conversions in Lower Manhattan* (1987), and Sharon Zukin's *Loft Living* (1982), in order of usefulness. Later guidebooks include Alexandra Anderson and B. J. Archer's *SoHo: The Essential Guide to Art and Life in Lower Manhattan* (1979) and Roland Hagenberg's *SoHo: A Documentary* (1986).

Henry Miller's memoir of Beauford Delaney on Greene Street appears in his *Remember to Remember* (1947); John Gruen's of Oscar Williams in *The Party's Over Now: Reminiscences of the Fifties* (1972); Calvin Tomkins of Robert Rauschenberg's from *The Bride and the Bachelors* (1964); and Donald Barthelme's of "Lower Broadway Windows" from his *Not-Knowing* (1997). The artists of Coenties Slip are remembered in a 1993 catalog of that title (Pace Gallery). For the Whitney Museum in Greenwich Village, see Avis Berman's *Rebels on Eighth Street* (1990). Other informative books on earlier American avant-gardes include Dickran Tashjian's *Boatload of Madmen* (1995), Steven Watson's *Strange Bedfellows* (1993), my own *Master Minds* (1969), and *The Theatre of Mixed Means* (1968). The Lucy R. Lippard quote about SoHo noise comes from page 199 of her *The Pink Glass Swan* (1995); John Canady's about 10th Street galleries from *Embattled Critic* (1962); Irving Sandler's testimony on the Tanager Gallery from *The East Village Scene*, a 1984 catalog from the Institute for Contemporary Art at the University of Pennsylvania.

Articles probably influencing my own move to SoHo include Joan Kron's "Lofty Living," and Dorothy Seiberling's "SoHo: The Most Exciting Place to Live in the City," both in *New York* magazine (May 20, 1974). The influential guide to loft renovation was James Stratton, *Pioneering in the Urban Wilderness* (1977). Newer, slicker loft renovations, none of which I've ever seen firsthand, are featured in Mayer Rus's *Lofts* (1998). *The International Book of Lofts* (1986) by

Suzanne Slesin and others documents the influence of the SoHo rev-
olution in interior design.

The richest survey of the arts in early SoHo is the bilingual catalog of an exhibition, *SoHo: Downtown Manhattan* (1976), organized
in West Berlin by the Akademie der Kunst, typically recognizing an
American avant-garde long before comparable native institutions did;
the quotes by Douglas Davis and Lucy R. Lippard come from it.
Never reprinted, neither here nor in Germany, this book commands a
healthy price from Antiquariats, as used bookstores are called in
Germany.

Regarding the alternative spaces of Artists' SoHo, see *The Kitchen*
(1992), mentioned before, and Claudia Gould and Valerie Smith's
5000 Artists Return to Artists Space: 25 Years (New York: Artists Space,
1999), which publishes on its large pages small-print interviews with
many artists and curators who participated in its generosity, incidentally telling much, especially between the lines, about the changing
artistic climate in downtown Manhattan from the early 1970s to the
pre- mid-1990s. Robin Brentano with Mark Savitt edited *122
Workshop/Greene Street: History, Artists & Artworks* (New York
University Press, 1981) mostly to document exhibitions. In 1982, the
co-op 55 Mercer Street published an eponymous retrospective
newsprint catalog titled *Twelve Years*.

For the Performance Group, see *Dionysus in '69* (Farrar, Straus,
1970). Richard Schechner remembers it at length in *Environmental
Theater* (1973; revised ed., 1996). David Savran's *The Wooster Group*
(TCG, 1988) is a premature retrospective. On Hannah Wilke, see
Amelia Jones's *Body Art: Performing the Subject* (1988). Robert
Wilson has been the subject of several books. The classic pioneering
study is Stefan Brecht's *The Theatre of Visions* (1978), which was pub-
lished in Germany in English, along with Brecht's *Queer Theatre*
(1978) on other downtown performance. Also see Trevor Fairbrother's
Robert Wilson's Vision (1991), Craig Nelson's *Robert Wilson: The
Theatre of Images* (1980); Laurence Shyer's *Robert Wilson and His
Collaborators*; and *Robert Wilson* (1997) by Franco Quadri and
Robert Stearns. Wilson's text for *The King of Spain* (1969) appears in
the third volume of William M. Hoffman's *New American Plays*

(1970); his *I Was Sitting on My Patio* (1977) was reprinted in my anthology of *Scenarios* (1980).

The best current source on George Maciunas is *Mr. Fluxus* (1997), lovingly edited—no, composed—by Emmett Williams. On Fluxus itself are several books, including exhibition catalogues from museums around the world. For literature of SoHo, see the anthology of that title I edited for *Shantih* magazine (1982). Sam Wiener's *Splendors of the SoHites* is still available from its author/artist at 186 Sachems Head Rd., Guilford, CT 06437. For e. e. cummings as proto-SoHo, see my anthology *AnOther E. E. Cummings* (1996). The best critical introduction to Richard Foreman's work is Gerald Rabkin's anthology, *Richard Foreman* (PAJ-Johns Hopkins University, 1999), which contains reviews of individual productions, "overviews," and interviews (including the 1982 one with me), in addition to a selection of Foreman's own writings. His scripts along with occasional prose have been collected in *Plays and Manifestos* (ed. Kate Davy, 1976), *Love and Science: Selected Librettos* (TGG, 1991), *Unbalancing Acts* (Pantheon, 1992), *My Head Was a Sledgehammer* (Overlook, 1995), and *Paradise Hotel and Other Plays* (Overlook, 2001). *No-Body* (a novel) appeared in 1997 (Overlook). A trio discussion among John Cage, Foreman, and myself appears as "Art in the Culture," in Bonnie Marranca and Gautam Dasgupta, eds. *Conversations on Art and Performance* (Johns Hopkins University, 1999). Kate Davy has published *Richard Foreman and the Ontological-Hysteric Theater* (1981).

Regarding downtown theater in general, see Arnold Aronson, *American Avant-Garde Theater: A History* (2000). Deborah Jowett edited a critical anthology on Meredith Monk (1997), who is also featured in K. Robert Schwartz's book *The Minimalists* (1996). Sally Banes wrote the introduction to the exhibition catalog *Meredith Monk: Archeology of an Artist* (1996), an exhibition catalog published by the New York Library for the Performing Arts. Contemporaneous reviews of SoHo avant-garde music performances are reprinted in Tom Johnson's *The Voice of New Music* (1989). The fullest survey of American avant-garde music is Kyle Gann's *American Music in the Twentieth Century* (1997). Roselee Goldberg's *Performance: Live Art 1909 to the Present* (1979; revised ed., 2001) is a standard survey.

Regarding photography, the Michael Kirby remark comes from
his *The Art of Time* (1969), reprinted in my *Esthetics Contemporary*
(1978, 1990). Among the Cindy Sherman monographs are, in no particular order, Rosalind Krauss, *Cindy Sherman 1975–1993* (Rizzoli,
1993); Amanda Carr et al., *Cindy Sherman Retrospective* (Los Angeles
Museum of Contemporary Art, 1997); Els Barents and Peter
Schjeldahl. *Cindy Sherman 3* (Schirmer/Mosel, 1987); Amanda
Cruz, *Cindy Sherman* (Thames & Hudson, 1998); Elisabeth Bronfen,
Cindy Sherman Photographic Work 1975–1995 (Schirmer/Mosel,
1995); Peter Schjeldahl and Lisa Phillips, *Cindy Sherman* (Whitney
Museum, 1987); *Cindy Sherman* (Museum of Modern Art, Shiga,
Japan, 1986); Arthur Danto, *Cindy Sherman: History Portraits*
(Rizzoli, 1991); Catherine Abrams, *The Essential Cindy Sherman*
(Abrams, 1999); Marco Meneguzzo, *Cindy Sherman* (Padiglione
d'Arte Contemporanea, Milan,1990); *Cindy Sherman* (Museo
Nacional Centro de Arte Reina Sofia, Madrid, 1996); *Cindy Sherman*
(Stedelijk Museum & Schirmer/Mosel, 1982); Betty van Garrel et al.,
Cindy Sherman (Museum Boijmans Van Beuningen, Rotterdam,
1996); Thomas Kellein, *Cindy Sherman* (Edition Cantz, 1991);
Catherine Morris, *Essential Cindy Sherman* (Abrams, 2001). Whew. I
challenge anyone reading through all these books not to put them
aside after seeing the same choice images reproduced too many
times. Nonetheless, though Sherman hasn't published any books
under her own name, an argument could be made that coffee-table
volumes will ultimately become the most appropriate repository for
her work. Peter Hutchinson's work is remembered in Christopher
Busa's *The Narrative Art of Peter Hutchinson* (1996); Bill Beckley's in
an eponymous catalog (1986).

No other SoHo artist has generated as much literature as Nam
June Paik. The distinguished German curator Wulf Herzogenrath,
prepared *Nam June Paik: Werke 1946–1976 Musik-Fluxus-Video* for a
1977 exhibition at the Kölnischer Kunstverein. For its pioneering retrospective, the Everson Museum in Syracuse produced *Nam June
Paik: Video 'n' Videology 1959–1973*. John Hanhardt produced two
catalogs in conjunction with museum exhibitions he curated—*N.J.P.*
(Norton, 1982) and *The Worlds of N.J.P.* (Abrams, 2000). *Nam June*

Paik: Du Cheval à Christo et autres Écrits (1993) is an homage mostly in French, with some English, edited by Edith Decker and Ermeline Lebeer. *Nam June Paik: eine DADA base* (c. 1993), edited by Klaus Bussman and Florian Matzner, was prepared for Paik's participation as a German in the Venice Bienale. Two German-speaking curators, Toni Stooss and Thomas Killien, edited *Nam June Paik* (1991), a catalog for an exhibition that traveled only in Europe, that was translated into English as *Video Time—Video Space* (1993). Jean-Paul Farbier's *Nam June Paik* (1989) is an illustrated monograph entirely in French, while *Nam June Paik. Lo sciamano del video* (1994) is an anthology in Italian and Edith Decker's *Paik Video* (1988) is a verbally denser monograph in German. The Michael Rush appreciation comes from his *New Media in Late 20th Century Art* (1999). For the renovations of Richard Gluckman, see *Space Framed* (Monacelli, 2000).

The most relevant Sonic Youth album is *Goodbye to the 20th Century* (SYR 4, the letters identifying their own label). Several Alan Vega CDs have recently been in print, mostly from Infinite Zero Archive: *Power to the Zero Hour* (1985), *New Raceion* (1994), *Deuce Avenue* (1990), *Dwang Prang* (1995), and *Cubist Blues* (1996). The richest retrospective, selected from several earlier records, is *Suicide/Alan Vega Anthology* (213cd), which is not yet commercially available. Bernard Gendron's *Between Montmartre and the Mudd Club* (2002) offers historical intelligence on popular music in avant-garde art worlds.

The Meredith Monk epigraph comes from an interview by Andrew Shapiro published in *21st Century Music* (May 2002). Monk gets a chapter in Sally Banes's *Terpsichore in Sneakers* (1980) and a section in Kyle Gann's book on contemporary American music mentioned before. Other quotations come from her website: www.meredithmonk.org, which incidentally has complete lists of her releases in various media. Deborah Jowett's *Meredith Monk* (1997) is an anthology mostly of criticism.

Carl Glassman's *SoHo* (1985) is a photograph book mostly not about art or even artists' lofts but street scenes with an equally misguiding introduction by the cultural journalist John Leonard, who reportedly lives on the Upper East Side. (Books so worthless inevitably make you wonder how they were published.) As a general rule, may I suggest that the best first books on new culture are written by participants; absentee scholars are better down the road. The entry on SoHo in Kenneth Jackson's *Encyclopedia of New York City* (1995) barely acknowledges the artists whose presence gave the downtown area its current name.

Many individuals and terms mentioned here are discussed in isolation in my *A Dictionary of the Avant-Gardes* (1992; second ed. 1999).

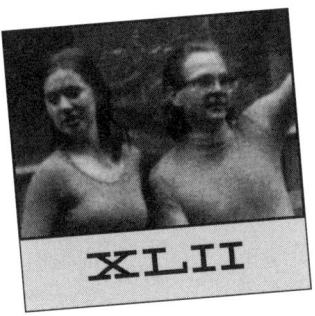

XLII

Appendix

S INCE NO INITIAL list of recognizable American artists residing in and near SoHo for some consequential time can be definitive, I resisted making one. One fear was the sorts of errors, beginning with misspellings, that might creep in to such a list. On the other hand, nothing less than a large inventory can convey so persuasively my sense of it as a hothouse. Many of these professionals are already acknowledged in the critical histories of their arts; others no doubt will be, not just because they lived in SoHo. In the following alphabetical order, I used genre tags not to define an individual's work but to give their names a professional context. My swimming-pool buddy Sean Sweeney, incidentally a SoHo community activist, contributed several names.

Douglas Abdell, visual artist

Vito Acconci, poet/performance artist/architect

Olga Adorno, performance artist

Joanne Akalaitis, theatre director

Richard Alcott, architect

Frances Alenikoff, choreographer

Laurie Anderson, media artist

Jonathan Andrews, painter

Suzanne Anker, painter

Stephen Antonakos, light artist

Janine Antoni, sculptor

Carl Andre, sculptor

Ida Applebroog, visual artist

Robert Ashley, composer

Alyce Aycock, sculptor

Beth B, filmmaker

Donald Bacheler, visual artist

Amy Baker, art archivist

Rudolph Baranik, painter

Jared Bark, painter/framemaker

Elliott Barowitz, visual artist/writer

Burt Barr, video artist

Jack Barth, painter

Jennifer Bartlett, painter/writer

Tosun Bayrak, performance artist/Sufi

Betty Beaumont, sculptor

Bill Beckley, sculptor

Connie Beckley, performer

David Behrman, composer

Lynda Benglis, sculptor

Jake Berthot, painter

Obie Benz, film director

Scott Billingsly, video/performance artist

Mel Bochner, visual artist

Andrew Bolotowsky, musician

Power Boothe, painter

Lizzie Borden, filmmaker/writer

David Bowie, pop musician

Scott Billingsly, filmmaker

Dara Birnbaum, video artist

Eric Bogosian, playwright

Paul Brach, painter

Joe Brainard, artist/writer

Trisha Brown, choreographer/director

Robert Buecher, instrument-maker

Henry Buhl, photographer

Nancy Burson, photographer

Jim Burton, composer/visual artist

David Byrne, musician

Peter Campus, videographer

Rosemarie Castoro, sculptor

John Chamberlain, sculptor

Rhys Chatham, musician

Lucinda Childs, choreographer

Daryl Chin, playwright

Ping Chong, performance artist

Christo and Jean-Marie, sculptors

John Clem Clarke, painter

Francesco Clemente, painter

Chuck Close, painter

Maxi Cohen, media artist

Orenette Coleman, musician

Dick Conette (aka A. Leroy), composer

Maureen Connor, sculptor

Elizabeth Cook, visual artist

Phillip Corner, composer

Petah Coyne, visual artist

William Creston, filmmaker

Jason Crum, sculptor

Willem Dafoe, actor

Steve Dalachinsky, poet

Alan Daugherty (aka Red Spot), visual artist

Jaime Davidovich, videographer

Bevan Davies, photographer/retailer

Douglas Davis, videographer/writer

Edit de Ak, art writer

Carmen de Lavallade, dancer

Walter de Maria, sculptor/installation artist

Claudia de Monte, visual artist

Robert De Niro, director

Robert De Niro, painter

James Dee, photographer

Agnes Denes, visual artist

Anne Deon, performance artist

Stuart Diamond, visual artist

David Diao, painter

Charles Doria, poet

Rackstraw Downes, painter

Tan Dun, composer

Carol Dunham, painter

Douglas Dunn, choreographer

Jean Dupuy, sculptor/performance artist

Martha Edelheit, visual artist

Mary Beth Edelson, visual artist

Stefan Eins, visual artist/gallerist

Brian Eno, musician

Ralston Farina, performance/visual artist

Molissa Fenley, choreographer

Hebert Ferber, sculptor

Jackie Ferrara, sculptor

Joel Fischer, visual artist

Janet Fish, painter

Audrey Flack, painter

Henry Flynt, musician/conceptual artist

Richard Foreman, playwright

Simone Forti, choreographer

Linda Francis, painter

Peter Frank, writer

Chris Frantz and Tina Weymouth, pop musicians

Suzan Frecon, painter

Lynn Frehm, painter

Carole Gallagher, photographer

Mimi Garrard, choreographer

David Geary, filmmaker

Emmanuel Ghent, composer

Chris Gianakos, sculptor

Steve Gianakos, painter

Jon Gibson, composer/musician

Ralph Gibson, photographer

Davidson Gigliotti, videographer

Kathy Gilje, painter

Frank Gillette, videographer/visual artist

Madeline Gins, writer

John Giorno, poet/performer

Phillip Glass, composer

Richard Gluckman, architect

Robert Gober, visual artist

Michael Goldberg, painter

RoseLee Goldberg, art historian

Leon Golub, painter

Ron Gorchov, painer

David Gordon, theater artist

Stephen Jay Gould, writer

Dan Graham, media artist/writer

Nancy Graves, visual artist

Spalding Gray, writer/performer

Joel Grey, actor

Penelope Grill, visual artist

Red Grooms, visual artist

Julie Gross, painter

Mimi Gross, visual artist

Robert Grosvenor, sculptor

Art Guerra, visual artist

Don Gummer, sculptor

Marcia Hafif, painter

Janz Haimsohn, performance artist

David Hammons, visual artist

Ruth Hardinger, visual artist

David Hare, sculptor

Keith Haring, artist

Meg Harper, dancer

Susan Harris, sculptor/performance artist

Richard Hayman, composer

Al Held, painter

Michael Heizer, earth artist

William Hellerman, composer

Geoffrey Hendricks, painter

Jon Hendricks, art historian

Judith Henry, designer

Julia Heyward, performance artist

Dick Higgins, polyartist/publisher

Jene Highstein, sculptor

Chuck Hinman, visual artist

Lucy Hodgson, sculptor

Geoffrey Holder, performer

G. H. Hovagimyan, media artist

Robert Hughes, critic

Robert Huot, sculptor

David Hykes, filmmaker/composer

Robert Indiana, visual artist

Will Insley, visual artist

Suzanne Joelson, painter

Buffie Johnson, sculptor

Tom Johnson, composer

Joan Jonas, video artist

Donald Judd, sculptor/writer

John Kacere, painter

Daile Kaplan, photographer/art historian

Alex Katz, painter

Bill Katz, architect

Lila Katzen, sculptor

Pooh Kaye, performer

Tony King, painter

Alison Knowles, visual artist

Kiki Kogelnik, sculptor

Joseph Kosuth, conceptual artist

Joyce Kozloff, painter

Max Kozloff, writer/photographer

Lenny Kravitz, pop musician

Barbara Kruger, visual artist

Shigeko Kubota, videographer

Robert Kushner, visual artist

Joan LaBarbara, composer/singer

Richard Landry, musician

Ellen Lanyon, painter

Anna Lascari, visual artist

Elizabeth LeCompte, theater director

Barry Le Va, sculptor

Les Levine, artist/publisher
Mon Levinson, painter

Jacques Levy, theater director

Vared Lieb, visual artist

Maya Lin, visual artist

Lucy R. Lippard, writer

Liz-N-Val (Liz Clark and Val Goroskho), visual artists

Joan Logue, video artist

Jeffrey Lohn, musician

Alvin D. Loving, visual artist

Abraham Lubelski, painter/publisher

George Maciunas, Fluxus master

Jackson Mac Low, poet

Loren Madsen, visual artist

Andy Mann, videographer

Bryce Marden, visual artist

Gordon Matta-Clark, sculptor

Lynne Mayo(cole), visual artist

Jonas Mekas, filmmaker/writer

Barbara Mensch, photographer

Larry Miller, visual artist

Marilyn Minter, visual artist

Mary Miss, installation artist

Manfred Mohr, visual artist

Meredith Monk, singer/media artist

Robert Morris, sculptor/writer

Françoise Mouly, writer

Elizabeth Murray, painter

Judith Murray, conceptual artist

Robert Murray, visual artist

Verita Nemec, visual artist

Louise Nevelson, sculptor

Graham Nickson, painter

Kenneth Noland, painter

Richard Nonas, sculptor

Patsy Norvall, painter

Thomas Nozkowski, visual artist

Claes Oldenburg and Coosje van
    Bruggen, sculptors

Pat Oleszko, performance artist

Dennis Oppenheim, sculptor

Lawrence Osgood, playwright

Mary Overlie, dancer

Jack Ox, visual artist

Nam June Paik, visual artist

Charlemagne Palestine,
    performer/visual artist

Ray Parker, painter

Dave Pascal, cartoonist

Susan Pear, painter

Judy Pfaff, visual artist

Ellen Phalen, visual artist

Peter Pinchbeck, painter

Suzan Pitt, filmmaker

Maggie Poor, visaul artist

Stephen Posen, visual artist

Lucio Pozzi, visual artist

Jonathan Price, word artist/writer

Richard Prince, visual artist/writer

Larry Qualls, art archivist/historian

Bill Rabinovich, painter/videographer

Yvonne Rainer, choreographer/film-
    maker

John Reilly, videographer

Deborah Remington, visual artist

Rodney Ripps, painter

Corrine Robins, writer

Dorothea Rockburne, visual artist

Sal Romano, painter

Barbara Rose, critic

Jane Rosen, sculptor

James Rosenquist, painter

Barbara Rosenthal, polyartist

Stephen Rosenthal, painter

Phyllis Rosenblatt, visual artist

Charles Ross, sculptor

Frank Roth, painter

Barnaby Ruhe, painter

Meg Ryan, actress

Jerry Saltz, art critic

Andra Samelson, visual artist

Fred Sandback, sculptor

Alan Saret, sculptor

Miriam Schapiro, painter

Julian Schnabel, painter

Barbara Schwartz, painter

Richard Schwartzwald, sculptor

James Seawright, sculptor

Joan Semmel, painter

Richard Serra, sculptor

Valda Setterfield, dancer

Joel Shapiro, sculptor

Willioughby Sharp, media artist/pub-
    lisher

Ronda Shearer, sculptor

Cindy Sherman, visual artist

Charles Simonds, sculptor

Alison Sky, visual artist

Sylvia Sligh, painter

Jack Smith, performance artist

Mimi Smith, visual artist

Shirley Smith, painter
Susan Smith, painter
Kenneth Snelson, sculptor
Alan Sonfist, visual artist
Eve Sonneman, photographer
Steven Soreff, visual artist
Nancy Spero, painter
Art Spiegelman, graphic artist
Robert Stackhouse, sculptor
Ted Stamm, painter
Peter Stampful, post-folk musician
Lewis Stein, visual artist
Gary Stephan, painter
May Stevens, painter
Joyce Stillman, painter
Sting, rock singer
Elizabeth Streb, choreographer
Meryl Streep, actress
Alex Streeter, jeweler
Marjorie Strider, visual artist
Michelle Stuart, sculptor
Alan Suicide/Vega/Bermowitz
Elaine Summers, choreographer
Suzanne Tanger, painter
Ann Tardos, video artist/performer
Amy Taubin, writer/media artist
Carolee Thea, visual artist
Lynne Tillman, writer
Paul Tschinkel, videographer
Bernard Tschumi, architect
Twyla Tharp, choreographer
Gwen Thomas, photographer

Joan Thorne, painter
Hanne Tierney, puppeteer
Nancy Topf, dancer
Lun-Yi Tsai, painter
Wen-Ying Tsai, kinetic sculptor
Lyn Umlauf, painter
Peter van Riper, composer
Ted Victoria, sculptor
Yoshimasa Wada, composer
Paul Waldman, painter
Robert Watts, sculptor
William Wegman, videographer
Robert Wiegand, videographer
Grahame Weinbren, media artist
Roger Welch, conceptual artist
Robert Whitman, performance artist
Hanne Wilke, visual/performance artist
John Willenbecher, painter
Thornton Willis, painter
Christopher Wilmarth, visual artist
Susan Wilmarth, painter
Robert Wilson, theater artist
James Wines, architect
Jackie Winsor, sculptor
Robin Winters, visual artist
Marilyn Wood, choreographer
Nina Yankowitz, painter
La Monte Young, composer
Robert Zakanitch, visual artist
Marian Zazeela, visual artist
Rufus Zogbaum, visual artist

As mentioned before, artists from elsewhere in the world gravitated to SoHo's magnetism from its beginnings. I remember hearing sometime in the early 1970s that all of the Japanese artists selected for a Venice Bienale resided on Canal Street. Among the visual artists residing here, again for consequential time, were Zigi Ben-Haim, Kochi Doktori, Jacob El-Hanni, Joshua Neustein, Oded Halami, Osvaldo Romberg, Serge Spitzer, and Buky Schwartz from Israel; the video artist Jaime Davidovich from Argentina; Michael Snow and Joyce Wieland from Canada; Malcolm Morley, Bruce McLean, Lisa Béar, and Peter Gee from England; Nassos Daphnis, Anna Lascari, and Chryssa from Greece; Virginia Cuppaige from Australia; Max Gimblett and Billy Apple from New Zealand; Arman, Alain Kirili, Jean Dupuy, Christian Xatrec, François Morellet, Helene Valentin, Bernard Venet, Olivier Mosset, and Colette from France; Hilla and Bernd Becker, Manfred Mohr, Dieter Frose, Hans Haacke, and Hanne Darboven from Germany; Vanessa Beecroft and Gregore Müller from Italy; Stefan Eins from Austria; Jacques Bekaert from Belgium; Krishna Reddy and Natvar Bhavsar from India; Nam June Paik from Korea; Mihail Chemiakin, Ernst Neizvestny (who had been Khrushchev's favorite sculptor) and Vitaly Komar/Alexander Melamud from Soviet Russia; Ay-o, Arakawa, Ryozo Iwashiro, On Kawara, Yasano Tone, Taki Iimura, from Japan; Eugenia Barcells and Antonio Muntadas from Spain.

Should a second edition of this book appear, expect omissions to be repaired; corrections made.

About the Author

R ICHARD KOSTELANETZ, born in New York City in 1940, took his B.A. in American Civilization from Brown University and his M.A. in American cultural history from Columbia University with fellowships from the Woodrow Wilson Foundation and the International Fellows program. Later a Fulbright Scholar at the University of London, he also received fellowships from the Guggenheim, Pulitzer, Ludwig Vogelstein, and Pollock-Krasner foundations, in addition to ten individual grants from the National Endowment for the Arts particularly for his work in media and visual art. His art with words, numbers, and lines in several media have been exhibited around the world; *Wordsand* (1978–1981) was a traveling exhibition. His electroacoustic compositions have been aired over radio stations here and abroad; his videotapes presented in one-man exhibitions. His holograms and book-art books are selectively shown. He was recently featured in *ID/entities* (2001), an exhibition initiated by the MIT Media Lab.

Individual entries on Richard Kostelanetz's work in several fields appear in various editions of *A Readers Guide to Twentieth-Century Writers* (ed. Peter Parker, Oxford), the *Merriam-Webster Encyclopedia of Literature, The HarperCollins Reader's Encyclopedia for American Literature, Contemporary Poets, Contemporary Novelists, Postmodern Fiction, Merriam-Webster's Dictionary of American Writers, Baker's Biographical Dictionary of Musicians, Directory of American Scholars, Who's Who in the World, Who's Who in American Art*, and the *Encyclopedia Britannica*, among other directories. Though usually unaffiliated, he has been a Visiting Professor of American Studies at the University of Texas and of Theater at Hunter College, CUNY. His website is www.richardkostelanetz.com. After nearly three decades in SoHo, he relocated his books and papers, videotapes and audiotapes, art and music—all of Wordship, as he calls it—to the Rockaway Hamptons section of New York City.

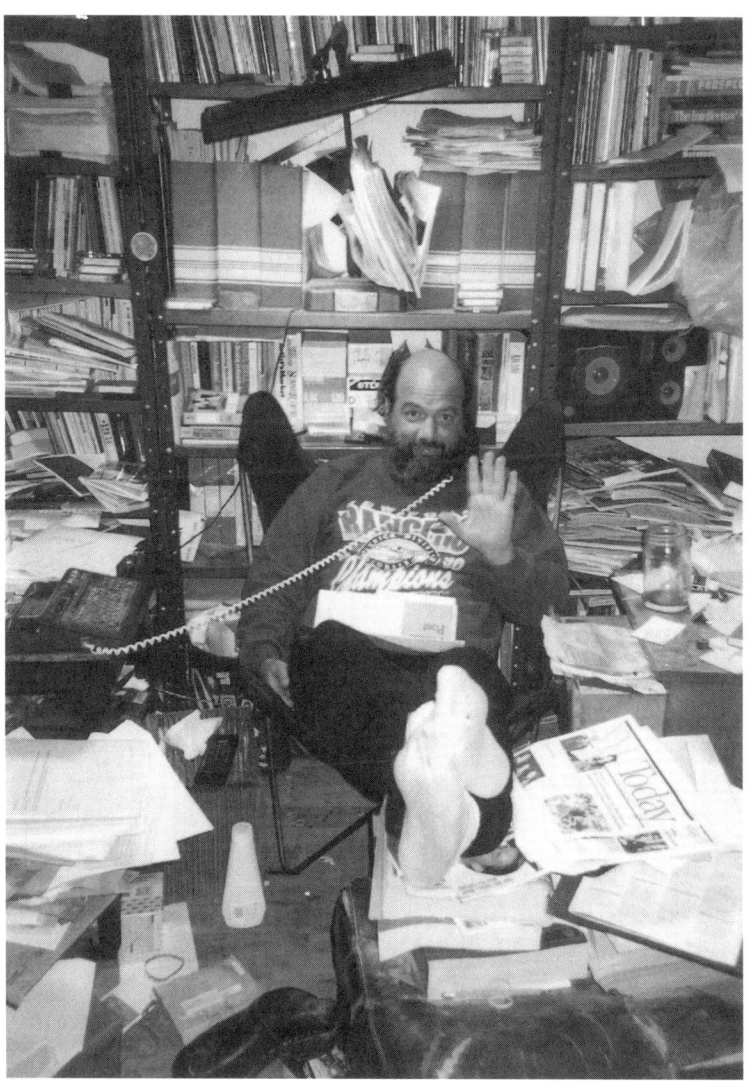

Index